The Best of
Santa Fe
and Beyond

Dear Ila and Stuart

Remember the dinner at
the Cooks and Peters!
Hope you find this 7
interest.

Love,
Elizabeth

The Best of Santa Fe and Beyond

By Elizabeth Thornton
Illustrated by Alban Butler

Adobe Publishing
Santa Fe • New Mexico

The Best of Santa Fe and Beyond

erved. No part of this book may be reproduced
in any form without written permission from the publisher.

All information in this book was correct and true to the best
of the author's knowledge at the time of printing. Please
contact Adobe Publishing with any errors or omissions.

Printed in the United States of America
First Edition

Library of Congress Catalogue Card Number; 97-77738
Includes index.
ISBN 1-878776-00-2

Cover: Alban Butler drawing of La Bajada Hill, the old El Camino Real
Cover design by John Tollett and Ford Ruthling
Tennis is my Racket by Gladys Heldman
El Pescador by Jules Heldman

There were countless entrepreneurs, museum directors, gallery directors, scientists, spies, politicos, divas in all fields, informants and friends and family to whom I owe special thanks, even for chapters that had to be deleted from the book but will appear in the next edition or sooner on my web site. My real gratitude to my mother and father and brother for their encouragement and support.

About the Illustrator—

Alban "Bud" Butler
1891–1949

The drawings in this book were done by my great-uncle Alban "Bud" Butler who frequently came to Santa Fe to visit his sister, my great-aunt, Gladys Butler. During these visits they took excursions to places around Santa Fe which Bud would document with humorous drawings. The illustrations in this book are Bud's drawings from those outings.

Bud, a graduate of Yale and Harvard Law School, was being groomed for the family oil business in Oklahoma. His senior year at Yale he was the chairman of the *Yale Record* and drew caricatures in the yearbook for each person in his graduating class of 1913. His Yale classmates described him saying, "there are few of us who have not been amused by his drawings." Bud said in the yearbook, "The cause of my wit is in other men."

I never knew Bud, but his drawings, which had been his hobby all his life, show the side of him I like most: his intelligent wit, fine-tuned humor, eye for detail, and technical skill as an artist. Bud drew for fun but with purpose. His drawings, sometimes humorous, sometimes documentary in style, always capture the emotion of the moment. From fear to embarrassment to indifference, Bud knew how to portray these emotions with humor.

In the drawings I have selected for this book Bud captures the essence of Santa Fe, adding a twist of insightful humor to the "City Different."

Bud's last trip to Santa Fe was in early January 1949 to care for Gladys who had taken ill. Two weeks later both died within hours of each other. An article in the *Santa Fe New*

Mexican on Monday, January 19, 1949 was captioned "Alban Butler and Sister are Dead Here" and reads:

> "Alban Bernard Butler Jr., Tulsa, Oklahoma died suddenly of a heart condition early Saturday afternoon while painting at the studio of Will Schuster, 550 Camino del Monte Sol. His sister, Gladys S. Butler, 1120 Canyon Road, who had been ill about two weeks and whom Butler and his wife had come to Santa Fe to care for, died early yesterday morning, about twelve hours later, at her home.
>
> Prominent in Santa Fe social circles, she had not been told of her brother's death. She is survived by a niece, Mrs. Drew Pearson, Washington, D. C., wife of the nationally known columnist, who flew into Santa Fe yesterday. Luvie Pearson was at one time a resident of Santa Fe.
>
> Alban Butler who was 58, was born in San Francisco. He was in the oil business in Tulsa, Oklahoma but for years he had made sketching a hobby: actually artists of high standing said that his craftsmanship was of professional status.
>
> When Gladys Butler was taken ill two weeks ago and he came to this city. Butler began studying with Schuster early last week for the first time in oils and similar media. He was working at an easel when he suffered the fatal attack."

His biography in the Yale yearbook in 1931, the year he graduated, said he was born in San Francisco on August 19, 1891, but in giving the list of many places he has spent his life, he becomes discouraged and ends up with an "etc."

About the cover: Alban Butler's "Scene from La Bajada": "The road to Santa Fe, the same road used by Oñate, the El Camino Real, now called La Bajada, where the road left the river from San Felipe and Santo Domingo Pueblos and began to climb toward the escarpment of La Bajada. There the narrow road led in precarious double curves up to a great plain, and they came in sight of the Sangre de Cristo Mountains twenty miles away, in whose foothills lay the ancient and famous cityof Santa Fe and the end of the journey." Paul Horgan, *Lamy of Santa Fe*

This book is dedicated to the memory of my niece and nephew, Wendy and George.

They broke hearts, dates, horses, bones and records. They brokered deals. They climbed the highest peaks. They were the fastest, they laughed the loudest and lived life to the fullest. Their lives were the shortest. They passed through Santa Fe to the great beyond

George Teagle Clements

1964 - 1988

Wendy Lewis Moore

1967 - 1997

Contents

Introduction

In most cities, the unique has a way of standing out—but in Santa Fe, unique is the rule. It's no wonder that the roads are not straight and the walls are not flat. In fact there is not a single straight line in the architecture of my own house!

What I like about Santa Fe is that it is such a small town and yet so steeped in culture and history. To think that all these different cultures and people call Santa Fe home. This city takes the best of everything and molds it into its own style.

Seemingly random events have shaped the character of Santa Fe in a fascinating way: In 1598, Oñate discovered the Indians instead of the fabled cities of gold, and decided to stay in the area. And in the 1920s, a chance mishap with an unruly wagon wheel in the mountains led a young community of artists to Santa Fe. The Manhattan Project in Los Alamos beckoned the nuclear scientists in 1943.

And so the melting pot of Santa Fe became miraculously rich with people well versed in a large variety of intellectual and spiritual pursuits. Somehow members of the community were connected with each other; there was a commonality of knowledge. But now that Santa Fe has expanded physically, we don't have the same common fund of knowledge, and sometimes people forget what made it great in the first place.

How could anyone live in Santa Fe or visit here and not know who Will Schuster is? He invented the annual gloom burning ritual, *Zozobra*. His murals are featured at the museum, and he was one of the five, fun, unruly bachelor painters, the *Cinco Pintores*. His house on Camino del Monte Sol is one of the "five little adobe huts built by one of the five little nuts."

I never visited Santa Fe before I·moved here in 1986, but I was told many tales of this magical place by my family members who lived and visited here. My great-aunt Gladys Butler started coming here in the 1920s. Her brother, Alban Butler, visited her off and on for over twenty years. Their mother, "Granny B," came here from San Francisco. All three of these relatives died in Santa Fe in 1949. My father's sister Luvie and her son Tyler Abel moved here from Washington before she married Washington columnist Drew Pearson. My father's other sister, Chess, came here to visit her relatives and she recollects that "When the house at 1120 Canyon got crowded, people would have to use the outside loo. Bud [her uncle, the illustrator of this book] painted a character peering in the outhouse window to surprise the occupant."

Outhouse humor aside, I am thrilled that this book has allowed me to cross the boundaries of time and space to collaborate with my great-uncle's vision of Santa Fe. My intention is to share the richness of this unique cultural landscape and provide an exploration of the nooks and crannies of Santa Fe's tight community of artists, athletes, eccentrics, spiritual guides, scientists, dogs, and more!

Elizabeth M. Thornton
Santa Fe, New Mexico

Downtown Santa Fe

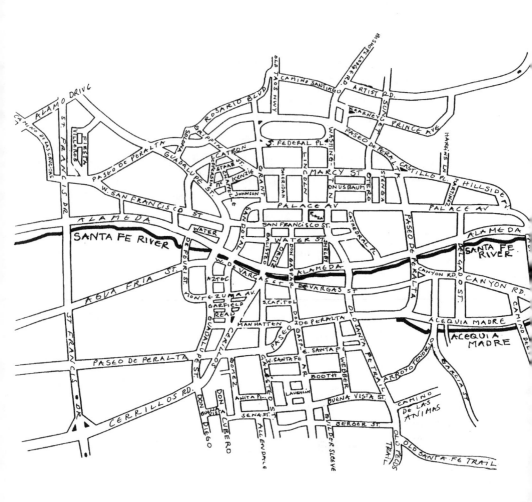

Arriving

Airports, Airlines & Shuttles

Albuquerque International Sunport
(505) 842–4379

Getting to Santa Fe can be a hassle. It's the only state capital without a commercial airport. Most people fly into the Albuquerque Airport, then rent a car or use one of the efficient, economical shuttle services for the sixty-four-mile drive north on Interstate 25 to Santa Fe.

Bus Shuttles to/from Albuquerque Airport

Greyhound Bus Lines
858 St. Michael's Drive, (505) 471–0008 or (800) 231–2222

The bargain fare for these scheduled shuttles to/from the bus station on St. Michael's Drive in Santa Fe to/from the Albuquerque Airport is $21.53 roundtrip.

Shuttlejack
1600 Lena Street, (505) 982–4311 or (800) 452–2665

You can call the 800-number to make your reservation for Shuttlejack in advance. Friendly, helpful drivers make twelve trips a day each way. This shuttle service will pick you up or drop you off at two hotels in central Santa Fe—the Eldorado or the Inn at Loretto—and take you to the Albuquerque Airport. Each one-way fare is $20.

Twin Hearts Express and Transportation
(505) 751–1201 or (800) 654–9456

A pick-up from any downtown hotel at 10:30 A.M. and 12:30 P.M. is for $15 one way.

The Santa Fe Municipal Airport
Manager, Mike Halpin, (505) 473–7243 or (505) 995–4708 to get info

Santa Fe has one of the most elegant, least-used small-town airports in the country. There is a restaurant in the main terminal—**Santa Fe Airport Grill Restaurant** (505) 471–5225. For many reasons,

Santa Fe residents have resisted regular commercial air service to the city, but the airport has gradually expanded from merely housing and servicing private planes. There are two fixed-based facilities to service airplanes—**Santa Fe Jet** (505-471-2525) and **Zia Aviation** (505) 471–2700, and **Avis** and **Hertz** rental cars. Commuter services are as follows:

Aspen Mountain—Air Lone Star Airlines
(800) 877–3932

This is the most convenient way to get to Santa Fe if you are coming from Dallas/Ft. Worth Airport. They offer non-stop, twice-daily service between Santa Fe and DFW Airport.

Mesa Airlines—United Express
(505) 473–4118 or (800) 241–6522

Mesa Airlines is a Farmington, N.M., based Mesa Air Group that flies United Express flights for United Airlines. Mesa provides service to Denver and Albuquerque from Santa Fe Airport three times a day except Sunday.

Transportation to / from Santa Fe Airport
Avis Rent-a-Car, (505) 471–5892
Hertz Rent-a-Car, (505) 471–7189
Roadrunner Shuttle, (505) 424–3367

Buses

The Only National Bus Line
Greyhound Bus Lines
858 St. Michael's Drive, (505) 471–0008 or (800) 231–2222

Greyhound has regularly scheduled bus transport all over the country, including major sites in New Mexico. Buses run three times daily to the Albuquerque Airport.

City Transport For Senior Citizens for $ .25
City of Santa Fe, (505) 984–6731

The city provides transportation for people 60 or older as long as they register at the City of Santa Fe Senior Center and pay a small annual fee. One day notice before 3 P.M. is required.

Santa Fe Ride Paratransit for Handicapped & Seniors
City of Santa Fe, (505) 438–1474 for information about the program

A city transportation program is available seven days a week from 7 A.M. to 7 P.M. for two categories of local Santa Feans with I.D: Senior citizens (60 or older) can ride anywhere in Santa Fe for $4, disabled Santa Feans (you must fill out an application that shows why you can't ride the bus) can ride for $1.

First City Bus Powered by Compressed Natural Gas
Santa Fe Trail Bus Lines, (505) 438–1464

The Santa Fe Trail Bus Lines is the first bus line in the country completely powered by compressed natural gas and the only public bus line in the city; it has been awarded a grant from the U.S. Department of Transportation. The bus line has thirty buses on ten routes all over the city.

Cabs and Limos

The Only Cab Company
Capital City Cab Company
2875 Industrial Road, (505) 438–0000

Metered cabs operate twenty-four hours a day but don't expect to hail a cab, Santa Fe is not New York: call for a cab.

Limousine Services
Limotion, (505) 471–1265
Santa Fe Hotel Limo, (505) 988–3535

Train Service

Only East-West Train From New York To Los Angeles
Amtrak (800) 872–7245

Lamy Shuttle Service round trip from Santa Fe (505) 982–8829

You hear the "whoosh" of the West when the East-West and the West-East trains pass each other in Lamy, twenty minutes from Santa Fe, between 2:30 and 3 P.M. There is silence followed by a tremendous racket, followed by silence. The only restaurant in Lamy is an old-style saloon, the Legal Tender, right across the street from the train station. If you are meeting a train, plan to have lunch there before the train arrives.

The Only American "Orient Express"
T. C. Swartz Expeditions, (800) 727–7477 for a schedule

Plush, first-class, very expensive, and varied seven to nine day tour packages originate in Washington, D.C., the west coast, Denver, and Santa Fe with two-day stopovers in Santa Fe. Gourmet meals are served on fine china, renowned speakers lecture on board, and informed tours of Santa Fe and its environs are offered.

The Only Spur Line that Goes From Lamy to Santa Fe
Bob Sarr, Santa Fe Southern Railway, 410 South Guadalupe Street, (505) 989–8600

The only real Santa Fe train station is on Guadalupe Street. Santa Fe Southern offers excursions four or five times weekly from the Santa Fe railyard to Lamy. You have time for lunch at the Legal Tender or a picnic. Tickets are $21 roundtrip for adults, $16 for seniors, less for children. Locals use the trip as a clever way to entertain guests. If you want to rent a sleeper car or go to Lamy and back, contact the number above.

...and train lore

Santa Fe is one of the most interesting places for train buffs because it once was served by both the narrow gauge **Denver-Rio Grande Railroad** and the standard gauge railroads: the **Atchison, Topeka & Santa Fe** (the east-west train) and the **New Mexico Central** (the north-south train) railroads.

In the 1880s, Santa Fe's most the famous ecclesiastic, Bishop Lamy, was propelled into action when he found out that the Atchison, Topeka & Santa Fe Railroad had decided that it would not be economically feasible to haul the one freight car needed to supply Santa Fe each week. Lamy didn't want the railroad to bypass the state capital, so he sold two bond issues to the public for $75,000 apiece and built the spur line from Lamy to Santa Fe. In 1950, the railroad suspended passenger traffic. On March 12, 1992, the line was bought by the **Santa Fe Southern Railway.**

The Denver-Rio Grande, built in 1880, was the most reliable means of transportation in the mountains until World War ll. It transported mining supplies and passengers to mining camps before there were good roads. It came to the Santa Fe station, (now Tomisita's Restaurant) on Guadalupe Street until 1941 when they tore up the tracks from Santa Fe to Chama. In 1967, New Mexico and Colorado jointly bought for $500,000 the section of the old Denver-Rio Grande railroad between Chama and Antonito when it was about to be scrapped. They revived it for tourists and renamed it the Cumbres and Toltec Scenic Railroad. The Cumbres and Toltec now runs across the Colorado and New Mexico border from Chama, New Mexico, to Antonito, Colorado. The sixty-four- mile-long railroad climbs from 7,800 feet in elevation to 10,015 feet: it is the longest and highest narrow-gauge steam railroad in the United States. It is open daily from Memorial Day weekend until mid-October. An adult round-trip ticket from Chama to Antonito costs $49.10. For a taste of what it's like, see *Indiana Jones and the Last Crusade,* which featured this train. Antonito station (800) 654–9545; Chama station (505) 756–2151.

Accommodations

"No other lived-in place on the continent is as old as Taos Pueblo"—
Eric Sloane, *The Road to Taos*, published by Wilfred Funk

Unique and/or Cheap

Hotels and motels on Cerrillos Road or outside of the downtown area tend to be cheaper than the hotels closer to the Plaza. Big hotel chains, such as the Holiday Inn Express, Comfort Inn, Luxury Inn, Super 8, and Motel 6, are in the cheapest range, and sometimes can cost as little as $39 a night. If you are willing to go a little higher—still under $80—you can stay in the Comfort Suites, Travelodge South, Holiday Inn, Santa Fe Motel, or Garrett's Desert Inn. If you want the most luxurious hotel suites, the best and the most expensive that Santa Fe has to offer, try the Eldorado, the Inn at Loretto, La Fonda, the Inn of the Anasazi, or the Inn on the Alameda. Phone the agencies below for comprehensive listings of hotels in the price range you want.

Santa Fe Central Reservations, (800) 776–7669 or (505) 983–8200
Santa Fe Visitors Bureau, (505) 983–8200 or (800) 338–6877

Price Ranges

$	cheapest $10–$50
$$	cheap $50–$80
$$$	moderate $80–$179
$$$$	expensive $180–$249
$$$$$	most expensive $250–up

*Downtown or Historic District

The Most Time-Honored Hotel & Resort
Bishop's Lodge, Bishops Lodge Road, (505) 983–6377

The Bishop's Lodge has been consistently awarded the Mobil Travel Guide's Four Star rating for at least 10 years, the only New Mexico establishment to receive Mobil's highest rating. The land on which Bishop's Lodge was built was part of a land grant given to Urbano Montano by Governor Gaspar Domingo de Mendoza in 1743. In the 1860s, Santa Fe's first Archbishop, Bishop Lamy purchased the property for $80 and built a house—part of which is still standing. Lamy died in 1888. The Pulitzer family bought the property in 1915, but did not keep it long. Jim Thorpe paid $25,000 for the 152.8 acres and established a resort, which the family continues to run today. The lodge has a health club, a tennis club, and riding. $$$

The Second Largest Hotel in Town
The Doubletree Inn, 3347 Cerrillos Road, (505) 473–2800

The Doubletree Inn is the second largest hotel in town with 213 rooms that have been newly renovated and cost $99 per night. The three bedroom presidential suite costs $299 per night. Complimentary shuttle service is provided to the Plaza every two hours. The inn is equipped with an indoor heated pool, two jacuzzis, and exercise rooms. $$$

The Most Expensive Accommodation in Santa Fe
The Presidential Suite at the Eldorado Court, 309 W. San Francisco Street
(505) 988–4455

The most expensive accommodation in Santa Fe is the Presidential Suite at the Eldorado Court. The suite starts $975 a night, and it has patio space to entertain 150 guests. The Eldorado is the biggest convention hotel in town. It features good shops and piano music nightly with hors d'oeuvres in a large room full of out-of-towners. $$$$$*

The Oldest Locally Owned Motels on "Motel Row"
El Rey Inn, 1862 Cerrillos Road, (505) 982–1931

One of the most popular motels with the locals since 1935, the El Rey Inn is close to the Animal Shelter (an instition in itself). The motel is nestled between the downtown hotels and the Cerrillos Road "Motel Row." The inn recently bought a motel next door and added thirty rooms. El Rey has a pool, complimentary breakfast, and four acres of landscaped gardens. $$

The Essence of Santa Fe
Owner, Sam Ballen
La Fonda Hotel, 100 E. San Francisco Street, (505) 982–5511

La Fonda, at the end of the Santa Fe Trail, was always the place for old-timers to celebrate after months on the trading trails. La Fonda is the oldest hotel in Santa Fe and the only hotel on the Plaza. This lively hotel attracts a constant flow of locals and visitors. Its decor and mood reflect the entire scope and history of the Southwest, especially the Anglo, Hispanic, and Indian mix unique to this area. La Fonda's earliest written records only date back to 1822, but there is evidence that it may have been operating as an inn as early as 1610.

Myths meet at La Fonda. It was the U.S. headquarters for General Kearny's staff in 1846. Billy the Kid may have worked in its kitchen. Errol Flynn and President John F. Kennedy have been welcomed in its best "suites." Its older incarnation (then known as the Exchange Hotel) was demolished in 1919; the Fred Harvey organization leased the present building from 1926 to 1969. The present owner, Sam Ballen, maintains the Southwestern flavors and sense of fun that are the hallmark of La Fonda. The bar is always one of the most lively hotel bars in town. There is always a fun band. **$$$***

The Motel with the Largest Outdoor Parking Lot
Garrett's Desert Inn, 311 Old Santa Fe Trail, (505) 982–1851

If you are traveling in a camper or mobile home, Garrett's large parking lot makes it ideal. Garrett's motel rooms have no particular charm, but its convenient location (only two blocks from the Plaza) and its very reasonable prices give it an edge over some other hotels in its area. The Avis Rental Car agency, a travel agency, and even a nice French restaurant are located inside. **$$***

The Most Luxurious Inn
The Hacienda del Cerezo Inn, 100 Camino del Cerezo, (505) 982–8000

A ten-suite inn owned by Barbara and Steven Kirchenbaum is on three hundred acres of land northwest of Santa Fe. The hefty $600 a day fee provides full amenities—beautiful rooms, each with king-sized beds, jacuzzis, fireplaces, and stunning mountain views. Three gourmet meals a day and use of the riding facilities and tennis courts are part of the package. **$$$$$**

The Historic Casa de Ortiz
The Hilton of Santa Fe, 100 Sandoval Street, (505) 988–2811

The Casa de Ortiz was built by a prominent early Santa Fe family. Nicolas Ortiz I accompanied Don Diego de Vargas during the 1693 reconquest. This restored historic house, now the Hilton of Santa Fe, provides reliable Hilton service. Two blocks from the Plaza.$$$*

The Most Innovative Joint Venture
The Hotel Santa Fe, 1501 Paseo de Peralta, (505) 982–1200

Here you witness the only Native American/Anglo joint venture on non-Indian land in New Mexico. When Congress passed the Indian Finance Corporation Act to encourage economic development, real estate developers Paul Margetson, William Zeckendorf, and Joe Schepps built an $11 million hotel with a $9 million guarantee from the Bureau of Indian Affairs through the Picuris Pueblo. The 131-room hotel is staffed by personnel from the Picuris Pueblo and other reservations. The Picuris Pueblo tribe owns 51% of the hotel; they perform tribal dances on the patio every Saturday evening and bake native bread every Sunday morning. The Hotel Santa Fe has a cozy lobby, and the only Native-American restaurant in town, the Corn Dance Cafe. The hotel is six blocks from the Plaza. $$$*

Listed on the National Register of Historic Places
Hotel St. Francis, 210 Don Gaspar Avenue, (505) 983–5700 or (800) 529–5700

This historic inn with eighty-two guest rooms is just one block from the Plaza. Completely renovated in 1986, it has unique charm. High tea is served daily in the lobby and reproductions of period furnishings enhance the hotel's ambiance. The outdoor patio was voted "the best" by the *Santa Fe Reporter.* $$$*

The Smallest "East Side" Hotel
The Inn on the Alameda, 303 E. Alameda, (505) 984–2121

The Inn on the Alameda, either Santa Fe's smallest hotel or Santa Fe's largest B & B, is on the east side of town two blocks from the Plaza. This cozy hotel serves a very good complimentary breakfast. Dogs are welcome. $$$$*

The Only Hotel With a 4 Diamond Restaurant In It
The Inn of the Anasazi, 113 Washington Street, (505) 988–3030

This keenly elegant contemporary inn, one block from the Plaza, evokes the wonder of a pre-historic site. Its fifty-nine rooms have gaslit fireplaces and four-poster beds. The library is a cozy place to read in the daytime or to dine at night. $$$$$*

The Most Beautiful Window Boxes
The Inn of the Governors, 234 Don Gaspar Avenue, (505) 982–4333

Here each room has Southwestern furnishings, a wood-burning fireplace, and a balcony whose window boxes spill over with flowers. The heated pool is open year-round. The Inn of the Governors has a restaurant and a quite lively piano bar. $$$$*

The Only Hotel Connected to a Museum
The Inn at Loretto, 211 Old Santa Fe Trail, (505) 988–5531

The inn adjoins the Loretto Chapel and museum. The "Miraculous Staircase" of the Loretto Chapel was the scene of one of TV's *Unsolved Mysteries* series. Still unsolved is the question of who long ago designed and carved this magnificant circular staircase out of one piece of wood. The owner of the chapel/museum rents the chapel for weddings and conferences. The recently renovated Inn at Loretto has some of the best hotel shops in town. $$$$*

Stay With The Most Famous Ghost
La Posada de Santa Fe, 330 E Palace Avenue, (505) 986–0000

Legend claims that the famous ghost of Julia Staab lurks in Room 256 at the top of the stairs. Her family, early German Jewish immigrants, was among Santa Fe's earliest merchants and related to the *Spiegelbergs* and the *Zeckendorfs* of Santa Fe fame. They were among the most socially prominent families in town. Abraham Staab built the mansion on Palace Avenue in 1883 for his wife Julia, who died on May 14, 1896 of mental illness at the age of 52. La Posada opened in 1934 and rooms were added in 1960 and in the 1980s. Olympus, the company that also owns the Algonquin

Hotel in New York, bought La Posada in 1997. The 120-room hotel, one block from the Plaza on six acres of beautifully landscaped gardens, has an outside restaurant patio and a swimming pool. $$$*

The Best Furnished
Seret's 1001 Nights, 147 East DeVargas Street, (505) 982–9480

One of the best furnished accomodations and in a good location, across from Santa Fe's "oldest church," Seret's has fully equipped kitchens and elegant baths. $$$$*

ABC Produced a Movie about this Popular Resort
Manager, Michael Cerletti
Rancho Encantado, State Road 22, (505) 982–3537

In 1968, Betty Egan from Cleveland, Ohio, bought the 160-acre Rancho del Monte guest ranch and renamed it Rancho Encantado. For the last thirty years it has been a preferred refuge for the famous—such as the Dalai Lama, Prince Rainier, Princess Grace, Henry Fonda, and Robert Redford. Don't miss the Rogues' Gallery of celebrity visitors in the bar. Rancho Encantado was the scene of ABC's 1993 TV movie, *Rio Shannon.* This popular, well-equipped resort has riding stables, a tennis court, and a swimming pool. $$$$

The Only International Hostel in Santa Fe
Santa Fe International Hostel, 1412 Cerrillos Road
(505) 988–1153 or (505) 983–9896

Men's and women's dorms range from $10 to $12 a night. A private room runs $23 per night. To reserve a room payment must be made in advance, otherwise it is first-come, first-served. $

Roadside Original
The Silver Saddle, 2810 Cerrillos Road, (505) 982–3551

The only New Mexico motel "authentic" enough to be featured in the movie "Motel" was the Silver Saddle, right next door to Jackalope, one of the best marketplaces in the state. $$

The Least Expensive Place to Stay by the Month
The Warren Inn, 3357 Cerrillos Road, Santa Fe, NM 87505, (505) 471–2033

If you can't afford the higher priced places, at $400 a month, the Warren Inn is ideal for longer stays. Be warned: they check you out before they check you in. Know the room number in advance if you wish to phone a guest. Rooms have kitchenettes. **$**

The Most Photographed House in Santa Fe
304 Delgado Street, (505) 988–2118

For the ultimate "native" Santa Fe experience, rent this charming, impeccably decorated adobe (full of English antiques and New Mexico folk art) facing Canyon Road at the corner of Delgado. A favorite of tourist photographers and postcard producers. Built by Carlos Vierra in the early 1900s, this 2,000 sq. ft. completely equipped two-bedroom house has two reception rooms, a large dining room, large kitchen, two bedrooms (one queen, one twin-bedded), and one bath. Full maid-service and optional catering, can be rented by the day, week, or winter months. **$$$$***

B & B's

Alexander's Inn
529 E. Palace Avenue, (505) 986–1431

Carolyn Lee has five guest rooms in a quiet, bright brick home on the historic eastside, a short walking distance from the Plaza, as well as two suites in the back, and two cottages, one of which has two bedrooms (which rents for $200 a night). Continental breakfast is served on the deck. A jacuzzi in the garden can be shared with other guests. **$$$***

Casa De La Cuma
105 Paseo De La Cuma, (505) 983–1717

Hosts Donna and Art Bailey are four blocks from the Plaza, close to Fort Marcy Park with its pool and walking-jogging field, near the road to the ski basin. They have four guest rooms with TVs, and serve an extended continental breakfast by a fire or out on the patio with views of the Sangre de Cristo Mountains and the city. **$$$**

El Paradero

220 W. Manhattan Street, (505) 988–1177

Thom Allen and Ouida MacGregor restored this old Spanish farmhouse with fourteen guest rooms near the Plaza. A full gourmet breakfast is served in a sunny dining room overlooking a charming patio. Eight minutes from the Plaza. $$$*

Four Kachinas Inn

512 Webber Street, (505) 982–2550, (800) 397–2564

The Four Kachinas is a charming, nicely decorated inn—probably because the owners display their Indian art collection. Each of the four bedrooms (three have patios) is named for a Hopi kachina doll. Breakfast is served to your room or patio at the time you request. The inn is within walking distance to the Plaza. $$$*

The Grant Corner Inn

122 Grant Street, (505) 983–6678

Since 1982, at this charmingly restored colonial house just two blocks from the Plaza, Louise Stewart has served a full gourmet breakfast with homemade breads and pastries inside or on the attractive verandah. The restaurant is open to the public; in addition to breakfast, they serve lunch daily. Located right next door to the Georgia O'Keeffe Museum. $$$*

Inn of the Animal Tracks

707 Paseo de Peralta Street, (505) 988–1546

Five rooms, "Eagle," "Deer," "Otter," "Rabbit," and "Wolf," with private baths in this historic ninety-year-old adobe. Each room has the Southwestern charm of vigas, hardwood floors, handmade furniture, and kiva fireplaces. A full breakfast is served in the morning and high tea in the afternoon. $$$*

Preston House

106 Faithway Street, (505) 982–3465

Owner/Manager Signe Bergman will show you to one of fifteen rooms in this historic house near the Plaza. This house is distinguished by Edwardian fireplaces, antiques, stained-glass windows, and fresh flowers. Full continental breakfast, fresh-squeezed juices. $$$*

Pueblo Bonito
138 W. Manhattan Street, (505) 984–8001

In an old estate with stables, Amy and Herb Behm's secluded adobe compound has eighteen "Southwest" rooms with corner (kiva) fireplaces, private baths, and TVs. A continental breakfast is served in a sunny dining room or on the patio. The twelve rooms and six suites, each named after an Indian Pueblo, have a kitchen, a bedroom, and a living room. $$$*

Territorial Inn
215 Washington Street, (505) 989–7737

This inn has ten rooms, some with fireplaces and private baths (except two rooms that share) in an 100-year-old house. Your innkeeper, Lela McFerrin, can assist you in any arrangements for various activities. There is a gazebo and an enclosed hot tub in the garden, cable TV, and laundry service. One block from the Plaza. $$$*

Water Street Inn
427 W. Water Street, (505) 984–1193

Getgood and Franklin have Southwestern and antique furniture in their restored adobe next to Vanessie's Restaurant. There are eleven guestrooms, private baths, and cable TV. A continental breakfast on a tray is served in your room and happy-hour wine and hors d'ouevres in the living room. Some rooms have fireplaces. Laundry facilities, homemade cookies, turn-down service, and a hot-tub are provided. $$$*

The Airborne Community

New Mexican Airborne Facts

"Pollen flies too!"
—**David Old,** Santa Fe Helicopter, (505) 983–8454

Twenty percent of New Mexicans suffer during the annual
allergy season. The local culprits are sagebrush, juniper, and
various weeds. Many New Mexicans plan their vacation cruises
during the allergy season which kicks off during the early spring.

America's first Air Force One,
a Lockheed Constellation used by President Eisenhower,
is at the Santa Fe Municipal Airport.

Ballooning
Big and Little

Hot-air ballooning in Santa Fe can be dangerous because of the mountains, the high altitude (7,000 feet), and the strong winds. The neighboring city of Albuquerque, however, is two thousand feet lower than Santa Fe and has the ideal mixture of balloon weather in October—clear days with cool temperatures and variable winds under ten m.p.h. The "Albuquerque Box effect" allows pilots to fly up and down with more precision. This unique combination of mountain formations and wind characteristics makes Albuquerque the undisputed ballooning capital of the world.

The Kodak International Balloon Fiesta
(505) 821–1000

This annual nine-day event, starting the first weekend in October, is the largest gathering of hot air balloons and the most photographed annual event in the world. The spectacular "mass ascension" held both weekends from 7:30–9 A.M. is the ultimate experience whether you are on the ground or in the air.

Balloon World
2127 Calle Tecolote
Santa Fe, (505) 988–1443

Owners Cynthia and Sandra Williams deliver helium balloons or balloon bouquets to any kind of function. They decorated the Sweeney Center for New Mexico Governor Johnson's Inaugural Ball.

Bird Watching

Birdwatching is the fastest-growing leisure activity in the U.S., and Santa Fe's bird population—both resident and migratory—is as diverse and fascinating as its human population. According to Lynn Mann, owner of **Wildbirds Unlimited** (505–989-8818), there are 480 verified bird species in New Mexico.

Bosque del Apache National Wildlife Refuge
Naturalist, Daniel Perry
Near Socorro, 154 miles from Santa Fe, (505) 835–1828

This refuge was established by the U.S. Fish and Wildlife Service in 1939 to provide habitat and protection for migratory birds, with particular emphasis on the then endangered greater sandhill crane. Today it has the largest winter concentration of these birds in the world—two-thirds of the world's population.

The fourteen to sixteen whooping cranes that wintered in the Bosque were part of an experiment in 1975–1988. Scientists and wildlife officials placed "whooper" eggs in the nests of sandhill cranes, hoping to bring out a new population of whooping cranes. Unfortunately, this mixture did not work because the juvenile whooping cranes did not figure out how to find each other in the large flocks of sandhills and consequently no mating occurred.

The annual fall migration of tens of thousands of sandhill cranes and snow geese is one of the most incredible sights of nature in New Mexico. The weekend of the **Festival of the Cranes** in mid-November through mid February is the best time to see the large flock of wintering birds—the best time to view the wildlife is sunrise and sunset. The refuge offers weekend tours to the general public from November 22–February. Tours begin at 9 A.M. on Saturdays and 1 P.M. on Sundays. The refuge offers weekday tours for school groups. Call for reservations.

The Wildlife Center
P.O. Box 246
Espanola 87532
(505) 753–9505

The Wildlife Center is the nonprofit Northern New Mexico Raptor Rehabilitation and Education Center. It was opened in 1985 by Dr. Kathleen Ramsey, head veterinarian at the **Cotton Veterinarian Clinic** (505) 753–3790. The Center is housed in the same building as the Clinic. Dr. Ramsey, who heals and rehabilitates anything "feathered, furred, or slimy" is considered one of the top bird doctors in the country. She is experienced in treating birds without human imprint so they can be returned to the wild. The Wildlife Center will schedule a school program with live birds of prey.

SAY "AAH."

Falconry
Frank Bond, General Counsel for the North American Falconers Association
(505) 984–2061 and (505) 988–4476

Falconry, is a medieval sport at least a thousand years old, it is regulated by the State Department of Fish and Game and the U.S. Fish and Wildlife Service. It takes years of apprenticing and licensing before one can become a "master" falconer. It is the "ultimate form of birdwatching" because, even though birds of prey cannot be tamed, they can be conditioned to hunt with their owners. Falcons have learned that their owners will scare up game for them, making them partners in this co-dependent gaming process. There are only two "master" falconers in Santa Fe: Michael Umphrey, (505) 988–2533, and Frank Bond, listed above.

Pigeon Racing
Willie d'Alessandro, President of the Rio Grande Racing Pigeon Association
(505) 473–1311

"Pigeons are a poor man's race horse," says Willie d'Alessandro, owner of Tony's Italian Restaurant. Tony has been raising and racing pigeons since he was nine years old. In this sport, birds are bred to race around a course, sometimes 600 miles away, and then return to their homes, or "lofts," instinctively. There is a schedule of races twice a year. The young birds race in the fall for seven weekends. The old birds race in April. The birds are banded with a different color band and an identification number each year. A "driver" takes the owner's pigeons to a predesignated loft release point. For the 600-mile race they are driven to a point near San Antonio, Texas. There is a formula, yards per minute, which determines who wins the race. The birds will travel thirteen or fourteen hours, about forty or fifty miles an hour, to their home loft. Immediately when they arrive home, a rubber band is removed from their leg and put in a machine that records the time of arrival. There are twenty-two members in this club which takes in Northern New Mexico. D'Alessandro's birds live in his backyard.

Randall Davey Audubon Society
1800 Upper Canyon Road, (505) 983–4609

This old historic house and grounds was bought by Randall Davey, one of the "Cinco Pintores" artists, in 1920. He lived in this house until 1964, when he was killed in a car accident. The National Audubon Society bought the property and maintains the 135-acre grounds as an environmental education center and a wildlife refuge. The annual Audubon Christmas Bird Count, which began around 1900, uses volunteers to estimate the number of birds seen in one day. The center offers bird walks and classes for children.

Aerial Sightseeing

Southwest Safaris
Bruce Adams, (505) 988–4246 or (800) 842–4246

Bruce Adams, a knowledgeable natural historian, takes groups on air and land combination sight-seeing trips to Monument Valley, Grand Canyon, Canyon de Chelly, Mesa Verde, Arches, Chaco Canyon, and Aztec. The half day and full day tours leave from the Santa Fe Airport in a high-winged Cessna. The current cost for two people is $249 for a half day, and $349 for a full day.

Santa Fe Soaring
Frank Sage
Zia Aviation at the Santa Fe Airport, (505) 470–4571

Frank Sage of Santa Fe Soaring takes people in self-launched, motorized gliders. Once in the air, the motor is turned off and the wind currents do the rest. Aerodynamics at its best! The price is $125 for approximately an hour's trip.

Emergency Aircraft

Civil Air Patrol
(505) 471–5784

The Civil Air Patrol, a paramilitary group (an auxiliary of the U.S. Air Force), was founded in 1941. Nationwide they conduct 85 percent of all "searches" in the U.S.

The Commander of the Santa Fe squadron of 50 volunteers, runs the air-search group. They look for lost skiers, hunters, hikers, and downed aircraft. The squadron communicates with ground personnel like **St. John's Search and Rescue.** A downed aircraft's "ELT" on board sends out beeps; the air patrol picks up the signal through a satellite that circumnavigates the globe every sixty-three seconds pinpointing the exact location of the aircraft.

Helitack
Cibola National Forest, (505) 761–4650

Helitack is an emergency firefighting crew sent to inaccessible areas. A fully-equipped crew can hike into the area or be dropped into the area from a helicopter.

Smoke Jumpers
Gila National Forest, (505) 388–8350

"Smokers" are the "Navy SEALS" of firefighting. They are trained in Montana and dispatched to Silver City, New Mexico during the firefighting season. They are a "national resource" available to anyone who lives in an inaccessible area. Smokers jump from fixed-wing airplanes with all the equipment they need to put out a fire. They also carry communications systems, equipment and water for survival. Santa Feans learned about this elite group of firefighters during the famous drought and fires in 1996.

Air Ambulance Services
Air West Aviation, (505) 471–4500

Air West has an ambulance service, a charter service and an airplane rental service. They also give flying lessons, including crucial ground school.

Flight Instruction

Fantasy Fighters of Santa Fe
Larry Salganek
3662 Cerrillos Road, (505) 471–4151

This is the only dedicated training facility in the world for aerobics and "warbirds" (old military planes). The warbirds' inventory includes a T-34 (a Korean vintage warplane), a YAK -52 (a modern Soviet trainer), an L-29 (a navy trainer), a MIG-15 (a Korean warjet trainer), a Siai Marchetti (an Italian military trainer), and a jet Provost (a British jet trainer). People come to Santa Fe from all over the world to learn to fly these military planes, considered the finest collection of vintage aircraft in the country. Larry Salganek, a flight instructor since 1961, is the only pilot qualified to fly all of these planes. He taught Santa Fean Laurie Rollings to fly. She subsequently became the first civilian woman in the world to fly the MIG-29 and the SU-27 as well as the first American woman to be weightless with the Russian cosmonauts, "and also the first one not to throw up and to get a shot of vodka as a reward."

Zia Aviation
Santa Fe Municipal Airport, Airport Road, (505) 471–2700

Flight instruction from private pilot to instrument to commercial licensing. Ground school can be taken at Santa Fe Community College.

Jail Birds Escape Program

Santa Fe Penitentiary

There have been more escapes from the Santa Fe Penitentiary than almost any other prison in the U.S. (at least ten prisoners have escaped since 1987). But never fear!! They usually get recaptured, and it only shows that "the City Different" is loved by inmates, too! The most spectacular escape in U.S. prison history was on July 12, 1988, when a lovesick woman, Beverly Shoemaker, hijacked a helicopter and ordered its pilot, Charles Bella— who was handcuffed to the "joy stick"—to pick up her lover, Dan Mahoney, at the Penitentiary. The helicopter swooped down, grabbed Mahoney and two other inmates from the compound and took off, narrowly making it over the fence. They were recaptured within twenty-four hours. Later, when Bella became a suspect, his helicopter was confiscated. F. Lee Bailey, who successfully defended Bella, got the helicopter in lieu of legal fees.

Air Show

Santa Fe Air Show

Ken Mock, (505) 471–5111

The Santa Fe Air Show is one of Santa Fe's favorite family events and considered one of the major air shows in the country. The entire New Mexico airborne community—the armed forces, private pilots, and the Fantasy Fighters of Santa Fe—join in the fun!

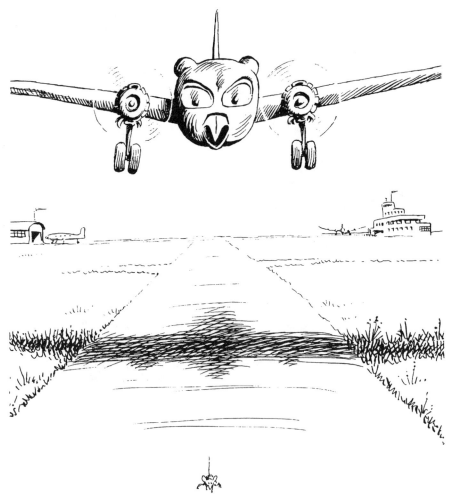

Annual Events

The Rodeo de Santa Fe

Most community-spirited

The Santa Fe Plaza, which was laid out by Don Pedro de Peralta in 1610, was and still is where most of the ceremonies important to this city's culture are staged.

Community Day in Santa Fe
Spring Event

This is an annual spring event held on the Plaza with continuous music, exhibits, and activities all day. Patti Bushee, its perpetrator, conceived the event to bring the Santa Fe community together.

A steady stream of performers appear free-of-charge at the all-volunteer, city-sponsored event. From the National Dance Institute to belly dancers, flamenco dancers to Eddy Swimmer, the world renowned Indian hoop dancer, everyone comes for the fun.

Earth Day
Spring Event

Earth Day, held the end of April, is the best time for environmental groups to air their ecological values in public. Some attendees dress up as your favorite species. One year at the *All Species Day Event* a man was shot out of a cannon. He disappeared into the sky in a puff of smoke, then parachuted right to the center of the stage at Marcy Park to protest the state of the sky. It has been one of the most amusing annual events put on in Santa Fe. Unfortunately, since the organizer of the event, Chris Wells, moved away the event has lacked solid community organization.

Fiesta de los Luminarias
Christmas Eve

A Santa Fe Christmas has many tri-cultural (Hispanic, Indian, and Anglo) events that can make you feel you are in a foreign country. In Santa Fe, Christmas is celebrated the same way it was one hundred years ago under Spanish rule—not a planned tourist event but a local tradition. On Christmas eve *farolitos* (brown paper

29

bags, each with sand and a candle stuck in it) decorate the roof edges of each house along the Christmas-stroll route on the historic east side. At sunset the candles are lit. In the old days, *farolitos* and *luminarias* (small bonfires) had a religious significance because they were thought to light the way for the Virgin Mary. In 1938, artist Will Shuster revived the ancient tradition of lighting the *farolitos*. It's the biggest and most beautiful event of the year on the east side. It brings people together, it's spiritual, and it's fun for people to be with their families and friends on that night. People keep warm at various *luminarias* along the route and visit friends along the way.

Fiestas de Santa Fe

Amalia Sanchez, who was 105 years old on December 8, 1997, was the first Santa Fe Fiesta Queen crowned in 1927.

Started in 1712, the Fiesta de Santa Fe is the oldest community celebration in the country. It commemorates Don Diego de Vargas' "reconquest" of Santa Fe from the Indians who had ousted the Spanish in the Pueblo Revolt of 1680. The so-called reconquest is a misnomer. The Spanish retook Santa Fe with no resistance.

Fiesta-related activities begin in May when the Fiesta Council puts on a competition for the Santa Fe Fiesta Queen and for the role of Don Diego de Vargas. These are very prestigious positions steeped in Santa Fe history. In June, the Fiesta Council carries the statue of "La Conquistadora," the sixteenth-century madonna credited with the military success of the Spanish conquerers, in a procession from her permanent home in St. Francis Cathedral to Rosario Chapel. The first night of Fiesta weekend in September begins with the annual burning of Zozobra, a sixty-foot-tall effigy who represents Old Man Gloom. The original Zozobra was designed by famed "Cinco Pintores" artist Will Schuster in 1926, along with Jacques Cartier, the creator of the fire-dancer. "Shus" awarded Zozobra to the Downtown Kiwanis Club in 1964. The Kiwanis sponsor the Fiesta event at Marcy Park and use the proceeds for scholarships. In 1969, the year Schuster died, Jacques Cartier danced his last firedance and Chip Lilienthal took over his role. Everyone, tourists and residents alike, get caught up in the excitement of the fire-dancers and the moaning and groaning of Zozobra. Go early with friends and a picnic dinner so that you will be primed when the event starts. When Zozobra is set on fire with a torch, there is mass hysteria and everyone chants "Burn him! Burn him!" Then your problems for the year are supposed to be purged. One year there was lightning and thunder, groaning and chanting all at the same time—scary, but thrilling! After the burning there is a mass exodus to the Plaza where street dancing continues until the early morning. **The Boo and Hiss Show** and the **Hysterical Parade** with Jay Miller and friends pokes fun at Santa Fe and its "City Different" foibles. **The Children's Annual Pet Parade** is a very popular event on Saturday morning. This is the chance for children (and adults) to be creative and to dress up their animals for the most bizarre pet parade in the country.

Fourth of July Pancake Breakfast
On the Plaza on the Fourth of July

The very popular mass feeding event, from seven a.m. to noon is sponsored by "Los Compadres," ambassadors for the Santa Fe Chamber of Commerce. Volunteers ("floaters, dippers, and runners") flip pancakes, pour orange juice, and help with the labor. Everyone in town shows up for this community event which raises money for United Way and Partners in Education. You get a good breakfast for $5, you see a lively crowd, and local bands play on the platform. **The Vintage Car Club** takes this opportunity to show off their old restored cars.

Girls, Inc.
On the Plaza in August, (505) 982–2042

This popular juried arts and crafts show held the first week in August just had its twenty-fifth annual show in 1997. Vendors from all over the U.S. may apply for the 234 spaces available in pottery, sculpture, jewelry, painting and photography. One-third of the proceeds from this show go to Girls, Inc., which offers programs for girls 6–12 years old. Girls, Inc., established in 1957, is a national program for girls from low-to-middle-income families. Their summer school is popular. Tuition is based on income

Mountain Man Rendezvous
Palace of the Governors

"Mountain Men" come to town in August for the Museum of New Mexico's annual buffalo roast. The rendezvous is known for its *Rocky Mountain oysters* (sliced, breaded, and fried bulls' testicles!) and *bourbon hailstorms* (a mountain man mint julep). Costumed mountain men ride into town on horseback in full regalia. The three-day event commemorates the early trappers (Kit Carson was one of them) who in the early 1800s traveled the West on horseback looking for beaver pelts.

Pelts sold in Santa Fe and Taos were transported to St. Louis, the center of the beaver pelt market. The trappers represented a broad cross section of men from every walk of life. They were brave, adventurous, and had a fierce freedom of spirit that was necessary for those who faced the constant challenges of the new Western frontier. The buffalo roast is held at the Palace Hotel where trappers once renewed their trapping licenses. Events include a trade fair which features all the "manly" things mountain men did in the early 1800's—trapping, black powder shooting, and tomahawk throwing. The buffalo roast raises money for the endowment for the Palace of the Governors.

The Rodeo de Santa Fe Parade
(505) 471–4300

The parade on the Plaza in July marks the beginning of the annual four-day rodeo at the rodeo grounds. The big parade passes through the historic downtown with "El Toro," a white fiberglass bull designed by Will Schuster. All the participants of the rodeo announce the arrival of the Rodeo de Santa Fe. For more information about being in the rodeo parade, call Joe Ortiz at (505) 983–7701.

The Rodeo de Santa Fe, the oldest, and most skilled professional rodeo in New Mexico, features many of the most expert riders in the world. Bull riding is one of the most popular events because it is the ultimate ego trip—man against beast. When a cowboy is thrown, bullfighters are on hand to protect the cowboy. In 1999, the rodeo will celebrate its fiftieth anniversary. A rodeo's size is judged by how much prize money it offers. Santa Fe ranks in the top ten percent of 800 rodeos in the country. All entrants must be members of the Professional Rodeo Cowboy Association (PRCA).

One of the reasons people come to Santa Fe is to get a feeling of the old West. **Western Days** is a week-long Southwestern cultural event held in conjunction with Rodeo de Santa Fe Association. Organizers of the event are Robert Stovall and Rosanne Gain. Activities and social events focusing on the West will take place throughout the city. El Rancho de las Golondrinas, a history museum, offers talks, reenactments, and cowboy demonstrations. The Santa Fe Southern Railroad operates special trains from Santa Fe to Lamy. Remember that there is always the risk of a holdup on a Western train!

WestMUTTster Dog Show
Santa Fe Animal and Humane Society, (505) 983–4309

Anyone who attended the First Annual WestMUTTster Show (for shelter dogs only!) held in June know that it's the most popular social event for dogs and people in Santa Fe. The competition is fierce. Ford Ruthling's dog, Mollie, was bitten while trying to compete in the "Most Beautiful" event. Mollie had to be taken to the hospital, and the biting dog was disqualified. Nancy Dickenson's dog, the only three-legged dog in the event, won the "Most Urine" contest. The "Old Dog New Trick" category was won by Dawn Douglas who taught her dog to yodel.

Annual Film Festivals

Margaret Mead Traveling Film and Video Festival
Santa Fe Community College, 1600 Richards Avenue, (505) 438–1668

The largest cultural documentary film festival in the country presents a variety of documentary and ethnographic works by anthropologists and independent filmmakers. Sixteen films, which range from eight to eighty-eight minutes, will be presented, and are followed by a discussion at the conclusion of each session.

Native Americas International Film Exposition
Director, Virginia Manion
P.O. Box 5034, Santa Fe 87502 (505) 983–5220

An annual film festival in October which includes Native American filmmakers from the entire Western Hemisphere. Prominent producers, writers, and directors present workshops. The film exposition is sponsored by the Southwestern Association for Indian Arts (SAIA).

Taos Talking Film Festival
Director, Josh Bryant
126M North Pueblo Road #216, Taos, NM 87571 (505) 751–0637

The Taos Talking Film Festival, held in Taos at the end of April, is one of the most important networking events for independent movie producers, directors, and screenwriters. The festival has seminars, panels, and tributes to major motion picture stars. It presents a most unusual contest that boosts entries in the event: the Special Innovation Award for the most innovative feature film of the year. In 1996, Gary Walkow, the director of *Notes from Underground,* won the First Annual Award and received five acres of local land as the prize.

Shows & Auctions

Santa Fe has annual shows and sales that attract dealers and tourists from all over the country. For more information call the Sweeney Convention Center (505) 986–6901.

Alterman & Morris Art Auction
225 Canyon Road, (505) 983–1590
Held in November

This is one of two very popular auctions that take place the same weekend in November: the Alterman & Morris Auction and the Gerald Peters Auction. Alterman & Morris hosts a private cocktail party the night before for participating artists and collectors. It's the best annual opportunity to buy paintings by the Taos Artists and Cinco Pintores as well as other well-known artists. The location is announced in the catalogue.

Antique Indian, Tribal and Folk Art
M.C.M. Produtions, Kim Martindale
38 W. Main St., Ventura, CA, (805) 652–1960

Kim Martindale presents a series of shows: the Winter Antiquities show at the end of December; then the Antique American Indian Show; the Tribal Antique Show; and an Antique Folk Art Show from the end of June through July 6.

ART Santa Fe
Megan Fox, (505) 989–9141

National and international galleries display contemporary art for sale in local hotel rooms. In 1997, ART Santa Fe was held at the Hotel Santa Fe. The fair is held in conjuction with the Second SITE Santa Fe Biennial. Exhibitors pay $1,000 for participation and advertising fees in addition to the cost of their hotel room.

Bead Expo
Recursos de Santa Fe
826 Camino de Monte Rey, (505) 982–9301

The annual five-day bead event held in March is one of the largest bead bazaars in the country. This show has everything from rare Venetian beads to Tibetan turquoise, old amber, contemporary hand-blown glass beads, Zuni fetishes, antique netsuke, and ojime. About 6,000 people come to Santa Fe learn all about beads at the symposiums and workshops held in hotels all over town. In addition, one hundred and thirty vendors sell their beads from all over the world. The director of the Center for Bead Research coordinates the expo with Recursos' Giesela Happe.

Channing's Annual Indian Market Summer Auction
53 Old Santa Fe Trail, (505) 988–1078

William Channing has an annual sale and auction at the Eldorado Hotel before Indian Market in August. It is oriented toward Navajo and Pueblo silver jewelry and Navajo blankets. Sometimes a portion of the proceeds goes to **Wings of America,** an organization that encourages American Indian youth to become involved in cross-country running competitions. In 1991, Channing auctioned off the contents of Greer Garson's Forked Lightning Ranch.

Contemporary Hispanic Market
Santa Fe Council for the Arts, 806 Faldas de la Sierra, (505) 988–1878

At the Plaza, on Lincoln Avenue, during Spanish Market in July. Exhibitors must show proof that they are at least one-fourth Hispanic and residents of New Mexico. The market has incredible silver and jewelry.

The Santa Fe Doll Art Show
Jean Riley
La Fonda, on the Plaza, (505) 820–0992

This annual international show and exhibition of one-of-a-kind dolls attracts people from all over the country. Jean Wiley, the American representative, and Peter Coe, the international coordinator, also present a weekend symposium on dollmaking with master class workshops throughout the weekend. The Edith Lambert Gallery has their very popular annual doll show in conjunction with the Doll Art Show.

Eight Northern Pueblo Artists and Craftsmen Show
8 Northern Indian Pueblo Council and Art & Craft Show
(505) 852–4265 or (800) 793–4955

The largest local Native American craft show is a consortium of the eight pueblo tribes north of Santa Fe. They decide each year where the event will be held. It is the largest Indian-owned and-operated juried show, held the third weekend in July, of more than 1,200 artists in the United States. San Ildefonso Pueblo is the home of the famous potter Maria Martinez whose reputation as a great artist originally contributed to the art show's drawing power. Many collectors enjoy this show more than Indian Market. Go early on the first day to avoid crowds and have a tamale for breakfast at the Pueblo.

Whitehawk August Show
Sherry Maxwell and Nikki Rivera
P. O. Box 1272, Santa Fe, NM 87504, (505) 992–8929

This series of August shows—The Old West and Country Show, the Antique Ethnographic Art Show, and the Antique Indian Art Show, are very popular. Held just before Indian Market in August, the Antique Indian Art Show is one of the largest and longest-running shows in Santa Fe.

Furniture Expo
John and Deborah Oliver
(800) 299–9886

Furnituremakers from New Mexico show their Santa Fe-style furniture in June.

Indian Market
Southwestern Association for Indian Art, (505) 983–5220

Started in 1922, and held in August, Indian Market is the largest and finest Indian market in the world. Each of the American Indian tribes is invited to participate. Since Indian Market is a juried art show, it is also the best in terms of quality and diversity. In order to enter, exhibitors must be of Indian ancestry and must submit their wares to a panel in order to insure that it meets the high standards set for the market. Membership in the Southwestern Association on Indian Affairs is international and open to all who have an interest in preserving Native American culture through its arts and crafts. The judging and preview takes place on Friday night and Saturday. Indian artists who have shown at Indian Market for at least five years and have won awards can exhibit in the "Master Artists" show.

Plaza Arts and Crafts Show
Challenge, New Mexico, (505) 988–7621

"One of the top 200 shows in the U. S."—**Sunshine Artist Magazine**

This is a juried annual fund-raiser art show in June that benefits Challenge, New Mexico and provides services for the disabled. Local and out-of-town applicants must apply for the maximum of 235 spaces that are available. The show includes all crafts, painting, jewelry, sculpture, photography, and clothing.

Santa Fe Art Auction Limited Company
Organized by Gerald Peters Gallery
P.O. Box 2437, Santa Fe, NM 87504, (505) 988–5049

This very popular art auction sponsored by the Gerald Peters Gallery takes place the same weekend in November as the Alterman & Morris auction. The preview is held at the Gerald Peters Gallery the night before the auction. This is a great time for art collectors to pick up some really fine Western American art like Remingtons, Russells, W. Curtis photographs, or works of the "Taos School of Artists" and the "Santa Fe School." This is the Southwest's largest auction of classic Western American art and is very popular with dealers.

Spanish Market
The Spanish Colonial Arts Society
239 1/2 Johnson Street, (505) 983–4038

Spanish New Mexico: Spanish Colonial Arts Society Collection, a two-volume book, highlights the society's spectacular Spanish colonial art collection. It has been called "a museum on paper." Spanish Market is the largest annual collection of Spanish colonial religious art in the world. The three-day event on the Plaza, held the end of July, is dedicated to preserving the art forms developed during the state's Spanish colonial era. Exhibitors must be native New Mexicans. There is music and dancing and many booths of food. Enjoy the pageantry on the grandstand, shop and eat, and look at the hundreds of traditional Spanish artists and exhibitors. **Winter Market**, held the first full weekend in December in the

La Fonda Hotel, is the best place to get traditional New Mexican Christmas gifts. There is a full weekend of performances by local artists. The vividly costumed *matachines* dance on the Plaza. They wear fez-like head dresses and decorated pillow cases on their legs. This is perhaps the only ceremonial dance performed by both Hispanic and Native Americans.

Martha Struever's Annual Pottery Exhibition
P. O. Box 2203, Santa Fe, 87504, (505) 983–9515

The annual show and sale during Indian Market weekend held at the Hotel Plaza Real is a major exhibition of some of the most renowned Pueblo potters of the twentieth century. Martha, a specialist in American Indian art for more than twenty-one years, also leads very interesting travel study seminars on Native American Art of the Southwest.

The Wheelwright Museum Indian Auction
704 Camino Lejo, (505) 982–4636

This is the largest fund-raiser for the private, not-for-profit Wheelwright Museum, which brings quality exhibits and events to the public free of charge. The auction takes place on the Friday before Indian Market in August.

ARTISTS

San Ildefonso Pueblo

Architecture

CAMINA DEL MONTE SOL — SANTA FE.

Odon Hullencramer, Will Schuster, and Oliver La Farge

Santa Fe Style

"Whoever designed this town did so while riding on a jackass, backwards and drunk."
—**Will Rogers** on his first visit to Santa Fe.

The "Santa Fe Style" of architecture has its origins in the indigenous Pueblo dwellings. When the Spanish arrived they found Indian settlements of "puddled" adobe, or adobe mortared stone work. The Spanish introduced the concept of a sun-dried mud brick as a building material.

In 1821 the Santa Fe Trail opened trade with the East supplementing the long route to Mexico City over the Camino Real. With the arrival of easterners new technologies came into use. Kilns to fire brick and saw mills to cut finished lumber were built. Greek Revival style, popular in the East, was locally expressed as "Territorial" style with fired brick cornices and pedimented window frames.

The arrival of the railroad in 1880 provided quick access to a wide variety of materials and architectural styles, so by the time New Mexico became a state in 1912, Santa Fe was rapidly taking on the appearance of other towns across the West.

Edgar Lee Hewett, founder of the School of American Archeology, was intstrumental in developing in 1912 the city's first general plan. Its focus was to boost the local economy by promoting the unique indigenous architecture to tourists who came to enjoy the romance and history of the area. This preservation movement was encouraged by a group of archeologists, artists, and writers that included Jesse Nusbaum, Carlos Vierra, and Sylvanus Morley, among others.

Carlos Vierra House

Carlos Vierra came to New Mexico in 1904. By 1912 he was a staff member of both the Museum of New Mexico and the School of American Archeology and became involved with the restoration of the Palace of the Governors under the supervision of archeologist Jesse Nusbaum. This project launched the revival of Spanish-Pueblo architectural style in Santa Fe. In 1918 he bought a plot for $1 and began construction of a large two-story adobe home. Its design demonstrated his zeal for the integrity of the Pueblo and Spanish colonial architecture. The house, on Coronado and Old Pecos Trail, is now owned by Julius and Gladys Heldman. He also built the house on the corner of Canyon and Delgado—the oldest part of which was built in the early 1900s. 304 Delgado is one of the most photographed houses in Santa Fe because the softly contoured lines of adobe go around its corner and its rickety gateway door embodies chic, authentic Santa Fe style.

"New Mexico adobe architecture looks like melted chocolate ice cream."—**Henriette Wyeth**

The "Five Nuts in Adobe Huts"
Camino del Monte Sol

The "Cinco Pintores" (Five Painters) came from the east and worked cooperatively in their art and real estate projects. Freemont Ellis, Will Schuster, Josef Bakos, Walter Mruk, and Willard Nash bought adjacent parcels of land on Camino del Monte Sol —then called Telephone Hill because the town's only phone line was there. Together they built adobe houses adjacent to each other. Their walls kept tumbling down until they learned to perfect their building techniques. These artists' homes on Camino del Monte Sol are a unique grouping of Pueblo Revival buildings in a neighborhood of mostly owner-built Revival homes. Their closeness to Canyon Road influenced the conversion of Canyon Road from a purely residential street to a thoroughfare lined with studios and galleries.

The Oldest Church
Chapel of San Miguel
At Old Santa Fe Trail and DeVargas Streets

The Chapel of San Miguel is the oldest church in Santa Fe. Originally built in 1626 for the laborers that the Spanish leaders brought with them, it was damaged during the Pueblo Revolt of 1680 and rebuilt in 1710. In 1859 Archbishop Lamy and the Christian Brothers bought the chapel and it became St. Michael's College.

John Gaw Meem Designed It
Cristo Rey Catholic Church
Upper Canyon Road

One of the most important landmarks in Santa Fe and probably the largest adobe church in America, Cristo Rey exemplifies New Mission architecture. Renowned architect John Gaw Meem was commissioned to design the church to commemorate the 400th anniversary of Coronado's 1540 explorations. Cristo Rey Catholic Church was dedicated on June 27, 1940. The large carved stone altar screen commissioned in 1760 is the most famous Spanish work of colonial ecclesiastical art in New Mexico and was brought from "La Castrense," the old chapel on the Plaza, prior to the chapel's demolition. The altar screen is recognized in the *National Register of Historic Places.*

The Santuario de Guadalupe
The Guadalupe Historic Foundation
100 Guadalupe Street

The Sanctuatio de Guadalupe is a world-famous landmark in Santa Fe and the oldest church still standing in the United States dedicated to Our Lady of Guadalupe. It stands at the terminus of the Camino Real, or the Guadalupe Trail. The exact date the church was built is unknown but its *licensia* was granted in 1795. The Guadalupe Historic Foundation was founded in 1975 to organize the much-needed renovation that took place in 1989.

The Oldest Continuously used Public Building
Palace of the Governors
100 Palace Avenue, (505) 827–6483

Territorial Governor Lew Wallace wrote most of Ben Hur *there during his term from 1878 to 1881.*

The Palace of the Governors, built by Governor Pedro de Peralta in 1610, is the oldest continuously used public building in the United States. It has been the seat of government under Spain, Mexico, the Confederacy, and the Territorial U.S.

"There was a passageway from our basement to the Palace of the Governors."—First Chief Engineer of La Fonda and Sam Ballen, Owner of the La Fonda

A Pioneer in Passive Solar Design
William Lumpkin

Bill Lumpkin popularized contemporary Territorial architecture with solar architecture. A transcendental artist whose group started in the 1930s to show their art, Lumpkins decided to become an architect when as an artist "he learned to like to eat." Bill has a great sense of humor and is a Renaissance man. "I paint just about every day. I never have a plan. I work as a Buddhist, with an empty mind, and see what happens." He is a popular Santa Fe artist who knew everyone in the Santa Fe Art Colony, including the Cinco Pintores. Examples of his architectural work are Rancho Encantado, parts of the La Fonda and the Inn at Loretto.

Archbishop Lamy's Crowning Achievement
St. Francis Cathedral
North of La Fonda Hotel

"We at La Fonda paid for exterior lighting of St. Francis Cathedral so that when Fray Angelico Chávez was asked what kind of lights they were, he answered Israel-lites."—**Sam Ballen,** Owner of La Fonda Hotel.

Built in 1869 and designed in the French Romanesque style, this is one of Santa Fe's greatest landmarks. It was built from stone from local quarries. Portions of the original church, La Parroquia, houses La Conquistadora, the sacred statue of the Virgin Mary first brought here in 1625 to symbolize the conquest of New Mexico by the Spanish.

The Miraculous Staircase & the Disappearing Carpenter
Loretto Chapel
219 Old Santa Fe Trail

Loretto Chapel was designed to serve the spiritual needs of nuns Archbishop Lamy brought to New Mexico. When the chapel was completed, there was no way for the nuns to ascend to the choir loft. A carpenter appeared and built a stairway without nails or support, hence the name "miraculous staircase;" then he disappeared without getting paid.

Sena Plaza

This historically important plaza, whose buildings are now dominated by shops and two restaurants, was part of a parcel granted in the late-seventeenth century to Captain Arias de Quiros by General Diego de Vargas. It eventually passed to Don José D. Sena, who married Isabel Cabeza de Baca, and they amplified the building into a thirty-three room hacienda. In the late-nineteeth century, the second-floor ballroom housed the New Mexican legislative asssembly.

Commemorates the Link between Spain and Santa Fe
Executive Secretary, Bill Friedman
The Scottish Rite Temple (at Paseo de Peralto and Bishops Lodge)

This pink landmark must be Santa Fe's best-kept secret: nobody understands what it is. It was built in 1911 as a meeting place for the ancient fraternal order, the Masons, whose membership of 4,000 gathers in Santa Fe for two annual reunions that last for three days. A mural on the wall depicts January 2, 1492 when Queen Isabella expelled the Moors from Spain. During the preceeding ten-year siege on the Alhambra, the catholic Kings built a town called Santa Fe. Coincidently, this was the same year Isabella commissioned Christopher Columbus to sail to the New World. So, the Masons chose Moorish architecture to commemorate Santa Fe's link with Spain. The Viceroy under King Ferdinand III decreed in 1610 that the Plaza be modeled to resemble Santa Fe Granada. Today Santa Fe in Granada is our sister city.

Five Tiffany chandeliers, each weighing 1,500 pounds, dazzle the dining room. The auditorium seats 404 people, and recitals take place on the 80-foot stage whose ceiling holds 97 drops that can create thirty-seven different scenes within in minutes!

A Territorial House with Faux Brick Exterior
Pinckney R. Tully House
136 Griffin Street

Built in 1851, the house has mortar and brick painted on its plaster to simulate the brick exteriors popular elsewhere.

Preservation

"You must improve your lands and develop and make the most of the resources that your location affords you, and get rid of your burros and goats. I hope ten years hence there won't be an adobe house in the Territory. I want to see you learn to make them of brick, with slanting roofs. Yankees don't like flat roofs, nor roofs of dirt."—**General William Tecumseh Sherman**, *Santa Fe Daily Democrat*, October 29, 1880.

First Historic Ordinance

In 1957 Oliver LaFarge and Irene Von Horvath wrote and enacted the first historic ordinance that recognized and regulated the Santa Fe style of architecture.

Historic Design Review Board
Planning and Land Use Dept. in City Hall
Box 909, (505) 984–6657

In 1992 the city added preservation standards to the design review ordinance because so many historic buildings were being lost. Now in addition to the design restrictions, the city categorized each building in the historic district and recognized their status as "significant, contributing, and or noncontributing." The "H-Board" meets twice a month. For information about design review applications or a copy of the city ordinance, call the Planning and Land Use Department in City Hall.

The Historic Santa Fe Foundation
545 Canyon Road in El Zaguan, Unit 2, (505) 983–2567

The foundation was formed in 1961 to receive tax-exempt donations for historic preservation. The foundation conducts research to identify buildings worthy of preservation and engages in other activities to preserve and maintain historic landmarks and structures in Santa Fe and its surrounding areas. The foundation has plaqued over fifty buildings, four of which it owns. This organization publishes *Old Santa Fe Today* and the *Bulletin*.

The National Park Service, Department of the Interior
Southwest Regional Office
1100 Old Santa Fe Trail, (505) 988–6004

The National Park Service sets standards for all aspects of preservation from research and documentation to repair work. They publish the *National Register of Historic Places* as well as regular reports. Built in 1933, it is America's largest-known adobe office building and one of the best examples of Spanish Pueblo Revival architecture. It was placed on the *National Register of Historic Places* and is a National Historic Landmark.

Old Santa Fe Association
922 Canyon Road, (505) 988–1059

This group was founded in 1926 out of concern for the future of Santa Fe. It is the only organization with a permanent member on the City of Santa Fe's Historic Design Review Board. The association has given awards for restoration and remodeling judged to be faithful to the city's architectural heritage.

1766–68—The "Oldest House"
215 East de Vargas Street

Tree ring specimens date the vigas as being cut about 1740–67, and a structure is shown on the Urriuta map of 1766–68. Archbishop Lamy sold this, the Chapel of San Miguel, and some property in 1881 to the Brothers of Christian Schools. It once had two stories but the poorly preserved second one was removed in 1902 and around 1926 a new second story was added. The western part of the building is typical of early crude buildings: low-ceilinged with a dirt floor and thick adobe walls.

1768—Juan Jose Prada House
519 Canyon Road

Maps dating from 1768 show the house, and the first owner of record was Juan Jose Prada. It had two sections joined by a corridor. Prada deeded the west section to Altagracia Arranaga in 1869, and his widow deeded the east part to her son-in-law, Miguel Gorman. These deeds stated that the front door of the corridor be left open to allow access to a dance hall in the rear and that the well in the front (still standing) be available for use by both sections. In 1927 Mrs. Margaretta S. Dietrich bought the east wing, added some rooms, and updated the interior. Then she acquired the western end and joined the two but without the "connecting corridor." This is now the residence of Santa Fe art collectors Nedra and Richard Matteucci.

Architectural Glossary

acequia–irrigation ditch

adobe–mud brick dried in the sun and used to build houses

alameda–a road

arroyo–a riverbed

banco–an adobe bench covered with plaster

canale–a roof spout that carries water off a flat roof

corbel–a decorated angle support for a beam

horno–an adobe outside oven still used at the pueblos

kiva–round religious chamber found in Indian pueblos

latillas–small branches laid on top of vigas

lintel–wooden beam over window or door

nicho–a small shelf or nicho carved into a wall

portal–porch or portico attached to a home

vigas–round logs used as beams in the ceiling

Body
Enhancements

Fitness Centers

Santa Fe was known in the old days as a center for wellness. Northern New Mexico is known for the healing, dry air of the Sangre de Cristo mountains. Some of the early artists arrived, some on stretchers, at Sun Mount Sanitorium in Santa Fe hoping to get relief from debilitating respiratory illnesses. Many of these artists then stayed and developed their art and became important artists.

Carl and Sandra's Physical Conditioning Center
510 Montezuma, (505) 982–6760

Carl Miller, a former U.S. Olympic weightlifting coach, and his wife, Sandra Thomas, run one of the best individualized weight-training centers in Santa Fe.

Club at El Gancho
Old Las Vegas Highway, (505) 988–5000

El Gancho is a complete indoor, outdoor tennis, swimming and racquetball facility, with a health club.

Club International Family Fitness Center
1931 Warner Avenue, (505) 473–9807

This health club has racquetball, Nautilus, weightlifting, a pool, a basketball court, a tanning booth, massage, a nursery, and a punching bag.

Fort Marcy Recreation Center
490 Washington Street, (505) 984–6725

Fort Marcy is a city facility with a YMCA flavor. It has a one-half mile jogging trail, a baseball field, and a very popular indoor lap pool.

Momentum
Shelly Geyer and Sue Perley
1807 Second Street #28, (505) 982–8000

Santa Fe is the official training base for teachers of the Pilates' Method. The Pilates' workout develops strength, flexibility, and endurance through a series of stretching exercises that improves posture and body alignment and gives a lean look.

Quail Run
3101 Old Pecos Trail, (505) 986–2222

Quail Run is the most expensive and the most luxurious of all the health clubs—except Las Campanas where the requirement for membership is to buy a $200,000 lot. It has a country club feeling with golf, indoor pool, weight room, aerobics room, and a friendly atmosphere.

Santa Fe Gold
708 W. San Mateo Street, (505) 988–2986

This is a serious body-building place with no frills and no social atmosphere.

Santa Fe Spa
786 N. St. Francis Drive, (505) 984–8727

Santa Fe Spa is a full-service facility that offers yoga, free weights, Nautilus, a 40-foot indoor pool and classes. Ask about their one-year membership, paid in advance, which includes all the facilities and the attention of a personal trainer seven days a week. In 1997, the price was $399.

Studio East
332 Camino del Monte Sol Road, (505) 988–3597

Studio East, formerly Gotta Dance, is the only dance studio in Santa Fe that crosses over and becomes a fitness center. They have a very popular after-school dance program for children and an adult day-time aerobic dance workout. In addition, they have yoga, weighted workouts, and the very popular Argentine tango on Sundays. New owners are Carlos Requejo and Frank Dangelo.

Spas

Ojo Caliente Mineral Springs
Located I hour away on U.S. 2, (505) 583–2233

A resort since 1860, Ojo Caliente is well known for their therapeutic mineral springs. You can soak in the geothermal waters and drink the mineral waters which supposedly have curative powers. The springs, with temperatures of 90 to 122 Fahrenheit, have been frequented for thousands of years. One of the oldest health resorts in North America, it was considered a sacred spot by the Indians who once lived there.

Ten Thousand Waves Health Spa
Ski Basin Road, (505) 982–9304

This spa offers public and private hot tubs, massage, shiatsu, rolfing, aromatherapy, and other exotic treatments by appointment in a beautiful setting with a Japanese feeling. They also offer "watsu," a water massage very popular with the skiing set. "The best place to blow off steam when your computer system crashes," says the *Santa Fe Sun.* Lodging is offered in seven nearby guest suites called Houses of the Moon.

Beauty Treatments

"All experience gained elsewhere fails in New Mexico."
—Governor Lew Wallace

Despite Santa Fe's reputation as a wellness center, the intense ultraviolet light at this elevation and the lack of moisture in the air conspire to make you look like a prune. People who live here have to make a conscious effort to drink lots of water and use lots of moisturizers. Site-specific places to go for help are as follows:

Aesthetics Skin Care Salon
Jill Jenkins, 489 Camino Don Miguel Street, (505) 982–5883.

The best pedicures, manicures, and facials are done by Jill, a talented woman who wears many hats. Jill participates in a white-water rafting company and has a talent agency, and she places principal actors and actresses in films, commercials and television in co-star or guest-star roles. Amazingly enough, she wears all three hats beautifully!

Concepts
Sanbusco Market Center, 500 Montezuma, Suite 110, (505) 988–3840

"Mommy?" No, the word's Egyptian—it's "mummy" in this luxurious full-service salon that even provides detoxifying body wraps. Make-up lessons, treatment series, and days of indugence are available.

Sterling Silver Beauty Institute
402 Don Gaspar Street, (505) 984–3223

The institute started in 1986. It focuses on skin care. They offer facials, cosmetic peels, massage therapy, aromatherapy, cellulite treatments, waxing and eyelash and brow treatment. Director Marian Urban, a skin expert, is a hydrotherapist who uses water to accentuate health and beauty practices.

Cafe Society

The Downtown Subscription

The Most Popular (with limited food)

Remember the Beatnik era? Well, guess what, it's back—or at least the coffee shops are. It's more complicated now because instead of plain coffee it's designer coffee. Going to a favorite Santa Fe coffee shop is a very important daily routine for Santa Feans. People go to coffee shops to smoke, hangout, people watch, read, flirt, and talk. Coffee houses are a good place to go to have a cheap date, see art, hear music, and enjoy poetry readings.

Aztec Street Cafe
317 Aztec Street, (505) 983–9464

This is a wonderful all-day meeting place for the younger idle rich and poor intellectuals. Here they play chess, smoke cigarettes, and eat healthy foods until 9 P.M.

Off the Wall
616 Canyon Road, (505) 988–5323

Coffee and baked goods lure you in to see (and perhaps to stay) the wonderful contemporary crafts and ceramics. Off the Wall has outdoor seating (no indoor seating) in a sculpture garden.

Downtown Subscription
376 Garcia Street, (505) 983–3085

This is the largest magazine store in town and one of the most delightful indoor people-watching places. They have readings by various authors. They have a hold list for *The New York Times,* which is available every day. When the weather is warm, the patio is always full.

French Pastry Shop
La Fonda Hotel,100 E. San Francisco Street, (505) 983–6697

This is a popular coffee house that serves French pastries at the La Fonda Hotel, the oldest hotel in town. Though the food and service are very good, locals tend to go to places with easier access to parking.

Galisteo Corner Cafe
Water and Galisteo Streets, (505) 984–1316

The Galisteo Corner Cafe is a local downtown hangout that has some magazines and numerous out-of-town newspapers. Space is limited, but they serve a terrific continental breakfast.

Java Joe's
2801 Rodeo Road, (505) 474–5282

A very popular coffee shop that is full all the time. Tables are set up for backgammon and chess. There is have another Java Joe's at College Plaza on Cerrillos Road.

New York Bagel Cafe
204 Montezuma, (505) 989–4300
720 St. Michael's Drive, (505) 474–5200

The cafe on Montezuma is especially popular with government and city workers.

Rocky's on Water
in the Hotel St. Francis, Water at Don Gaspar, (505) 983–5700

The only British high tea in town. Finger sandwiches, scones, and tea are served from 3:00 to 5:30 P.M.

Crafts and Artifacts

Archie Roosevelt bartering for a rug

A Navajo wearing-blanket sold for $522,500
at a Sotheby's auction in 1989.

Tribal and Indian Artifacts

The Elkhart Collection—Antique American Indian Art
Robert Ashton, 924 Paseo de Peralta Street, Suite 9, (505) 820–7211

Bob and Mark Winter acquire Navajo textiles, Pueblo pottery, pawn jewelry, and other unusual and interesting Indian items. They work with the historic Toadlena Trading Post (60 miles north of Gallup) on the Navajo reservation, and they have Two Grey Hills textile museums there. Bob and Mark also give lecture at museums and appraise Indian art.

Real Mummies!
Axis Mundi, 112 W. San Francisco Street, Suite 104, (505) 982–3096

Here you can shop for authentic Egyptian, Roman, and Greek artifacts (including real mummies!); antique medical art books and instruments; and the most exotic insect and butterfly specimens you can imagine.

Largest Selection of Classic and Late Navajo Blankets
Joshua Baer and Company, 116 1/2 E. Palace Ave., (505) 988–8944

Josh Baer and Company specializes in nineteenth-century Navajo blankets. The gallery has the largest selection of classic and late classic Navajo blankets for sale anywhere in the world. In addition to buying and selling Navajo blankets, the gallery also provides clients appraisal and restoration services. Joshua Baer is an authority on Navajo blankets and has been a consultant to museums and auction companies. He is the author of two books, *Collecting The Navajo Child's Blanket* and *Twelve Classics*.

Antique Indian Art & New Mexican Modernist Paintings
Canfield Gallery, 414 Canyon Road, (505) 988–4199.

Owners Ken and Barbara Canfield show antique Plains Indian beadwork and weapons, and Southwest cultural artifacts along with early New Mexico Modernist paintings. All this is in an historic adobe compound believed to be one of the oldest homes on Canyon Road.

Ten Years of Tribal Arts on the Plaza
Taylor Dale, 53 Old Santa Fe Trail, (505) 984–2133

Prior to opening the gallery in Santa Fe, Tad spent ten years collecting and researching antique tribal arts in Europe. He personally selects each piece for its artistic quality, age, and rarity, whether it is a mask, sculpture, ceramic, textile or painting. The gallery is located upstairs on the east side of the Plaza in the historic Catron building. The gallery shows a diverse selection of fine antique works of art from Africa, the South Pacific, Australia, and the Americas.

Stunning American Indian and Spanish Colonial Art
Dewey Galleries, Ltd., 53 Old Santa Fe Trail, 2nd floor, (505) 982–8632

The Dewey Gallery is located on the 2nd floor of the historic Catron building on the Plaza. This distinguished gallery represents private collections and estates and also offers consultation and appraisal services.

Unique and Eclectic Variety Museum Pieces
Economos Works of Art, 225 Canyon Road, (505) 982–6347

Jimmy Economos is known as the "Mayor of Canyon Road" because he owns so much Canyon Road real estate and because his desk is equidistant from a window on Canyon Road and a window on Delgado, allowing him to monitor all traffic and activities on that corner! His gallery is unique because of the eclectic nature of his one-of-a-kind collections of art objects that includes Pre-Columbian ceramics, African and Oceanic primative art, Native American art, and museum-quality North West Coast Indian and Eskimo objects.

He has colonial furniture from Mexico and South America and colonial paintings and European furniture.

Priced for the New Collector
Andrea Fisher Fine Pottery, 221 W. San Francisco Street, (505) 986–1234

Museum-quality ceramics priced for the established and new collector. They are exclusively dedicated to Native American pottery.

For the Major Innovators in American Indian Art
Gallery 10, Inc., 225 Canyon Road, (505) 983–9707

This is one of the most important centers in the country for collector quality American Indian art. Offerings include historic and contemporary ceramics and weavings, historic baskets, kachinas, paintings, and jewelry.

Ethnic Art
Gallery Tiqua, 812 Canyon Road, (505) 984–8704

Here you'll find antique American Indian art, pottery, Navajo rugs, paintings, santos, kachinas, and ethnic art.

The Best Native American Basketry—the Gamat
Kania-Ferrin Gallery, 662 Canyon Road, (505) 982–8767.

The basket inventory here is almost entirely in the antique line. Since many tribes don't produce baskets anymore, it is extraordinary that Kania-Ferrin has baskets from all the major basket-producing regions in North America.

Handles the Collection of Forest Fenn
Nedra Matteucci's Fenn Gallery, 1075 Paseo de Peralta, (505) 982–4631

There is a whole room devoted to historic Pueblo pottery, Southwest baskets, Plains Indian beadwork, and Northwest Coast totem poles and bone items. In addition, there are a number of pieces from the book *Spirits in the Art,* which details the vast collection of Forest Fenn, former owner of the gallery.

His Mentor Was Isamu Noguchi
Greg Lachappelle, 7722 Old Santa Fe Trail, 87505 (505) 983–3766

Greg works exclusively with basalt stone, the hardest and most resistant stone. He was first encouraged in this direction by sculptor Isamu Noguchi, who was for many years years a friend and mentor. His works are minimal and intense, and vary greatly in scale. He has also collected African art extensively, showing various areas of his collection in museums here and abroad.

Antiquities in an Historic 18th Century Adobe
Ron Messick Fine Arts, 600 Canyon Road, (505) 983–9533

One of Canyon Road's oldest historic homes provides the perfect showcase for this eclectic mix of antiquities and ethnic arts from the Americas and around the world. Ron sells santos and retablos, pottery, textiles, paintings, sculpture, furniture, jewelry, and more.

Museum-Quality Antique Native American Art
Henry C. Monahan Works of Art, Ltd., 526 Canyon Road, (505) 982–8750

Henry Monahan Works of Art offers a wide selection of musuem quality antiques from North and South America, including ceramics from the Southwest; textiles and beadwork from the Plains, wood sculpture from the Northwest coast and Great Lakes region, and select offerings from major Pre-Columbian cultures.

The Largest Selection of Historic American Indian Art
Morning Star Gallery, 513 Canyon Road, (505) 982–8187

The largest gallery in the country dealing with museum-quality antique American Indian art is located in an old hacienda building on Canyon Road. Their emphasis is on Plains beadwork, quillwork ledger drawings, parfleche, and Southwest pottery, baskets, textiles and jewelry. At present they have pottery by Maria Martinez and her family, jewelry by Charles Loloma and Hostien Goodluck, and engravings by Karl Bodmer.

Contemporary Native American Pottery
Robert F. Nichols Gallery, 419 Canyon Road, (505) 982–2145

The gallery is known for its outstanding selection of Southwest Indian pottery and traditional Southwestern Indian paintings.

The Largest Assortment of Tribal Rugs in Santa Fe
Seret and Sons, 149 E. Alameda Street, (505) 988–9151
224 Galisteo Street, (505) 983–5008

Owner Ira Seret has the largest assortment of rugs of all kinds including Turkish, Afganistan, and tribal rugs. Their Galisteo Street gallery features carved architectural pieces from all over the world. They custom-make armoires and tables and design couches, chairs and chaises with rugs, which you choose from their very large selection.

Navajo Rugs 1890-1930
Streets of Taos, 200 Canyon Road, (505) 983–8268

Owner, Hilda Street has antique Navajo rugs and Indian jewlery, pottery, and some New Mexican furniture from the 1930s. She owned the Taos Inn for 20 years. Hilda decided the name for her store was appropriate because when she came to Santa Fe everyone said, "here come the Streets of Taos!" Hilda's daughter Elizabeth McGorty and her husband Jim sell WPA art in the same building.

World Class Collectors of Antique Textiles
Textile Arts, Inc., 1571 Canyon Road, (505) 983–9780/989–9073

Owner Mary Hunt Kahlenberg is a museum consultant and world class collector of antique textiles from around the world. She was instrumental in bringing the Neutrogena Collection to the International Folk Art Museum, and she edited the Neutrogena catalogue.

Crafts

Santa Fe alchemically draws superb crafts persons into its orbit. Space allows me to mention only a few—for current exhibitions, consult *Pasatiempo* each Friday.

The Most Unusual Fused Glass
Debora Clare, Korinsky Fine Jewelry at Waxlander Gallery, 622-B Canyon Road (505) 820–7756.

Debora Clare makes highly unique enamel painted fused glass artwork. For the discerning hostess, Clare's glass place cards are highly distinctive and each one is different. She makes window panes that look like a lace curtain is hanging in the window.

The Best European Ceramics
The Clay Angel, 125 Lincoln Avenue, (505) 988–4800

The Clay Angel, located one block from the Plaza, carries all manner of pottery from Portugal, Italy, Spain, Ireland, and Hungary. The store has the largest collection of traditional European Majolica tableware in the country. While most of their pottery is utilitarian, they have many decorative things as well.

Chainsaw Art—The Best

Ron McDowell has been carving for twelve years and has won many contests. His friend Doug McWilliams is his protégé. They set up shop on Cerrillos Road next to Jacalope, and side by side they create wooden coyotes, cacti, and Indians.

Most Exquisite Dolls

Jean Cooley (505 474–8615) has Santa Fe's smallest gallery: one single window displays her doll art at La Fonda Hotel.

*The late **Helen Cordero**, the Cochiti Pueblo potter who invented the storyteller doll in 1977, revived the abandoned practice of making figurative ceramics, an art that dates to about 400 BC. The* *museum of International Folk Art owns more than one hundred Corderos.*

The Best Ceramic Tile Gallery
Counterpoint Tile, 320 Sandoval Street, (505) 982–1247.

They represent the best tile artists. Many of the best bathrooms and kitchens in Santa Fe were done by these talented artists.

The Best Contemporary Craft Galleries
Kent Gallery, 130 Lincoln Avenue, (505) 988–1001

They show ceramics, furniture, paintings, jewelry and glass. Maggie Muchmore's pastel paintings are popular.

The Moved to S.F. the Chinese Year of the Rabbit
Rabbit Art Works, (505) 471–3671
179A Calle Estrellas, SF 87505

Tina and Bob are a husband and wife ceramic team—he throws the pots and she does the designing and painting. They sell from their studio and also show at Kent Gallery. Most of their pieces have a rabbit motif. Their most recent commission was a mural for a family on Nantucket Island. The mural portrays the family members as rabbits going about their chores and hobbies with the Nantucket lighthouse in the background. One rabbit is wearing a Lilly Pulitzer dress and another is carrying a Nantucket basket.

His Ceramic Flower Gardens Become Dinnerware
Munson Gallery, 225 Canyon Road, (505) 983–1659

A set of Eddie Domenquez dinnerware has a specially designed base in which he can insert his plates vertically to look like leaves sprouting from the base. Between these *"leaves,"* stacked cups form stems for bowls. In fact, it is a functional as well as amazing dinner service which when doubles as a beautiful piece of sculpture!

The Best Glass Gallery
Garland Gallery, 125 Lincoln, Suite 113, (505) 984–1555.

Local glass makers who are represented by the Garland include Lucy Lyon, Charles Miner, Henry Summa (perfume bottles), Peet Robison, and John Bingham.

Animal Images
Pricilla Hoback, (505) 466–2255

Priscilla, the daughter of Pink Adobe owner Rosalia Murphy has been an artist in Santa Fe since the 1960s. She uses animal images in her ceramic murals. She lives in Galisteo and digs the clay from around her home. She raises horse and has "too many dogs to count!"

One of The Most Famous Blacksmith in the Country
Tom Joyce, Route 9, Box 73J, (in Arroyo Hondo) 87505, (505) 982–0485

Tom is one of America's premiere blacksmiths. He exhibits in museums here and abroad, and lectures in universities around the country. His Arroyo Hondo workshop houses three thousand tools of which about one-third were made by Joyce.

1997 Distinguished Artist Award Winner
Nancy Youngblood Lugo

Santa Clara potter Nancy Youngblood Lugo comes from a long line of distinguished Santa Clara pueblo potters. She learned her technique from watching her grandmother, Margaret Tafoya, a famous potter.

Maria Martinez was a legend in her own time. She was known as the most skilled potter of the San Ildefonso. She made the black - on-black pottery.

One-of-a-Kind Architectural Ceramicist
Shel Neymark, Embudo Station, (505) 579–4432

Shel Neymark is a tilemaker and a potter, one of the best ceramicists whose work is nice to incorporate into your house. He also has done incredibly creative bathroom sinks! He has to canoe across the Rio Grande to get to his house in Embudo.

One-of-a-Kind Neon
Joyce Nicholson, 3164 Plaza Blanca, (505) 473–4994

Joyce is the only Santa Fe woman neon artist creating both architectural and sculptural works of art.

Find a Gift and have Coffee at the Same Time
Off the Wall, 616 Canyon Road

Beautiful and playful ceramics are sold here and on Saturdays you can have your Tarot cards read by Lumari.

The Best Sampler of local Ceramics
See "Culinary Accoutrements."

The Best Place To Watch Glass Blowing
C. Miner and Co., P.O. Box 146, Tesuque NM, (505) 988-2165.

Charlie Miner of C. Miner & Co., established in 1975, has been blowing glass more than seventeen years, and he has a reputation for perfection and unique design. Since his studio and gallery are located in the same building, you can watch him blowing the glass then see the finished product and buy!

Paint Your Own Pottery
The Painted Dish, 105 E. Marcy, (505) 995–1165

This is a wonderful place to go when want to be creative and make your own designs. The store provides the paints, brushes, stencils, and kiln firing. Pick out the pottery, select your paint colors, and paint whatever you wish!

One of the Best Local Glass Artitsts
Flo Perkins

Flo is one of the most talented glass artists I have ever met. She makes large pieces as well as glass bouquets. She makes glass vines that will hang on a surface such as a window or a trellis. She blows the glass flowers, combines metal with the flowers, and the third challenge is putting this on the found object like a window or trellis. She shows at Cline Lewellan Gallery.

Lifelike Casts of Body Parts
Willa Shalit, (505) 983–2599 or (212) 255–3684

Willa Shalit has made thousands of life casts of people's body parts, legs, and faces. Many of the casts are of famous people, including presidents. She is known for her work in many cities. All of her casts are "touchable." Shalit's Touch Foundation for the Blind, a result of her life cast of Stevie Wonder, is an organization that encourages the blind to participate in the arts.

Miniaturist
Chris Thomas, (505) 982–4557

Chris creates entire Southwestern scenes in handmade miniature rooms complete with *vigas* and *kiva* fireplaces. It is like walking into a miniature gallery with silver candlesticks and jewelry, drums and moccasins. Chris shows at Nedra Matteucci's Fenn Gallery.

He Works at the Train Station
Peter Vanderlaan, Studio (505) 471–1194, Gallery, (505) 820–1050
Santa Fe Southern Train Depot at 410 S. Guadalupe Street

Peter has a gallery right in the Santa Fe Southern depot. He blows glass in an open-air gazebo right next to the station where you can watch him work.

Ice Carver—The Best
Maurice Zeck at the La Fonda, On the Plaza, (505) 982–5511

This international competitor in ice carving for the past ten years and executive chef at La Fonda creates ice sculptures with culinary students of the Santa Fe Community College bringing the outdoor artform to Santa Fe. Maurice makes and displays on the Plaza a large ice scupture for the Christmas season.

Folk Art

A folk art that originated in the mid to late 1700s in New Mexico is the art of the *santero*. A *santero* is a painter and carver of images of saints. *Santos* are depictions of religious figures in the form of a *bulto,* a small sculpture. Catholic priests began carving *santos* to decorate their missions. To recognize the saints in churches or to empower saints with the capacity to answer your prayer, you have to be able to identify them, and you do this by knowing their symbols. For example, Our Lady of Guadalupe is shown within a radiating mandorla, wearing a mantle, and standing on a crescent moon. Images of her frequently feature roses. Saint Francis of Assisi is shown bearded, dressed in a blue habit, and engaged with birds.

The late Elizabeth Boyd, a local art historian and scholar, said that one of the problems in identifying the saints was that many New Mexicans "gave the saints new clothes or repainted the old ones." —*Saints and Saintmakers of New Mexico*

There are many Hispanic artists from Santa Fe who show at Spanish Market and whose pieces are collected by museums around the country. They pass the tradition on to their children thus sustaining the continuity of talented artists trained in the traditional arts forms. Some of these families, along with non-Hispanic folk artists, are as follows:

The Father of the New Mexican Animal Carving
The late Felipe Archuleta, his students, son and grandson

"As a sculptor of wooden animals, Felipe Benito Archuleta has carved out one of the fastest growing reputations in contemporary folk art history. He is both pleased and troubled by this sudden fame. 'Maybe I quit this tomorrow,' says the 66-year-old sculptor, shaking his craggy, expressive face. 'If I want to go to the cemetery, I just keep making these things. Too many people come out and want this and that. I can't satisfy the whole world!'—**Davis Mather**, *The Clarion, America's Folk Art Magazine,* 1977

His Works are Made With Natural Pigments
Charles M. Carrillo, (505) 473–7941

The first book to document the work of a contemporary New Mexican *santero* was written about Charles Carillo. His *santos* are in the permanent collections of many museums including the Museum of International Folk Art in Santa Fe and the Millicent Rogers Museum in Taos. He created the fourteen stations of the cross in *retablo* form at Santa Maria de la Paz Catholic Church.

Painted Stations of the Cross at St. Francis Cathedral
Maria Romero Cash, 295 Lomita Street, (505) 988–2590

Maria Cash, an award-winning Spanish Market *santera* since 1975, was selected to paint fourteen pictures depicting the condemnation, crucifixion, and burial of Christ. The *retablos* were installed in St. Francis Cathedral on Ash Wednesday of 1997 and were blessed by Archbishop Sheehan in a special ceremony. Maria's parents, Emilio and Senaida Romero, are nationally known master tinsmiths. They have helped preserve the craft of tinsmithing

by passing the skill on to their daughter, Anita Romero Jones, who is also a skilled *santera*, and to their sons, Robert and Jim Romero, also tinsmiths.

Five Generations of Tinsmiths—The Delgados

Angie Martinez, the matriarch of Santa Fe's Delgado family, has a five-generation tinsmithing tradition. Old tin chandeliers in my house on Delgado Street were probably made by members of the Delgado family. They lived on Delgado Street, a street named after their family.

The Best Painted Doors
Monica Sosoya Halford, 850 El Caminito Road, (505) 982-4175

Monica Halford's mother was the sister of Father Fray Agelico Chávez's mother. Monica has exhibited in Spanish Market since 1979 and has been the recipient of many of their awards including the Master's Award—the best of the show. Her work was featured in the 1997 Spanish Market poster. Anyone who dines at Geronimo

Restaurant on Canyon Road can admire three doors she painted—the restroom doors and the door behind the bar.

The Best Hispanic Folk Art Collection In The World
Hispanic Wing of the International Folk Art Museum & Spanish Market

One of the best collections of colonial religious folk art in the world is in the Hispanic Wing of the International Folk Art Museum. If you are still interested, come in July for the annual weekend of Spanish Market—the largest assemblage in the world for Hispanic folk art.

Recipient of the National Heritage Award, 1997
Ramon Jose Lopez
Custom orders by appointment (505) 988–4976

Ramon Lopez, a *santero,* silversmith, and furniture-maker, has been chosen as one of twelve artists in the country to receive the prestigious 1997 National Heritage Fellowship Award from the National Endowment for the Arts. He has been instrumental in the revival of Spanish New Mexican silver hollowware, a craft that can be traced back nearly two centuries. Ramon began making contemporary jewelry in silver and gold in 1974, and he carves and paints *santos* in the New Mexican folk tradition in his own sanctuario next to his home off of Hyde Park Road. His work is represented in museums, private collections, and at Spanish Market, where he has been the recipient of several first place awards. (Ramon has passed the family traditions on to his twin sons.)

Won the Grand Prize at Spanish Market in 1997
David Nabor Lucero, 1924 Hope Road, (505) 983–1635

David Lucero is one of the most important emerging artists in New Mexican. During a three-year recovery from a motorcycle accident, he was inspired to paint. In a very short time he started winning awards, including the grand awards for Spanish Market in 1996 and 1997, and first place in the New Mexico State Fair in both 1996 and 1997.

The Best Moving Folk Art
Ed Larson, Yellow Bear Studio at *The Stables* on Canyon Road

Ed makes icon images of heroic characters such as Billy the Kid, Uncle Sam, and Saint Francis of Assisi. He has made mobile wind toys of Newt Gingrich and Santa Claus that move in the wind. Ed shows at Cline-Llewellan Gallery.

The Best Folk Art Stores

If you are interested in colonial religious art there are several places to go: Gloria List of **Nonsuch Arts** (505) 988–4002 is one of the best dealers in colonial religious antiques. **Pachamama** at 223 Canyon Road (505) 983-4020 is one of the best places in Santa Fe to find Latin American folk art and antiques. **Omar Clayborn**—Jill Clayborn's brother—has one of the best places to go for antique Mexican furniture. **Hampton Gallery**, 236 Delgado Street, (505) 983–9635. Here you'll find vintage Mexican silver jewelry and fabulous Mexican religious art. He handles the top Mexican silversmiths of the 1920s: Spratling, Aguilar and Frederick Davis. **Davis Mather Folk Art Gallery** at 141 Lincoln Street, (505) 983–1660 has wonderful Oaxacan handcrafted and painted snakes, coyotes, and ceramics. **Jackalope Pottery** at 2820 Cerrillos Road (505) 471–8539 has a large collection of folk art. **Doodlet's Shop** at 120 Don Gaspar (505) 983–3771 is one of the best places in town to get wonderful folk art gifts.

The Only Outsider Art
Leslie Muth Gallery, 131 W. Palace Avenue, (505) 989–4620

Leslie Muth deals in contemporary outsider, visionary, and self-taught American contemporary art with an emphasis on artists of the Southwest.

The Famous Hispanic Sculpture Of Tree Trunks
Ben Ortega family, in Tesuque, (505) 982–3020
El Dulcehogar Art Gallery

Ben Ortega is the patriarch of a family of woodcarvers—five sons and five daughters are carrying on his folk art tradition. He carved the wood scupture on the corner of Delgado and Canyon of St. Francis of Assisi. His wife Belle Ortega makes the best *sopa,* at Christmas. Her recipe for a crowd is as follows:

Sopa

Toast 4 loaves of bread

Grate 2 or 3 lbs of longhorn cheese

Soak 2 boxes of raisins in water

Boil 3 boxes of brown sugar and 3 cups white sugar in water in a skillet

Add some red wine to the sugar mixture

Add 2 tbsp. of vanilla

Soak peeled pinons in water—get these at Murphy's candy store on Canyon Road. Put everything together in a serving dish

Let it sit for a day. Serve hot or cold with ice cream.

The Best Straw Appliqué

Eliseo and Paula Rodriquez, 1027 Camino San Acacio Street, (505)

Eliseo and Paula Rodriquez learned the art of straw appliqué—the art of gluing small pieces of straw ("poor man's gold") together to form patterns on larger pieces. The Work Projects Administration (WPA) paid them to learn the craft. Today their crosses are in collections throughout the country. Eliseo Rodriguez's name is on one of the plaques on the sidewalk in front of' the Museum of Fine Arts. They have won many awards and show each year at Spanish Market.

The Most Innovative

Ford Ruthling, 313 Berger Street, (505) 982–2241

"Archbishop Lamy substituted imminently forgettable plaster of paris garbage saints from St. Louis for the beautifully painted saints he first encountered here which he thought were primitive, crude and obscene."—**Ford Ruthling**

Ford Ruthling is primarily an oil painter. U.S postage stamps featured his oil paintings of Indian pots in 1987. He creates unique embossed paintings—a type of monoprint. He has about forty-five monotypes, which are taken from his amazing life experiences and his incredible imagination. One of the best parts of buying one of his paintings is going to his house and hearing his presentation. His house and gardens are filled with his collections and his innovative and creative folk art—which has been written about in many magazines including a recent *New York Times* article. Ford also produces iron wall sculptures and tin on pots, and designs assorted furniture. His very popular large "Harvest Bowls" and his new line of plates are sold at Cookworks and are on display at the Eldorado Hotel. He collects and composes beautiful and spiritually resonant reliquaries.

VOCABULARY

bulto–a small religious sculpture.

exvoto–paintings on tin showing the calamity of the devoted with a written description of the incident. Exvotos arewhich is left at the church by the supplicants. Most are from Mexico but you can find them at the Santa Fe flea market as well as folk art stores.

milagros–frequently cast metal objects depicting body parts or other significant objects (house, dog, corn, etc.) to be left for the saint to which the pilgrim prays. These can be found at the Santa Fe flea market and folk art stores.

nicho–a small tin or wood cabinet to house santos.

reliquario–a shrine that contains various religious fragments.

reredos–large altar scenes (large *retablos*).

retablo–images of saints on pine panels.

santero–one who makes santos.

Santos–either bultos (carved in the round) or retablos (painted flat on wood or metal.

Creative Heritage

Jack Lambert   Dorothy Stewart   Craftsmen

Santa Fe, New Mexico
September, 1928

Creative Spirits in N.M.

Why is Santa Fe so Creative, Funky and Artistic?

"In no other state of this union is the trend of life so clearly shaped by art as in New Mexico. Art has rescued this state from the commonplace and made it conscious of its own fine character. The arts have kept Santa Fe from becoming an 'up-to-date' burg and made it unique and beautiful. Artists and writers constitute only a small percentage of the population, but their influence is wherever you look." —**Edgar Lee Hewett,** The Santa Fe New Mexican, June 26, 1940

New Mexico, Prehistoric Art Center

Santa Fe's rich literary history started with the Spanish chronicles of exploration. When Don Juan de Oñate came to the Rio Grande Valley north of Santa Fe, his chronicler-soldier, Villagra, observed that the Indians painted beautiful frescos on the walls where Onate and his troops were staying. More than three centuries later archaeologists discovered remarkable art in the ancient town of Kuaua which had also been chronicled by Villagra. Young Indians today still paint in this ancient tradition.

Hispanic Art, Here Long Before The Anglos Came

The arts and crafts of Spain were brought to the New World in the sixteenth century by the *conquistadores* and by the Spanish churchmen and settlers who followed. The great stone *reredos* (altarpiece) at Christo Rey Church is the finest example of early religious art in the United States. The Museum of New Mexico has ancient Spanish and Mexican paintings, an old altar with a painted *reredos, bultos,* and *santos* of saints painted during the Spanish conquest. These artistic traditions are still alive today.

The Taos Ten

In the late 1800s, Joseph Sharp visited Taos for a couple of weeks. When he and Ernest Blumenschein met in Paris as art students, they talked about his travels in New Mexico. Later when Blumenschein got an illustrating assignment in Taos, he talked his friend Bert Phillips into going back with him. In 1898, they found outfitters in Denver and, with no prior knowledge of horsemanship, the two started their journey in a light horse-drawn wagon. When they broke a wheel, they quickly discovered that their wagon was not sturdy enough for the treacherous country roads. They tossed a coin to see who would make the 40-mile trip by horse to Taos to fix the wheel. Blumenschein lost; it took him two days to get to Taos.

The "broken wheel" was the beginning of the Taos Society of Artists. Phillips and Blumenschein were the magnets who brought other up-and-coming artists from the east. They had their founding meeting at the site of the present-day Taos Inn in 1912. The founders were Blumenschein, Oscar Berninghaus, E. Irving Couse, W. Herbert Dunton, Bert G. Phillips, and Joseph Sharp. They were later joined by four other artists, Walter Ufer, Victor Higgins, Kenneth Adams, and E. M. Hennings, and they became known collectively as "The Taos Ten."

The Santa Fe Railroad And Fred Harvey

In the 1880s Santa Fe had long been a railroad town. Tracks had been laid for the Acheson Topeka and Santa Fe Railroad. The Fred Harvey Hotel and Restaurant chain, the finest hotel and restaurants in the Southwest, marketed New Mexico as a tourist attraction to other parts of the world. The Taos Society of Artists' circle grew. By 1915, over 100 artists had come to Taos lured to the area by the Society and the exhibitions they had mounted all over the country. The Exchange Hotel on the Plaza, which became the La Fonda Hotel, had always been the hub of Santa Fe activities. La Fonda, which was part of the Fred Harvey chain from 1943 to 1951, was the fanciest place in town. Celebrities, politicians, and Los Alamos scientists visited the hotel often, and the Harvey girls were synonymous with the best in service.

Trainloads of tourists who came via the Santa Fe Railroad were booked at Fred Harvey Hotels where the paintings of the Taos Society of Artists were displayed on the walls in the hotels and in ticket offices. These artists depicted this fascinating area in their canvases.

1917: Museum of Fine Arts Founded

The Museum of New Mexico and the School of American Research had been temporarily set up at the Palace of the Governors with Dr. Edgar Lee Hewett as its director. The new Museum of Fine Arts, founded in 1917, became an art center for works of both regional and international importance.

1920s: "Los Cinco Pintores " (five painters)

This group of five young (under 30) artists were Santa Fe's first cooperative art group. They banded together between 1920 and 1926 with their shared desire to be avant-garde—and to survive financially. They referred to the Taos School of Artists as the "derriere garde." Since there were then no art galleries in Santa Fe, they created an awareness of contemporary art which helped found the artist colony in Santa Fe in the early 20s. The group included Freemont Ellis, Will Schuster, Josef Bakos, Walter Mruk, and Willard Nash. Together they bought land from fellow artist Frank Applegate on Camino Monte Sol without knowing anything about building. They hand-built their houses through the "trial-and-error" method, which often ended in "error." These individuals were magnetic, and each had a great sense of humor. People called them "the five nuts in the adobe huts." They held their first group show at the Fine Arts Museum in 1921.

1920s and 1930s: Santa Fe Creative Colony

Writers found the same kind of inspiration here that attracted artists—the climate, geography, and the diverse social milieu. In the 1820s and 30s, New Mexico was an artistic and literary community similar to Paris in the 20s. It was cheap, beautiful, and intellectual; the mix of culture attracted a diverse and interesting society. Santa Fe was a melting pot of artists, writers, intellectuals, and easterners. The Santa Fe Art Colony artists Frank Applegate, Gerald Cassidy, Andrew Dasburg, William Penhallow Henderson, Albert Schmidt, John Sloan, Theodore Van Soelen, Carlos Vierra, Raymond Jonson, and Alfred Morang were part of the creative thread of Santa Fe.

Oliver La Farge (1901–1963), who won the Pulitzer Prize for his 1929 novel *Laughing Boy,* was also a famous anthropologist and an activist for Indian rights. His son, John Pen La Farge, lives in the same house on Old Santa Fe Trail in which his father wrote.

My father would have said Santa Fe was unusually open minded and welcoming, and therefore, was the perfect place for creative people, be they artists, poets, homosexuals, eccentrics, or raw-boned New England Yankees."—**John Pen La Farge**

Poet Witter Bynner, one of the great salon-keepers of Santa Fe, lived in Santa Fe from 1922 until his death in 1968. January 15th, 1949—the day Gladys Butler and her brother, Alban Butler, died—Bynner gave a memorial service for them at his house. Today that is a bed and breakfast called the **Inn of the Turquoise Bear** (505) 983–0798. Pulitzer Prize winning novelist Willa Cather, whose novel *Death Comes to the Archbishop* is based on the life of New Mexico's first Archbishop, Jean Baptiste Lamy, wrote portions of her book at Bishop's Lodge. Mary Austin, who wrote twenty-seven books in her lifetime, built Casa Querida (now the Gerald Peters Gallery on 439 Camino del Monte Sol) in 1925. D.H. Lawrence, who spent time in Taos between 1922 and 1925, wrote, "I think New Mexico was the greatest experience from the outside world that I have ever had. It certainly changed me forever."

1925: The Spanish Colonial Arts Society (SCAS)
239 1/2 Johnson Street, (505) 983–4038

SCAS was founded in 1925 to help to collect and revive the traditional folk art of the Spanish colonial period dating from 1690. By the early 1900s these traditional arts started to die out. The SCAS collection is now part of the permanent collection of the Hispanic Heritage Wing in the Museum of International Folk Art, the best collection of Spanish colonial art in the world.

1930s: New Deal Art

In November 1933, Will Schuster wrote a letter to his friend, John Sloan: "The merchants here," he wrote, "are now beginning to feel the pinch and are consequently pinching the other fellow." A month later, he wrote to Sloan to say that the government had offered to pay him $42.50 a week to paint.

During the Depression, President Roosevelt created the federal Works Project Administration, an art program designed to support starving artists while decorating public buildings at the same time.

SANTA FE, N.M.

John Sloan (left) in his studio

Organizations that benefitted from the artists' work had to contribute financially. Some 167 artists were involved in this project in New Mexico, and their work chronicles the history of the state. Among the famous artists in this program were Allan Hauser, Bill Lumpkins, Gene Kloss, Will Schuster, and Olive Rush (who painted two frescos in the old Santa Fe Main Library). A good reference source for the New Deal art is the book *Treasures on New Mexico Trails: Discover New Deal Art and Architecture* by Kathryn Flynn.

Indian Research and Market

Drawings of Navajo sandpainting at the Wheelwright Musuem show the age-old native Indian traditions still practiced today.

Edgar L. Hewett, an anthropologist, recognized the importance of the remains of Anasazi culture in Chaco as early as 1921. Upon the foundation of the School of American Research in 1907, he and his associates set up on-the-job training programs for students allowing them to work in Chaco Canyon for twenty years.

The New Mexico Association on Indian Affairs (NMAIA) was propelled into existence when it tried to defeat the federal Bursum Bill that had been designed to take land away from the Indians. At the same time that these political issues were being addressed, the Southwestern Indian Fair Committee formed in 1922. They held their first annual Indian Fair in 1923 in an effort to revive Indian arts using traditional techniques. One of the first people brought into Indian Market was San Idelfonso's famous Maria Martinez. The first official Indian Market was held in 1936. The Indian Fair Committee then merged with NMAIA.   In 1960 they changed their name to The Southwestern Association on Indian Affairs (SAIA). The annual Indian Market has grown into the largest assemblage of Indian artists in the world.

Culinary
Accoutrements

A cooking class at Cookwork's

Catering, Take-out, mobile

During Santa Fe's fast-paced summers, food can be catered, taken out, or brought to you on a bicycle. Grocery stores and delicatessens all have take-out sections. In addition, I recommend the following short list.

Adobo Catering
Ron Messick
1807 Second Street, Studio 7, (505) 989–7674

Adobe Catering specializes in contemporary Southwestern food style, but they have the flexibility to prepare classical French cuisine and traditional holiday menus, as well as elegant and very festive country barbeques.

Brown Bag Lunch
Catherine Wade
(505) 988–7549

A lunch-delivery service which brings sandwiches and snacks to galleries, local museums and downtown offices. Call ahead for their sandwich list which range in price from $4.50–$5. Free delivery.

Walter Burke Catering
P.O. Box 914, (505) 988–5001

Walter has helped Santa Feans plan parties since 1981. *Town and Country* says: "With entertaining a year-round happening and a high-pitched summer phenomenon (all without benefit of country clubs), the caterer is an important element. New York restaurant-trained Walter Burke has established his credentials and culinary skills for parties of a thousand or twelve."

The Chocolate Maven
222 N. Guadalupe Street, (505) 984–1980

Owner Mandy Clark's most famous exploit: she made Robert Redford a beautiful pink pig birthday cake during the filming of *Milagro Beanfield War.*

Cliff Simon
725 W. Manhattan Avenue, (505) 820–0231

"For every Jewish cakeman, there is a mother who stands behind him and says BAKE! BAKE!"—**Cliff Simon**

Cliff Simon is the best cake decorator with the best sense of humor in the country. He is a speaker, writer, and a cake-maker for all occasions. He "paints" his cakes so that they look like exact replicas of any of the great masters. The edible gilded framed pictures look like they should be hanging in the Louvre. He wrote *They Ate my Cake* about the celebrities for which he has baked. One of his celebrity cakes was made for hostess Katherine Walker on the occasion of the birthday of Agnes Gund, President of the Museum of Modern Art.

Porter Dillon
P. O. Box 2442, Santa Fe, NM 87504, (505) 982–6774

Porter, who has lived in Santa Fe most of her life, will cater anything for two to two hundred people. She is noted for her green chile canapés.

Edible
323 Aztec Street, (505) 983–4699

A wonderful catering company that is constantly good, especially at preparing gourmet dinners to take home and serve to guests for dinner. No one has to know your secret!

Gourmet Gazelle
209 Polaco Street, (505) 984–1430

Owner Scott Packer has a menu list of local Santa Fe restaurants from which you can pick and then have your selection delivered to your door. Great for businesses or hotel-bound visitors who don't want to go out.

Hors d'oeuvres de Soleil
Francie Vaughan
842 Camino de Jemez, (505) 989–8182

Francie specializes in hors d'oeurves which she delivers to your house. Her fantastic pot stickers are a staple in Santa Fe's most discriminating kitchens.

Kokoman Circus
301 Garfield Street, (505) 983–7770

Kokoman is a gourmet food and wine shop with a great variety of services for the gourmet. Catering is one of the biggest components of their business. Shirley Pisacane and Robert Witcher of **Circus Catering** are two of the owners. They have a take-out counter with a meat and cheese deli, and an area where you can have lunch. Keith Obermaier, the other owner, also owns **Kokoman Wines and Liquors** in Pojoaque. Their roof deck with great views can seat ninety people for private parties.

Metro Foods Catering Company
2754-C Agua Fria Street, (505) 438–7127

Owner Jason Aufrichtig tells us that he will cater all functions. Free deliveries for orders called in before noon. He also owns **Cafe Counterculture** on Baca Street which is a cross-cultural deli-soup-take-out shop.

Mucho, The Gourmet Sandwich Shoppe
135 W. Palace, Suite 200, (505) 988–2223

Sandwiches, soups and salads are delivered free to your door. Ask them to fax you their menu. Open nights.

Someone's in the Kitchen
Richard Derwostyp
1274 Calle Commercio, (505) 424–8209

This group will cater for any number between two to five hundred people, including weddings. They specialize in ethnic foods and chic Southwest food.

El Merendero Posa's Tamales
907 W. Alameda Street, (505) 982–7672
1945 Cerrillos Road, (505) 820–7672

The "best tamales in Santa Fe" are made with white corn dough filled with shredded pork or beef or chicken flavored with red chili and then wrapped. Sometimes you have to wait in line. Their two restaurants are open until 6 P.M.

Charities, Cookoffs, and Tastings

The Santa Fe Restaurant community is always very generous when it comes to giving food to charities and to the poor. Cookoffs are an opportunity to show of your cooking and perhaps win a prize.

Amnesty Day (A Memorial)
For twenty years—until 1995, when he was forced to stop—former Judge Fiorina annually exchanged traffic tickets just before Thanksgiving if offenders provided the makings of Thanksgiving dinners for needy families. Two hundred dollars worth of parking tickets was satisfied by paying a fine of $15 plus two delivered turkey-with-all-the-trimmings dinners as well as participation in a neighborhood food drive. CBS News once gave Judge Fiorino the accolade of "fairest traffic judge on the planet."

Annual Santa Fe Wine and Chile Festival
Executive Director; Greg O'Byrne
(505) 982–8686

There are more restaurants that participate in this event than in any other restaurant event in Santa Fe. It is a weekend event which promotes Santa Fe as a culinary destination. Over sixty restaurants and wineries participate and the cost per guest is $60. Seminars, wine tastings and cooking demonstrations are scheduled during the festival, held the last weekend in September. The Fiesta is organized as a marketing event more than a fund-raiser but it operates as a non-profit and all proceeds after expenses goes to charity.

Bean Tasting
Elizabeth Berry
(505) 685–4888

Elizabeth is a gardener and a bean gourmet of monumental proportions. Each winter, Elizabeth holds a bean-tasting event for thirty of the best chefs in Santa Fe to taste new varieties of her "heirloom" beans to see which ones they like best. Each chef picks four of their favorites. In the spring she will grow only those beans that the chefs have selected. Her hundreds of varieties of beans are sold nationwide.She also grows specialty vegetables and chiles at her farm in Abiquiu.

Souper Bowl (Saturday)
(505) 471–1635

This daytime soup cookoff, held at different places each year, benefits the Food Depot, which collects and distributes food for the needy. At least sixteen different soups are donated by some of the best restaurants in town. For only $5 you can slurp as much soup as you want. It is one of the most affordable and most popular eating events.

Taste of Santa Fe
(505) 982–4258

An annual "culinary cook-off" which benefits **Open Hands**, a non-profit organization that serves the elderly, the disabled, and the poor. Santa Fe's best restaurants participate and are judged. There is dancing and the "Essential Non-Essential Auction" of things that would be fun to have but you can live without. The cost is $25 per person, and you can eat as much as you like of food, all of which is made and donated by Santa Fe's best restaurants.

Kitchen Angels
(505) 989–3900 to volunteer time or money
(505) 471–7780

A group of about three hundred volunteers provides free, delicious meals to Santa Feans with cancer, AIDS, and other life-threatening diseases. The "angels in the kitchen" cook a full meal: soup, salad, an entree, bread, and a dessert. Food donations come from restaurants and businesses. Some restaurants have "five percent days" when Kitchen Angels receives that percentage of the day's sales.

Meals on Wheels
City of Santa Fe, Senior Services, (505) 984–6735

Meals are distributed through this indispensible charity group to eligible elderly people who are not able to cook for themselves.

Santa Fe Pro-Musica Winefest and Auction
(505) 988–4640

The annual Pro-Musica Auction and fund-raiser usually takes place at the La Fonda Hall Ballroom. Music is provided by the Pro-Musica Ensemble. You can sip wine from twenty-three wineries, drink beer from fifteen microbreweries, and eat hors d'oeuvres and desserts from twenty-three fabulous restaurants, all for $25.

Taste of the Nation
(505) 471–1633

Twenty five local chefs offer their restaurant's best cuisine. It is a fund-raiser for the Food Depot, St. Elizabeth's Shelter, and La Luz Family Shelter. Also, they will serve beer, wine and tequila for the same price of $40. The Food Depot is the storage and distribution center for Food in Santa Fe, the Food Brigade, and Kitchen Angels.

Chiles (red or green?)

A bundle of chiles (which hang more as decoration than as a method of drying the chiles to use in cooking) is called a ristra.

Chile is a pungent pepper, harvested in the fall, which is roasted, then peeled, and served in a variety of dishes which gives the state a distinctive cuisine which is called "Native New Mexican." It is hotly disputed who has the *hottest* or the *mildest* or *best* chile, but the degree of radioactivity in your nose and mouth will help you answer this burning question.

Chile is something that is taken very seriously by tourists, locals, and restaurants where the question is asked hundreds of times a day "Red or green?" If you can't make up your mind then order "Christmas"—a combination of both red and green.

The state legislature wanted to make "Red or green?" the "Official Question" by statute, but Governor Johnson vetoed it because it was "a waste of time and paper." Chile is, however, the state vegetable along with frijoles (pinto beans).

Chile is one of the most important staples in New Mexico cuisine, New Mexico is the eighth largest producer of chiles in the world and the largest producer in the United States.

Cooking Schools

La Fonda Hotel
Maurice Zeck, (505) 982–5511

Maurice Zeck, the chef at the La Fonda Hotel runs the only three year cooking apprenticeship program in Santa Fe. Apprentices get paid $6.50 an hour to learn to be expert professional cooks. Pupils take classes at Santa Fe Community College under the auspices of the American Culinary Federation. They learn "fifteen different stations" in the kitchen, and after three years they take a test that allows them to become a certified cook. Maurice Zeck makes the beautiful ice sculpture on the Plaza during the Christmas season.

Santa Fe School of Cooking
Susan Curtis
116 West San Francisco Street, (505) 983–4511

Here you will find the best Southwestern cooking classes in Santa Fe. Each class lasts about two and a half hours, and includes instruction, demonstrations, recipes, and then, of course, the pleasure of eating the meal. Call for their schedule of classes. Their store has a complete selection of local spices and sauces.

Santa Fe Community College
Richards Avenue, (505) 471–8200

The school has a two-year hands-on course teaching theories and techniques of cooking. In addition, they have regular cooking classes throughout the school year. Bill Weiland, the culinary arts instructor, was formerly the chef at Rancho Encantado and at Quail Run.

Wild Oats
1090 St. Francis Drive, (505) 983–5333

This natural food grocery store holds cooking classes and seminars in their community room on the southwest corner of the building. Classes are available in everything from sushi to juice-making. The schedule is posted on the community table next to the check-out counter.

Culinary Stores

Cookworks
316-318-322 Guadalupe Street, (505) 988–7676

Cookworks has three stores. The gourmet cookware shop has the fanciest of cookware, the tabletop store has porcelain, linens, china and candles, and the third building in a row has gourmet food. They are the exclusive reps for William Poll deli products from New York. Try taking a bite of any of these products and you won't be able to stop. Cookworks also puts on periodic cooking classes taught by famous visiting chefs. They also have an Albuquerque store (505) 837–9700.

Gift 'n' Gourmet (on the Plaza)
55 Old Santa Fe Trail, (505) 982–5953

This cookware shop on the Plaza has been in business for fifteen years and carries kitchen equipment, candles, cookbooks, gadgets, and everything that belongs in a kitchen.

La Mesa
225 Canyon Road, (505) 984–1688

This "table top store" is mostly stuffed with products from local artisans. It is a great place to buy wedding presents.

Nambe Mills
924 Paseo de Peralta Street, (505) 988–5528

Internationally known and locally made Nambeware has the elegance of silver and is functional as well. The downtown outlet has special reduced prices. Food prepared in advance can be taken out of the freezer and put in the oven and heated on one platter if you use Nambeware.

Farmers' Market
Pamela Roy
Sanbusco Center, (505) 983–4098

The Farmer's Market is one of the most popular social events of the year from June to October on Tuesday and Saturday mornings from 7:30 to 11:30 A.M. Food growers from all over Northern New Mexico sell their fresh produce here. It is one of the most successful and popular farmers markets in the state. The market is one of the few community activities that does not cater to the tourist market, but tourists love it for its display of active, natural foods that cannot be found anywhere else in the world (See *Market Places*).

Cultural Survivors

AUG. 8, '25.

"Except for Native Americans . . .
the rest of us are all immigrants."
President Clinton in Albuquerque on October 13, 1996

Gaming—it may be older than we think!

"Gambling was legal in New Mexico until early this century."
—**Marc Simmons**

Kathryn Gabriel speculates in *Gambler Way: Indian Gaming in Mythology, History and Archeology in North America,* that Chaco Canyon may have been one of the original gaming palaces of the Southwest. "Gambling is the great equalizer; in stories where body parts are wagered, an eye for an eye literally applies." Gambling has been a significant part of Native American culture since before Columbus..."I do not wish to glamorize, condone, or condemn gambling at Indian casinos. Instead, it is my intention to probe its sacred aspect, while raising the possibility that it is the origin of nearly all ancient religions."—**Kathryn Gabriel**, *Gambler Way: Indian Gaming in Mythology, History and Archeology in North America*

Dona Tules was considered the most notorious "monte" player in Santa Fe during the Mexican period (from 1821 to 1848).

The Oldest

The Acequia Madre ("Mother Ditch")
The Mayordomo, Roberto Moya
Chief Commissioner of the Acequia Madre
Phillip Bove, 922 Acequia Madre, (505) 983–3546

In the old days everyone along the Acequia Madre had to provide a wagon and a mule and so many peons per acre. Today $1 a year is assessed plus one day's labor on the ditch. If they can't provide the labor then they are charged one day's minimum wage.

The six-mile Acequia Madre is one of the most important cultural remains of the old Spanish farming communities, and it dates back to at least 1680. It stretches from the hills above Cristo Rey Church through the "Eastside," south of the Capital, and far out to Agua Fria. The *acequias* were and still are maintained by individual communities that chose a Mayordomo, or head, of the ditch. He oversees the traditional annual spring-cleaning and maintenance of the ditch and settles disputes arising from assertions about water rights. Today, even though only a handful of people irrigate from the ditch, it is an important cultural and historic part of the community. In 1990, it was argued in court that the water rights of the residents along the acequia predated the rights of the Public Service Company which was holding water in their reservoirs. The judge ruled that PNM had to release water to the acequia. This happens during the spring and summer twice a week. The Acequia Madre is on the National Register of Historic Places.

Church Preservation
Cornerstones Community Partnership
227 Otero Street, (505) 982–9521

"We were trying to help restore community spirit. The only way to do this is to get people to work together, to share the effort."—**Susan Herter**

95

New Mexico's adobe missions are included on a list of the world's 100 most endangered monuments. The list was compiled by the World Monuments Fund, one of the oldest historic preservation groups in the country. The missions date back to the earliest Spanish colonization of New Mexico in the 1600s. During the Spanish Missionary Period of 1598–1821, numerous mud, straw, and wood churches were built by the Catholic church. These little churches all over northern New Mexico were the center of village life. Many of these churches, which are still being used as places of worship, are pure examples of Spanish colonial churches architecture, and they house some of the state's best religious art.

Cornerstones, a non-profit "Community Partnership," has restored 140 churches since it started. They restore the churches using traditional building practices and "sweat equity" from the community. At the same time they attempt to restore the cultural and traditional values that the church represents. Volunteers for Cornerstones help "mud" the churches—a messy but rewarding job and a lot of fun. The locals fix a fabulous New Mexican feast after the "mudding" and participants get a tee shirt that says, "Soy un Zoquetero."

La Conquistadora

"Our Lady of Peace," the sacred statue of the Virgin Mary in St. Francis Cathedral, was brought to New Mexico in 1625 by a Franciscan brother to symbolize the spiritual conquest of New Mexico by the Spanish. But in 1680 the Spanish were exiled for thirteen years after the Pueblo Revolt. When Diego de Vargas triumphantly returned in 1693, he carried with him La Conquistadora and promised to have a yearly celebration in her honor. This has been an annual event in Santa Fe ever since and marks the beginning of Fiesta season.

The modern-day version of Fiesta started in 1883. During the event, de Vargas is knighted and the Fiesta queen is crowned. For the procession, La Conquistadora wears a diamond cross and a crown of jewels made from jewelry donated long ago by Santa Feans. La Conquistadora stays for one week at Rosario Chapel and is returned to the cathedral the following Sunday where she stays for the rest of the year. She is the icon most revered by everyone who knows her. There is a society that takes care of her beautiful clothes and jewelry.

Two rituals that have endured since the late-seventeenth century are the devotion to La Conquistadora and de Vargas's entrada into Santa Fe.

Curandera

Curanderas are Hispanic spiritual and herbal "healers" who have been in New Mexico since their Spanish descendants came here in 1598. Their healing skills have been handed down from generation to generation.

A *sobardora,* who is under the umbrella of the *curandera,* massages and works on physical ailments. The *sobardora* was in danger of losing this ancient art because of new laws that have been passed for the licensing of massage therapists.

In 1993 the state legislature approved the practice of a *sobada* as a cultural healing art. It recognized that "the practice and art of the *sobada,* a traditional healing art in Spain and Spanish America, has been practiced for several hundred years abroad and for almost three centuries in New Mexico....It has been passed from one generation to the next through intense and lengthy personal training and private apprenticeship. Many New Mexicans interested in preserving traditions and customs are now concerned that the practice of the *sobada* will be forever lost in a thicket of state health regulations and through the fading of traditional ways. Therefore, be it resolved by the House of Representatives of the State of New Mexico that it recognizes the traditional practice of the *sobada* and the significant role its practice plays in traditional Indo-Hispanic culture." Juanita T. Duran, *sobodora,* was active in getting this recognition.

Descansos

Descanso, which means "resting place," is a place along the side of the road marked by a pile of rocks placed there in memory of someone who is deceased. Before mortuaries and cars, the body would be taken by wagon in a procession to the church and cemetery. On the way, the procession would stop along the side of the road and pray for the soul of the deceased. A pile of rocks would be gathered to commemorate this spot. If someone was killed on the highway and there was no one to claim the deceased, the body might be buried at the exact spot along the road where he died. *Descansos* in New Mexico are considered an art form. They are elaborately decorated with crosses and usually plastic flowers, and maintained by family and friends of the deceased. In recent times, *descansos* have been built to commemorate the spot on which a loved one died in an automobile accident.

Feast Day for San Isidro
Procession starts at Cristo Rey Church in May
(505) 983–8528

Northern New Mexico traditions are deep rooted and beautiful, involving liberal worship of saints. Groups have processions, and have a strong sense of family and community. The annual procession "El Velorio ha San Ysidro," which starts at Cristo Rey Church, recognizes the farmers who farmed this area in the 1800s. The ceremony and procession start at Cristo Rey Church then down to the Santa Fe River where they ask the blessing of the saint of farmers, San Isidro. Then they go up Cerro Gordo Road to a tiny chapel dedicated to San Isidro. The small stone shrine was built by Lorenzo Lopez, a *santero*, in 1933. After Lopez's death in 1949 interest in the procession waned and the shrine started to fall into disrepair. But his grandson, Ramon Jose Lopez, also a *santero*, kept the tradition going and restored the chapel and revived the tradition. His father before him had carved the *retablos* and *bultos*, but they had "disappeared." Ramon, with his father's tools, carved another *bulto*, which he gave to Cristo Rey Church. Every year in May this figure is carried by Ramon and his family and friends to the shrine.

The Legend Of La Llorona

The "Weeping Woman" legend is the most popular in the Hispanic world. Although stories about her origins vary, Cortez supposedly had a son by an Aztec princess. Cortez then told her he was taking the boy and returning to Spain without her. In despair, she sacrificed the son and committed suicide. Now she spends eternity searching for him along *acequias* and *arroyos*. Judy Beatty and Ed Garcia Kraul, who edited forty-seven stories about the legend in the book *La Llorona* wrote, "Generally, she confronts wrongdoers in her black and white cape and long, flowing dress, and sets them straight by scaring the hell out of them. The experience is terrifying because she screams and wails and then often disappears in thin air. Alcoholics have a particularly bad time with her, as do adulterers. The confrontations take place at night." It is said that the night maintenance workers at the PERA building, which is built on an old cemetery, fear her and refuse to work alone.

Low-riders

Low-riders are modified cars that are an important part of New Mexico's contemporary culture as well as a particularly Hispanic art form. Because of their hydraulics, they jerk erratically as they move forward and backward—demanding attention. They are often elaborately designed with murals painted on the car. Customized interiors may have velvet cushions and the passenger seat may be removed—a captain's chair often replaces it. The popularity of the low-rider culture has become an industry, with car clubs, competitions, art shows, and magazines such as *Low-rider, Orlie's Low-riding Magazine,* and *Low-rider Art.* Española has been proclaimed the low-rider capital of the world. One of the low-rider car clubs, "Another Bad Creation," prohibits members from drinking and using drugs. Manish Gaur, who works for **Life Center for Youth and Adults,** puts on an annual low-rider fund-raiser in September on the Plaza. Call Manish Gaur at (505) 424–1404.

Our Lady Of Guadalupe
Santuario de Guadalupe, 100 Guadalupe Street

Guadalupe Santuario is a world-famous landmark in Santa Fe and the oldest church still standing in the United States dedicated to Our Lady of Guadalupe. The *licensia*, or permission, for its status was granted in October 14, 1795. The exact date the original church was built is unknown. There was no recorded devotion to Our Lady of Guadalupe in Santa Fe until September 1692, after the Spanish returned from El Paso del Norte twelve years after the Pueblo Revolt. Many returning settlers had developed loyalty to Guadalupe probably because there was a Mission Church in El Paso del Norte which was dedicated to Our Lady of Guadalupe. When the Spaniards returned twelve years later with Diego de Vargas, they were already loyal to Our Lady of Guadalupe. In fact Diego de Vargas brought La Conquistadora and "thanked" Our Lady of Guadalupe.

The Guadalupe Historic Foundation began a series of renovations beginning in 1976. Jacqueline Dunnington, one of the leading authorities on Our Lady of Guadalupe in New Mexico, says the largest image of Our Lady of Guadalupe outside of Mexico is the altar screen at the Sanctuario here in Santa Fe. The painting by the Mexican painter José de Alzibar was finished in 1783 and was brought in several sections.

Pueblo Tour

The Anasazi had a developed civilization in New Mexico for more than a thousand years before the Spanish came. New Mexico has nineteen Pueblo Indian reservations with separate identities practicing their traditional religions in old mission churches built in Spanish colonial times.

Included below are the eight Northern Pueblos (see *Map,* page 255)as well as Acoma Pueblo, the most unique, and Cochiti Pueblo, one of the best places to play golf.

Acoma Pueblo

Feast day honors San Esteban, September 2
(505) 552–6606

Acoma, one of the oldest and most stunning pueblos, is a National Historic Landmark. Acoma Pueblo is known as the "Sky City" because its mesa sits 400 feet above a great plateau. In 1598, the nephew of Don Juan de Oñate was killed by the Acomas. Oñate avenged his death by staging a brutal, well-planned attack. Acoma pottery has fine black geometric designs on a white slip. The Acoma people allow visitors only on specially guided, paid tours during the summer season, but tourists are also allowed on the Feast of San Esteban and for three days during Christmas.

Cochiti Pueblo

Feast day honors San Buenaventura, July 14
(505) 465–2244

The church built in 1628 still stands. Cochiti Lake, a recreational community built on land leased by the pueblo, also runs the 18-hole golf course. Cochiti is known for the famous "Storyteller" pottery designs created by Helen Cordero as well as for dance drums.

Nambe Pueblo

Feast day honors St Francis of Assisi, October 4
(505) 455–2036/2037

This pueblo is a short drive from Santa Fe at the foot of the Sangre de Cristo mountains. Most of the architecture is twentieth century. Nambe Falls, one of the few waterfalls in the state, is where a festive annual Fourth of July party is held.

Picuris Pueblo

Feast day honors San Lorenzo, August 10
(505) 587–2519

With only 270 inhabitants, they are isolated in the "Hidden Valley." Picuris Pueblo was not discovered by the Spanish conquistadores until 1591.

Pojoaque Pueblo
Feast day honors Our Lady of Guadalupe, December 12
(505) 455–2278

Pojoaque Pueblo was wiped out by a smallpox epidemic in 1890 but was able to start a new pueblo in the 1930s. The pueblo property along the main highway is leased to many businesses.

San Ildefonso
22 miles northwest of Santa Fe
Feast day honors Saint Ildefonso, January 23
(505) 455–2273

San Ildefonso Pueblo, said to have been established by 1300 A.D., is known for its polished black-ware Martinez (and Julian) pottery. The Black Mesa is spiritually important. It was here that the villagers defended themselves against the Spanish during the re-conquest. San Ildefonso means "where the water cuts down through." Edith Warner, who befriended these spiritual people, was a subject of Peggy Pond Church's book, *The House at Otowi Bridge*. It was this house that Edith Warner entertained Robert Oppenheimer, director of the Manhattan Project. There was a spiritual connection between her friend, the scientist, and the Indians at San Ildefonso Pueblo.

Santa Clara Pueblo
State Road 30 southwest of Española
Feast day honors St. Clara, August 12
(505) 753–7326

The residents of Santa Clara are descendents of the Puye Cliff dwellers. The Puye Cliff cave dwellings may be seen about four miles south of the pueblo. The original site was abandoned in 1500, but its 740-room archeological site is open to the public.

San Juan Pueblo
Feast day honors St. John the Baptist, June 24
(505) 852–4400

In 1598, four hundred years ago, Spaniards under Oñate established their first capital of New Mexico at San Juan until orders led to the founding of Santa Fe in 1610. San Juan was the home of Popé, who led the Pueblo Revolt of 1680. San Juan ceramicists are known for their red or brown pottery.

Taos Pueblo
Feast day honors San Geronimo, September 30
(505) 758–9593

The northernmost of the pueblos and the most famous is the Taos Pueblo. The main part of the building was most likely constructed between 1000 and 1400 A.D. and it is older than any other residential structure in the United States. About 150 live at the pueblo full-time. Some 1,900 live on Taos Pueblo lands. Taos was declared a National Historic Landmark in 1965 and nominated to the World Heritage Society in 1987 (along with the pyramids in Egypt). Taos artists are known for their drums and moccasins.

Tesuque Pueblo
Feast day honors St. James, November 12
(505) 983–2667

Just north of Santa Fe, Tesuque was inhabited as early as 1250 A.D. These people, with the help of Popé and his men, led the famous Pueblo Revolt of 1680.

Dogs and Cats

(and their support systems)

The West MUTT ster Dog Show

Best Support Systems

Since grooming, boarding and veterinary services for pets are such personal services and there are so many qualified people, please consult the Yellow Pages or ask a friend you can trust. For what it is worth, my dog *Taco* goes to the following:

Grooming: **Petite Pet Grooming Shop**
1300 Hickox Street, (505) 982–1780.

Boarding: **Paw Print Kennels**
Racetrack Frontage Road, (505) 471–7194

Veterinarian: **Arrigihetti Animal Hospital**
1882 Plaza del Sur Drive, (505) 471–2888

Free Spay Neuter Clinics at Pueblos
Hugh Wheir
Animal Alliance, 320 Galisteo Street, Suite 205, (505) 986–6007

The non-profit Animal Alliance was founded in 1989 in Santa Fe by veterinarian Hugh Wheir. Each year they conduct free spay-neuter clinics at Indian pueblos and teach veterinary students the procedures. This veterinary service and their educational programs are crucial to reduce animal suffering in areas where there is the greatest demand. They also are working to preserve the endangered Mexican Giant Sea Turtle.

The Best Dog Dance
The Barkin' Ball, Santa Fe Humane Society

The Barkin' Ball, an annual event held each October at Sweeney Center, is for leashed dogs (no cats) and their owners. The $35 admission includes cocktails, dinner, a canine fashion show, and dancing. The latter can be tricky because a lot of dogs haven't been taught how to dance. There are prizes for the best owner-dog look-a-like contest in different categories. The party benefits the Santa Fe Animal Dog Shelter and Humane Society.

The Best On-Site Obedience School
Augusta Farley
Best Friends, Rt. 2, Box 305–F, S.F. 87505, (505) 471–6140

The advantage to this school is that they train your dog in your house where it needs the discipline, instead of at an off-site obedience school.

The Best Service Dogs
Susan Bloch, Canine Companions for Independence
2133 Paseo Ponderosa, (505) 983–3650

Canine Companions for Independence is a nonprofit organization whose mission is to serve the needs of people with disabilities by providing trained service, hearing and social dogs and by providing continuing support to ensure the success of the working team.

The Best Dog Day Nursery
Sylvia Marburger
Del Corazon Boarding Kennels, (505) 474–6703

Located one mile beyond Lone Butte Store on Highway 14, this is one of the few places anywhere where the bedroom for the dogs resembles a nursery. At night each pup sleeps in his own 10-x-10 foot room. During the day all the dogs play together outside in a large enclosed yard. Sylvia interviews both you and your dog to make sure your dog is socially adjusted. All dogs must be spayed or neutered. The cost is $20 a day.

The Best Designer of Dog Collars
Abby Davidson
Spirit Dog Productions, 63 Tano Road, (505) 988–9555

Abby Davidson designs dog collars and tags and has a free color catalogue of products for dogs. *"What is a dog spelled backwards?...God."*

The Only 24-hour Emergency Clinic
Emergency Veterinary Clinic
1911 St. Michael Drive, (505) 984–0625

Heart and Soul Animal Sanctuary
Director, Natalie Owings
For information on adopting (505) 455–2774

The Heart and Soul Animal Sanctuary is a place where abused and neglected animals go when they are not adoptable—this group takes over where the shelter stops. Currently they have 45 animals including dogs, chickens, goats, cats, and birds.

The Best Dog Village
Jackalope Pottery, 2820 Cerrillos Road, (505) 471–8539

Prairie dogs, actually in the rat family, are not dogs but they are awfully cute! Several years ago, Darby McQuade, the owner of Jackalope Pottery, relocated a colony of prairie dogs from DeVargas Junior High School's football field into a new 18-foot-deep concrete-lined burrow behind his store on Cerrillos Road. There they still live.

The Best Drug Detection Dogs
K-9 Canine Kennels

K-9 Canine Kennels was founded in 1987 under the supervision of Major Glenn Remby. They have sixteen dogs who detect drugs (black labs), perform crowd control (Rotweillers), and track (bloodhounds). They have found lost children, lost skiiers and hikers, and lost cadavers. They are also trained to track in the water. The K-9 dogs have reputedly "found $2,000,000 worth of illegal drugs" in the state.

The Best Places to Bond with Your Dog
Paw Clean Laundramutt
825 Early Street, Suite D (505) 989–1414 or 984–0814

There are many pet washing and grooming places in town that you can find in the phone book. But if you want to feel more connected to your dog, Laundramutt is the answer. Laundramutt will provide YOU with the shampoo, conditioners, nail clippers, matt brush, and the washing basin for a reduced cost (as though you were going to the laundramat). If you don't wash dogs (or windows), they are also a full-service dog grooming outfit. The

107

shop *Regarding the Animal* 1415 Alameda Street, (505) 820–7166 is another place where you have the option to wash your own dog. The price includes use of fresh towels, shampoo, nail clippers, and an apron.

The Best Rural Outreach For Spay Neuter

Pecos Animal Welfare Society (PAWS)
P. O. Box 704, Pecos 8755, (505) 471–3708

PAWS is a local animal welfare organization serving rural communities in Northern New Mexico. Its mobile outreach Pawsmobile goes to small villages and provides curbside "pick-up" for dogs and cats that need to be spayed and neutered. They also offer foster care for abandoned dogs and cats.

The Biggest Variety of Dog and Cat Food

Santa Fe Pet-Vet Supply
913 W. Alameda Street, (505) 988–2237

If it is important to provision a finicky pet with the last word in dog food, this is the place to go.

The Best Place to Get a Pet

The Santa Fe Animal and Humane Society
1920 Cerrillos Road, (505) 983–4309

It is Santa Fe "chic" to have a dog from the pound. Pound dogs have a "saved" mentality and are thankful for anything. One of the biggest goals of the shelter is to help change attitudes towards animals and to educate the public about animal abuse.

The Most Exclusive Dog Burial Site ("El Deliro")

School of American Research, 660 Garcia Street, (505) 982–3585

The most famous dog cemetery in the country is at the School of American Research where maiden sisters Elizabeth Amelia White and Martha Root White lived in the 20s and 30s and raised Afghans and Irish wolfhounds. The kennels were located in the current archeology building. Martha died in 1939 and Amelia died in 1972. During these years more than 30 exotically named dogs and one cat were buried with wooden crosses and nameplates.

Amelia White was instrumental in the founding of the Santa Fe Animal Shelter. When Amelia died, the land was donated to the School of American Research. If you make a sizable contribution, maybe you will be able to bury your dog there.

The Best Apparel Shop

Teca Tu, Sanbusco Market Center, 500 Montezuma Avenue, Suite 108
(505) 982–9374

This dog apparel shop is for discriminating dogs, cats, and owners. The shop has a "deli for dogs and cats." One of the most popular items is a portable dog dish to take on hikes.

The Best Animal Communicator

Kate Solisti
(505) 984–8876

Noboby knows the real truth about cats and dogs or people except those that can communicate with them!

The Best Place to Show Your "Shelter" Dog

WestMUTTster Dog Show

Anyone who attended the First Annual WestMUTTster Show (for shelter dogs only) know that its the most popular social event for dogs in Santa Fe. The competition was fierce. Ford Ruthling's dog Mollie was bitten while trying to compete for the "Most Beautiful" event. Mollie had to be taken to the hospital and the other dog was disqualified. Nancy Dickinson's three-legged dog won the "Most Urine" contest. Dawn Douglas and her dog won a yodelling contest .

The Most Endowed Cat

El Zaguan

The cat "Mischka" was owned by Sylvia Loomis who lived at El Zaguan for more than forty years and died in 1994. Sylvia was the secretary to Mrs. Dietrich who saved the house from demolition by buying it and converting it into rental apartments. After her death in 1961 the building was bought by the Historic Santa Fe

Foundation. Mischka attends all the meetings of the Foundation and is just as much a part of El Zaguan as was her owner Sylvia who made the endowment.

Let's dance? Wanna boogie? Scene from the Barkin' Ball

Fine Arts

Art is long and time is fleeting

FINE ARTS

The Eye of the Collector

Contemporary art is a thriving global business and Santa Fe has an enviable reputation as one of the top three U.S. centers. The museums, the galleries, and the broad cross-section of artists who work here, and the presence of patrons and collectors, make Santa Fe one of the world's most sophisticated places to visit if you are interested in art.

The recently opened Georgia O'Keeffe Museum—along with SITE Santa Fe, a non-commercial contemporary exhibit space whose second international biennial opened during the summer of 1997—alone attract enough attention from art critics, dealers, and the viewing public to put Santa Fe on the map of "don't miss" places. In addition there are internationally known contemporary artists who live and work in the area—Bruce Nauman, Susan Rothenberg, Agnes Martin, Louis Jimenez, and Meridel Rubenstein. The Santa Fe Art Institute at the College of Santa Fe also attracts well-known contemporary "masters in residence."

Contemporary art, ethnic art, ancient art...art past, present, future, and perfect...can be found in leisurely strolls through town. Most galleries cluster on Canyon Road, the "art and soul of Santa Fe," or near the Plaza. All of these galleries have rotating exhibits and a stable of artists. Send me *your* recommendations for other respectable and exciting local galleries I have not been able to include here—art is long, but pages fleeting—and you'll find them in the next edition of this book. The following is today's representative sampling.

Represents Joan Potter and Veryl Goodnight
Altermann & Morris Galleries, 225 Canyon Road, (505) 983–1590

Joan Potter's paintings are filled with light and she is well-known for her lace and tapestry backgrounds and her fruit and flower still lifes. She has won over thirty awards and belongs to the invitational groups; Artists in America and Oil Painters of America.

Veryl Goodnight considered a regional artist, did a monumental statue of several horses stampeding through the broken Berlin Wall and called it *The Day the Wall Came Down* to commemorate the freedom.

He Sold a Mary Cassatt for $1 million
Barclay Fine Art, 424 Canyon Road, (505) 986–1400
By Appointment Only

Rutgers Barclay sold Cassatt's *Thomas Standing with His Mother Sucking His Thumb* (1893) for $1 million. Founded in 1980, Barclay Fine Art has dealt in 19th and 20th-century paintings, drawings, and sculpture. By appointment only.

Represents the Most Famous 20th century Fiber Artist
Belles Artes, 653 Canyon Road, (505) 983–2745

The Belles Artes displays works by Olga-de-Amaral—considered one of the most important international fiber artist. They represent Judy Pfaff who does installations and works on paper. Entering it is like walking into a 3D abstract expressionist painting. The gallery shows international contemporary art; African and Precolumbian, fiber, clay, painting, and sculpture.

The Most Famous Buffalo (aside from Ted Turner's)
There was a big stir a few years ago when Nedra Matteucci's Fenn Gallery placed a six-foot-tall 1,600-pound sculpture of a buffalo by Dan Ostermiller on a city median in front of the gallery on the corner of Paseo de Peralta and Acequia Madre. The city ordered the sculpture removed claiming it was a dangerous distraction and a hazard to motorists. No issue in the last twenty years has drawn as swift and intense a reaction: school children had a sit-in, Indian groups and civic organizations started a campaign to Save Our Buffalo (SOB). There were more letters sent to the editor than on any other subject. The buffalo now roams on his new home with Peaches and Eddie Gilbert.

They Exhibited Robert Colescott's Work
Cline Lewallen Contemporary, 129 W. Palace Avenue, (505) 988–8997

In 1997 Robert Colescott was chosen to represent the United States at the 47th Venice *Biennale*, the oldest and most prestigious contemporary arts festival in the world. Colescott is the first African American painter and the first painter to represent the United States in this exhibition since Jasper Johns in 1988. Cline Lewallen worked in conjunction with SITE Santa Fe in this representation. A two-year U.S. tour of Colescott paintings starts at SITE Santa Fe in 1998. Cline Lewallen also represents popular local painters, John Fincher, Forest Moses, and Louis Jimenez.

Largest Collection of Peruvian and Bolivian Textiles
Conlon-Siegal Galleries, 702 1/2 Canyon Road, (505)820–7744

The Conlon-Siegal Gallery is a collaborative effort. Bunny Conlon and Bill Siegal are married to each other, and they have several galleries in the same location. Bunny presents cutting edge contemporary art in one gallery and Bill presents historic textile in another gallery. They recently opened a 10,000-square-foot sculpture garden.

Represents Local Emerging Artists
Linda Durham Contemporary Art, HC75, Box 601, Galisteo 87540, NM
(505) 466–6600

Linda Durham, who has been involved in all aspects of the contemporary art scene for twenty years, moved from Canyon Road to Galisteo and still has a great stable of local artists—it just takes a bit longer to get there. She represents Peter Sarkisian, a young video artist who does both big video installations and small video works. Linda also represents another very popular artist, Robert Kelly, a local Santa Fean who divides his time between New York City and Santa Fe.

The Most Beautiful Sculpture Garden in Santa Fe
Nedra Matteucci's Fenn Gallery, 1075 Paseo de Peralta, (505) 982–4631

Large sculptures are shown in a spectacularly landscaped garden surrounding a large pond. The garden is also the home of

Hamilton, a Vietnamese pig who was a gift from Roddy Burdine, who also roams the gallery during work hours. The gallery's one-acre garden is an exceptional setting for monumental works by internationally known artists such as Francisco Zuniga and local and regional artists such as Glenna Goodacre and Doug Hyde. Goodacre's most controversial work is the Women's VietNam Memorial in Washington, D.C , the first memorial to commemorate women's military service. Doug Hyde was voted local "Artist of the Year" in 1996. Santa Fe and the Fenn Gallery are also home to Clark Hulings and Gary Niblett.

Clark Hulings, recognized as one of the best realist painters in America, paints with incredible detail, rich color, and a keen sense of light. In 1982 he sold a painting called "kaleidoscope" at the Western Heritage Auction for $310,000—a record price for a living artist from the West.

Gary Niblett is the most renowned Western painter in Santa Fe. His regionally inspired paintings of pioneer families, cowboys, Indians, horses, wagon trains, and ghost towns have won many national awards. The book *Gary Niblett: A New Look at the Old West* tells amusing tales about his close family and being brought up on a ranch in New Mexico. One of his relatives said about people from other places, "If they're not from Texas, we don't embarrass them by asking them where they are from."

Nedra's other gallery, **Nedra Matteucci Fine Art,** 555 Canyon Road, (505) 983-2731 represents the estate of the legendary Tommy Macaione, the "Van Gogh of Santa Fe." Tommy was recognized not only for his political involvement but also for his presence as a painter on the historic Eastside. Before he died he had seventy-five cats and twenty-one dogs living with him.

The Most Widely Exhibited Polish Artist in New Mexico
Voytek Fongor, (505) 983–4968

Voytek has exhibited at the Guggenheim Museum, the Museum of Modern Art, and the Hirshhorn Museum at the Smithsonian Institute and others. Voytek paints still lifes, portraits, and nudes. His wife Magda is a well-known folk artist.

She Organized ART, Santa Fe 1997
Megan Fox Gallery, 311 Aztec Street, (505) 989–9141

Megan Fox ran the international art fair that included more than fifty dealers who exhibited important contemporary and modern art in the rooms of the Hotel Santa Fe. The fair coincided with the opening of SITE Santa Fe's second biennial. Although her doll house-sized gallery located in the Guadalupe area near the Aztec Street Cafe features contemporary photography, her best seller is Charles Thomas O'Neil—an emerging local artist whose work is popular with Santa Fe collectors.

His Father Was One of 29 Navajo Code Talkers
R. C. Gorman (in Taos), (505) 758–3250

R.C. Gorman is a well known Navajo artist who lives in Taos. Gorman's father foiled Japanese eavesdroppers during World War II by simply speaking their native language. The code talkers were a special communications unit formed to foil Japanese eavesdropping. The Navajo language was used as the basis of a battlefield code used during the 1942–1945 Pacific campaigns. For example airplanes became "birds" which were codenamed *tsidi*.

A 104-Acre Allan Houser Sculpture Garden
Allan Houser, Inc.
Route 14, (505) 471–9667

Native American Allan Houser was one of the most important international artists of the 20th century; President Bush awarded him a National Medal of the Arts. The Allan Houser Compound, open by appointment, is located 20 minutes south of Santa Fe on Route 14. It features a ten-acre sculpture garden, a visitors' center, an indoor showroom, and a scholarly archive of Houser's collection. To insure best quality, the studio added its own bronze foundry, which began casting in 1996. Other family members live at the compound, and works of art by Allan Houser's son, Bob Haozous, are also exhibited there. Bob's contemporary steel sculptures, which usually make a political statement, are considered among the best of the Native American political or environmental artists.

Represents "Concrete & Radical" Minimal Art
Charlotte Jackson Fine Art, 123 E. Marcy Street, (505) 989–8688

Charlotte Jackson is the only gallery in Santa Fe that represents "concrete and radical" painters from the United States and Europe. Concrete painting is a very strong movement in the European Art Community; it is expressive of an appreciation for the clarity and focus of monochromatic work that is uncommon in the United States. Charlotte Jackson is now an international dealer of monochromatic paintings. An example is the work of Marsha Hafif's pink monochromatic paintings. Florence Pierce from Albuquerque, one of the only surviving members of the Transcendental Painting Group, shifted to the minimalist monochromatic style of work and had a show at the Museum of Fine Arts in 1997.

The Only Latin American Contemporary Art Gallery
Meredith Kelly Latin American Fine Art
135 W. Palace, (505) 986–8699

"Latin American art is currently making its presence felt in many New Mexico galleries and museums. The artists now being shown are making demands upon our emotions and questioning our spirituality."—**Meredith Kelly,** Director

Greatest Space to Exhibit Serious Contemporary Art
Allene Lapides Gallery, 588 Canyon Road, (505) 984–0191

Allene Lapides has an incredible eye for architectural layout. It was her vision that the Marion's understood when they decided to buy her old gallery for the Georgia O'Keeffe Museum. The Allene Lapides Gallery now occupies the most beautifully renovated historic building on Canyon Road and a new building behind. The gallery represents national and international artists as well as several prominent local artists such as James Havard, Herb Ritts, and Alexandra Eldridge.

The Most Electrifying Contemporary Sculpture In N.M.
in Quemado, NM, (505) 773-4560 and (505) 842–0365

Lightning Fields, by American sculpture Walter De Maria, was commissioned by Dia Center for the Arts. Four hundred stainless steel poles in a rectangular grid array one mile by one kilometer. The ultimate visual and mental experience is to go with as few people as possible and stay at least one night during the summer when there are lightning storms. Dinner and breakfast the next day are provided, but bring your own liquid refreshments!

Perhaps the Most Well-Paid Living Woman Artist
Agnes Martin, (505) 758–9636 in Taos

Agnes Martin, the most famous woman "minimalist" in the world, is probably also the highest-paid woman artist. She is well-known here and abroad, and her work is in many museums and private collections. Her first showing in a museum took place in 1947 at the Harwood Museum in Taos when she was a graduate student at the University of New Mexico. This long-standing relationship has culminated in a gift of seven paintings which she gave to the museum in 1994. The Harwood Museum is building a special wing, the *Agnes Martin Gallery,* which will include an octagonal-shaped gallery to permanently house the seven paintings—a *series* which is to be exhibited as a set. (The only other series is owned by the Whitney Museum in New York). The Agnes Martin Gallery will be one of the most important exhibition spaces dedicated to a woman artist in the world. For more information call the Harwood Museum (505) 758-9826.

The Most Intimate
Ernesto Mayans Galleries, 601 Canyon Road, (505) 983–8068

Here you will find twentieth century paintings and sculpture. Many people like his photography by such artists as Kertesz and Mexican photograhpher Iturbide. David Barbero, a local colorist whose pictures hang in the window of the gallery, is a big draw.

One of the Oldest Art Galleries in the Country
Munson Gallery, 225 Canyon Road, (505) 983–1657

Larry Munson comes from three generations of established art gallery owners who started out in New Haven, Connecticut, in 1860. His gallery in Chatham on Cape Cod, Massachusetts, has been open since 1955, and his gallery in Santa Fe first opened in

1979 next door to The Compound Restaurant. In 1984, he opened his current gallery on Canyon Road. He represents popular William Lumpkins, one of the surviving members of New Mexico's Transcendental Painting Group (1938–1942) and Elmer Schooley from Roswell, New Mexico, who does colorful over-sized New Mexico landscape paintings in a pointalist style.

Two Local Internationally Known Artists
Bruce Nauman and Susan Rothenberg

"Looking at the Nauman restrospective is like walking through someone else's psychoanalysis; it's full of patterns and recurring wishes, anxieties, and obsessions."—**Andrew Solomon** in *The New York Times*

Bruce Naumann and his wife Susan Rothenberg are two of the most blue-chip artists who have settled here. Bruce Nauman was one of two Santa Fe artists who showed at SITE Santa Fe, 1995. Together they live a low-profile life on their Galisteo ranch. Her best-known paintings are large, subdued, and dark pictures of horses. They both avoid Western and Santa Fe clichés in their work.

An Indian Owned Art Gallery
Niman Fine Art, 125 Lincoln Avenue, (505) 988–5091

The gallery is one of only two Indian-owned art galleries in Santa Fe. The gallery is owned by famous Indian painter Dan Naminga's father. They represent Allan Houser, Fritz Scholder, and of course Dan Namingha, a 25-year resident of Santa Fe, and one of five generations of artists.

Represents Luis Tapia
Owens Dewey Gallery, 76 E. San Francisco Street, (505) 982–6244

Owens Dewey focuses on nineteenth and twentieth century American paintings, and sculpture as well as contemporary (Page Allen) and Spanish colonial art. He has represented Luis Tapia, whose carvings and religious images are in many museum collections. They provide consulting and appraisal services.

The Widest Variety of Art & the Most Quality Galleries
Gerald Peters Gallery, 439 Camino del Monte Sol, (505) 988–8961

The Gerald Peters Gallery has the widest artistic variety in Santa Fe, representing internationally known artists such as Helen Frankenthaler, Charles Ginnever, Beverly Pepper, George Rickey and Carlo Maria Mariani, and, of course, such local artists as Carol Anthony, Carol Mothner, Mark Spencer, Mary Neumuth, and George Fischer (from Taos). In addition he handles some of the finest paintings of the Taos Founders, the Santa Fe art colony, and Western painters and sculptors such as Frederic Remington and Charles Russell. He handled Georgia O'Keeffe's work during the last years of her life in addition to collecting her work. Gerry, who has been labeled the Donald Trump of Santa Fe, will soon relocate to a 32,000-square-foot gallery space next to Nedra Matteucci's Fenn Gallery on Paseo de Peralta. Gerald Peters also has galleries in Dallas and New York City.

Created "Critical Mass" for SITE Santa Fe, 1995
Meridel Rubenstein, (505) 471–3054
Cline Lewallen Contemporary, 129 W. Palace Avenue, (505) 988–8897

This exhibit was especially interesting if you read Peggy Pond Church's *House at Otowi Bridge* about Edith Warner and her connection both with the San Ildefonso Pueblo Indians and with scientists at Los Alamos, whom Robert Oppenheimer, director of the Manhattan Project, often brought to Edith Warner's house for dinner. It took Meridel Rubenstein six years to complete *Critical Mass*—a mixed-media work about the creation of the bomb and its fiftieth anniversary—in which Meridel examines interactions between the mysticism of native culture and the scientific approach of scientists. Her husband is Jerry West (505) 424–3959, a well-known painter whose 1989 mural is in the lobby at City Hall.

She Shows at Santa Fe's only Coop Gallery
Jane Chermayeff at Santa Fe Contemporary Art
901 W. San Mateo, (505) 988–5678

Jane Chermayeff works in oils, acrylics and watercolors and her subjects; landscapes, still lifes and abstracts, show her subtle to vivid sense of color. Her designs are often strong and exhuberant.

120

The Most "Rediscovered" Santa Fe Art Colony Artist
Albert Schmidt

Gerald Peters Gallery, 439 Camino Del Monte Sol, (505) 988–8961

Most of the original Santa Fe art colony painters who came here from big Eastern cities became established painters and today are well known. But when Albert Schmidt died (1885–1957), his widow Marjorie placed his work in storage where it remained for 35 years. When Marjorie died at age 98 in 1992, Karen Schmidt, granddaughter and heir to her grandparents' estate, found hundreds of his paintings in the garage of their Tesuque property. Karen enlisted Gerald Peters to help re-establish Schmidt's previous artistic reputation. Few people then knew that Schmidt had been well-known in Chicago in 1915 before he came to Santa Fe in 1922. The exhibit at Gerald Peters Gallery called the *Silent Partner* told the story of how the artist's early fame in Chicago was forgotten but regained in Santa Fe, until he died and was forgotten once more...before his most recent revival!

The Only Second Generation Gallery Owner
Laurel Seth Gallery, 1121 Paseo de Peralta Street, (505) 988–7349

Laurel is a second generation gallery owner who specializes in contemporary and representational fine art and folk art. Her mother, Jean Seth, opened a gallery at 710 Canyon Road in 1967. She was married to the late Oliver Seth, Appellate Court Justice and well known in all circles. Josette Delaharpe and Lisa Bemis show in this gallery.

One of the Best Foundries in the Country
Shidoni Scupture Foundry and Gallery, Bishop's Lodge Road in Tesuque
(505) 988–8001

An eight-acre garden shows large contemporary sculpture on consignment of artists who otherwise might not have any other place to show. Two outdoor fields and an indoor gallery has contemporary pieces. Tom Hicks has run the gallery and foundry for over twenty years—one of the best foundries in the country. The public is invited to see the bronze pourings.

Santa Fe's International Biennial
Director, Louis Grachos
SITE Santa Fe, 1995, 1997, 1606 Paseo de Peralta, (505) 989–1199

SITE Santa Fe, 1995 was the first international contemporary biennial presented in Santa Fe. The inaugural exhibition called *Longing and Belonging: From the Faraway Nearby*—played off the theme of how place and identity affect art and culture. Thirty-one artists were selected because of their "site-specific" themes which ranged from lowriders to the making of the bomb at Los Alamos. The second biennial was in 1997. Ongoing exhibits between biennials complement the local art scene by introducing internationally known works of art and literature.

She Is one of the Top Portrait Painters in the Country
Bettina Steinke

Bettina Steinke is considered one of the best portrait painters in the country but she isn't painting portraits anymore. She has painted Dwight D. Eisenhower, Irving Berlin, Arturo Toscanini, Walter Winchell, Wendell Wilkie, and many other notables. Her first job was Toscanini. She did such a good job that he was commissioned to paint all ninety-eight musicians in the orchestra. She started painting when she was twelve years old. One of her teachers was Norman Rockwell.

Space Allows Viewers to See An Entire Range of Work
Riva Yares Gallery, 123 Grant Avenue, (505) 984–0330

Her gallery in Santa Fe has been open for five years and her other gallery in Scottsdale has been in business for thirty five years in 1997. Her gallery space in Santa Fe enhances the viewing of monumental works of art, all from the center of the room. One of their well-known painters, Estaban Vicente, is 95 years old and still painting and teaching. They represent Hans Hoffman, the father of abstract expressionism and Milton Avery's work as well as Morris Lewis, Ed Moses; considered cutting edge in the 70s, and Robert Graham who is married to Angelica Houston. Elias Rivera is inspired by his trips to Guadamala and Central America.

He is well-known for his very large paintings of ordinary Guadamalen people captured in a brilliant explosion of light and color. His openings sell out quickly because his paintings are sought after by museums and collectors.

The Most Important Painting Dynasty
Director, Peter de la Fuente
Wyeth-Hurd Gallery, 301 E. Palace Avenue, (505) 989–8380

The late Henriette Wyeth was particularly known for her still life paintings and her portraits captured her subjects' inner spirit. She was the daughter of artist N. C. Wyeth and sister of Andrew Wyeth. She married artist Peter Hurd and established themselves at Sentinel Ranch in San Patricio, New Mexico. Their son Michael Hurd and daughter, Carol Rogers both became artists. The family has a gallery at their Sentinel Ranch in San Patricio (505) 653–4331. Peter de la Fuente, a grandson and painter, is the director of the Wyett-Hurd Gallery.

Historic New Mexico Painters
Zaplan Lambert Gallery, 651 Canyon Road, (505) 982–6100

The Zaplan Lambert Gallery show the "explorer painters" George Catlin and Thomas Moran, but their focus is on the Taos and Santa Fe Founders. They represent a local couple, Jim Asher and Joanna Arnet, who share a studio in a house built by the popular TV series *This Old House*. They both paint flowers—he in watercolors and she in oil. Zaplan Lambert Gallery also represents local horsewoman Star York; she sculpts horses and she also plays polo for the Santa Fe team.

Furniture & Furnishings

Santa Fe has a large selection of designers, furnituremakers, antique shops and local artists to choose from. Santa Fe style furnishings can be simple or elaborate, reflecting one or all the influences of the people who have lived here: Spanish, Mexican, Indian, missionary, cowboy, and Anglo. The style can be old or new, traditional, country, elegant, and casual. The following is a smattering of furnituremakers and stores that sell furniture. Four well-known, "resource"-ful local decorators are Barbara Pohlman (who decorates Jane Fonda and Ted Turner's ranches), Susan Dupépé, Shanna Gunn, and Mary Emmerling (she has written many books on decorating). For other possibilities, see Crafts and Artifacts.

Furnituremakers

William Penhallow Henderson and his wife, the poet Alice Corbin Henderson, were an important part of the Santa Fe art colony from the 1920s to mid-1940s. His hand-carved furniture became the protoype of Santa Fe style. Alice was diagnosed with TB in 1917 and was given a year to live. Alice Corbin entered Sunmount Sanitarium and Henderson then lived with his daughter Alice Oliver Henderson—Tish Frank's mother—who married Bob Evans, the only son of Mabel Dodge Lujan.

The Most Complete Home Furnishings Store
American Country Collection Inc., 620 Cerrillos Road, (505) 984–0955
On the Plaza, (505) 982–1296

Owners Carol Israel and Michael Needle have antiques from verywhere. They also produce their own line of furniture reproductions, and fabric and lamp lines. They also reupholster furniture. Their Memorial Day weekend sale is legendary.

The Best Cowboy Furniture
LD Burke's, 1105 Don Gaspar, Studio (505) 424–7322 or (505) 983–8001
Brandon Gallery, 235 Don Gaspar (505) 820–1400

LD, which stands for "Little David," makes one- of-a-kind cowboy furniture—some of his furniture even has hooves and antlers! Gorbachev and Ronald Reagan both own mirrors made by Burke.

Won First Place at Spanish Market for a Reproduction
David E. C'de Baca, 18 Capilla Vieja, Santa Fe NM 87505 (505) 438–3211

A traditional wood-carver, C'de Baca makes museum reproductions in the Spanish New Mexican style.

John Gaw Meem Designs
John Gaw Meem Designs, (505) 753–0460
Showroom: 227 Otero Street (in the Cornerstones Building)

Nancy Meem Wirth (daughter of noted architect, John Gaw Meem), works with partner George O'Bryan (grandson of Jesse Nusbaum, first director of the Laboratory of Anthropology) to manufacture furniture using Meems' designs. Meem designed more than eighty private houses and many public buildings, including Cristo Rey Catholic Church.

Thirty-five Years in Business—the Most Time Honored
Volker de la Harpe, 707 Canyon Road, (505) 983–4074

His custom-made, Northern European one-of-a-kind pieces are made of the finest walnut and cherry in the only furniture factory on Canyon Road. He also makes "elegant Southwest" pieces.

The "Teddy Roosevelt Look"
Carlos Machado, (505) 466–3237 in Lamy

Carlos Machado makes "hill country," leather covered, hand-tooled Victorian-influenced furniture that belongs in "a cattleman parlor with flocked wallpaper."

125

The Finest Local Custom-Made Furniture
Morrelli Fine Furniture and Custom Doors
540 S. Guadalupe Street, (505) 992–8867 or (800) 739–6886

Jerry Morrelli is an extraordinary Santa Fe-based architectural and fine furnishings designer-builder who creates a spectacular array of custom-designed, hand-made, hand-carved, heirloom-quality fine furniture, doors and entry ways, and architectural elements.

The Best Conference For Woodworkers
New Mexico Woodworkers' Conference at Santa Fe Community College
John Oliver, (800) 299–9886, in June

Local Home-Made Southwestern
Santa Fe Country Furniture, 1708 Cerrillos Road, (505) 984–1478

All of their very functional Southwestern furniture is made locally and according to your specifications and price range.

The Best Animal Furniture
David Ross Studio Gallery, 610 Canyon Road, (505) 988–4017

David has a working studio on Canyon Road where he has an inventory of furniture with animals painted on headboards, library stairs, and painted screens. He will do a commission of your favorite pet.

Santa Fe Heritage Furniture
500 Montezuma Street, Sambusco Center, (505) 983–5986

This outfit makes custom-made doors and furniture in the Territorial and Spanish colonial styles as well as ornately carved furniture.

The Oldest Furniture Maker in the State
Southwest Spanish Craftsmen, 328 S. Guadalupe Street, (505) 982–1767

Roger Nussbaumer owns Southwest Spanish Craftsmen which opened in 1927, where they make furniture and doors in the Spanish tradition, including reproduction museum pieces. They do any style from Spanish Renaissance to Spanish colonial and territorial.

Stores

The Largest Furniture Store In New Mexico
American Home Furniture, 901 St. Michael Drive, (505) 988–4502

Dennis McMillan shows his furniture lines from Old Santa Fe Furniture Company exclusively at American Home Furniture.

Nine Antique Stores in One!
Antiques on Grant, 136 Grant Avenue, (505) 995–9701

Antiques on Grant has nine antique stores in the historic Tully House. Collectively they sell everything from American and European antiques to ethnic furnishings and art.

The Biggest Downtown Mexican Furniture Operation
Artesanos, 222 Galisteo Street, (505) 983–1743

Artisanos' furniture operation is on Galisteo along with its glassware, light fixtures, and some tile. Their large tile operation is in a different location—1414 Maclovia Street.

Fine English & French Antiques
Mary Corley Antiques, 215 North Guadalupe Street, (505) 984–0863

Owned by David and Mary Corley, the store features fine imported French and English country antiques and accessories and occasional reproductions drawn from David Corley Designs inventory. Their dry-flower arrangements are magnificent one-of-a-kind designs.

Un-Southwest Look
Expressions, 607 Cerrillos Road, (505) 820–0025
Will Downey

This nationwide franchise makes custom upholstery for the home and has a broad variety of fabrics as well as a hundred and fifty frames to choose from.

Spanish Antiques
Elements, 1091 Siler Road, at Agua Fria (505) 474–7866

The six-thousand square foot showroom has a collection of antiques from sixteenth to nineteenth-century Spain.

Representative for David Marsh Painted Pine Furniture
Leslie Flynt Gallery, 225 Canyon Road, (505) 982–5178, (800) 743–8611

We carry handcrafted furniture all made from scratch,
Every few months we get a new batch.
We have lamps and frames for you and a friend,
A bundle of dough you won't have to spend.
So stop by, we're open seven days a week,
Chances are you'll find what you seek.

The Largest Mexican Furniture Store
Jackalope Furniture, 2810 Cerrillos Road, (505) 471–5390

See "Marketplaces."

Two Different Locations!
El Paso Import Company, 1519 Paseo de Peralta, (505) 986–0037
419 Sandoval Street, (505) 982–5698

El Paso Import sells Mexican colonial and ranch style antique reproductions. Their furniture in two locations is made in Juarez.

Doors!
La Puerta,1302 Cerrillos Road, (505) 984–8164

This is a good place to go if you want antique doors from Mexico. If you think the door is the most important thing about a house, you may be the kind of person who finds the door before you build the house. If so, this is the place for you!

History

The 400th Anniversary of Don Juan de Oñate's
arrival in New Mexico
1598-1998

10 stages of history

*1998 is an important year for New Mexicans because it is the **400th** anniversary of the Spanish arrival in the area, the **400th** anniversary of the El Camino Real. and the **150th** anniversary of the Treaty of Guadalupe-Hildago.*

Settling the west was a south-north movement; people came up from Mexico City to Santa Fe. El Camino Real—the Royal Road—was one of the world's greatest trade routes: it connected Mexico City to Santa Fe on 1,800 miles of highway for 400 years. This was New Mexico's only connection to European civilization until the 1820s when the Santa Fe Trail was forged. Interestingly enough, the Santa Fe Trail is always mentioned in history books, but the El Camino Real is often not.

Spanish Exploration: 1540–1598

In 1540 Francisco Vasquez de Coronado, a 29-year-old explorer, "borrowed" $1 million (in today's equivalent money) from his wife to help finance a trip to find the legendary Seven Cities of Cibola (gold) and Quivira. The expedition with 300 soldiers, livestock, and 1,300 servants turned out to be a bust. Instead of finding cities of gold they found a Zuni Pueblo in New Mexico. After a series of successful invasions on Pueblos, he returned broke and discredited to Mexico City in 1542. Other "entradas" were attempted by other Spaniards after Coronado's departure.

Permanent settlement was not achieved until 1598. Juan de Oñate, a prominent and wealthy citizen from Zacatecas, then led an expedition of ten Franciscans, 129 soldiers, many with their children, cattle and a "chronicler." He established the first Spanish colony in New Mexico on the Rio Grande, in San Gabriel, twenty-five miles north of Santa Fe near San Juan Pueblo in 1598.

"Zaldivar's men were impressed with the buffalo that 'have beards like billy-goats' and decided to take some of the animals back in

captivity. A stockade was erected and some buffalo directed into the trap, whereupon the Spaniards learned that herding buffalo was a little different from their previous experiences with four-legged animals. Gaspar Perez de Villagre, one of Oñate's captains, relates that 'they began to stampede, rushing about like a raging whirlpool, raising an immense cloud. Had our soldiers not been stationed on an eminence [hill] they would no doubt have been trampled to death beneath the hooves of these savage beasts.' With the stockade in shambles and the men thankful for their lives, no further attempts were made to herd buffalo. Could this have been the first roundup in the West?"—**Tom Chávez**, Director, Palace of the Governors

When Oñate became unpopular he was ordered back to Mexico City in 1609. While in New Mexico he stopped at El Morro (between Acoma and Zuni) and cut his name in stone on **Inscription Rock.** He was the first European to do this. Today it is a national monument off NM 53, (505) 783-4226.

Spanish Colonization: 1600–1680

When Pedro de Peralta was appointed governor and sent to New Mexico, he chose a spot which had more water and better protection, La Villa de Santa Fe—The City of Holy Faith. Santa Fe had already been founded earlier by Don Juan de Oñate, but Peralta got the credit for the 1607 founding of Santa Fe. Santa Fe was chartered as capital in 1610. Peralta followed the Ordinances of 1573 legislated by King Philip II of Spain calling for ordered development of New World settlements. These requirements are still visually engraved on Santa Fe's architectural layout: a central plaza, surrounded by street grids. An *acequia* system diverted water from the Santa Fe River to cultivate the fields. Peralta built the Palace of the Governors, the oldest continuously used public building in the United States. Santa Fe became the most northern Spanish outpost until 1821.

For seventy years churches were built with forced Indian labor as Franciscan friars tried to convert the Indians to Catholicism. Many pueblos disappeared. The Indians attempted a number of unsuccessful revolts because the Spanish were trying to outlaw their religious and customary practices. Then in 1675, Pueblo religious leaders were sentenced to death for witchcraft. One Indian religious leader, ironically named Popé, vowed revenge and he hid out for several years as he orchestrated a revolt of all the Pueblos.

Pueblo Revolt: 1680–1693

The Pueblo Revolt began at the Taos Pueblo. Popé was a key figure in the rebellion. He sent messengers who ran to other Pueblos carrying a knotted cord. The knots signified the number of days until the beginning of the uprising. Four hundred Spanish settlers and friars died. In Santa Fe, about 1,000 settlers sought refuge in the Palace of the Governors. Then they fled 330 miles to El Paso del Norte via El Camino Real after the Pueblo Indians drove them out. They remained exiled for thirteen years until 1693. During this time, some Spanish traditions persisted but Catholicism was almost completely obliterated.

Reconquest and Resettlement: 1692–1821

In 1692, Diego de Vargas marched up the Rio Grande "accepting submission" of the Pueblos all along the way. In 1693, he marched into Santa Fe with his Spanish military forces and laid seige on the Palace of Governors.

Santa Fe Trail Opens, Mexican Rule: 1821–1846

When Mexico became independent from Spain in the Treaty of Cordova, New Mexico became part of Mexico. The commercial growth of Santa Fe was augmented by the opening of the Santa Fe Trail in 1821. The 900-mile journey on the Santa Fe Trail from Missouri to Santa Fe took two months. Santa Fe became a gateway for U.S. traders who went from Independence, Missouri to Chihuahua and points south in Mexico. The trail was international until after the outbreak of the Mexican War in 1846.

U.S Military Occupation: 1846–1850

General Kearny and the Army of the West in 1846 marched unopposed into the Santa Fe Plaza on August 18, 1846, establishing American rule over the entire route. In August 1846, Kearny appointed Charles Bent as governor, with hardly any resistance from Mexico, whose last governor, Manuel Armijo, had fled. But in January 1847, New Mexicans revolted and scalped Governor Bent. According to local historian Marc Simmons, the "most famous scalp ever lost in New Mexico was that of Gov. Bent." In 1848, the Treaty of Guadalupe-Hidalgo officially ended the Mexican War and transferred New Mexico, along with vast areas of the Southwest, to the United States. Although theoretically protected by this treaty, Hispanic landowners found that the newly imposed American laws worked to their disadvantage. Many long-time residents were deprived of their previous titles to land grants bestowed upon them by previous Spanish and Mexican governments.

New Mexico Becomes a Territory: 1850

The American flag was raised over the Palace of the Governors and New Mexico became a territory of the United States on September 9, 1850.

Tready of Guadalupe-Hidalgo

Rise Of The Santa Fe Ring: 1850–1912

This latter part of the nineteenth century was marked by great expansion in trade and transportation. The Santa Fe Ring, a group of mostly Anglo lawyers with common political and economic interests, amassed land through undermining the legal legitimacy of Spanish and Mexican land grants. This battle over land grants continues unabated today.

New Mexico Became 47th State: 1912

As early as 1850, there were unsuccessful attempts to gain statehood, and Santa Fe's status as capital was equally threatened. The Santa Fe Trail lost its status as a primary trade route. "The Santa Fe Trail Passes into Oblivion," heralded the *Santa Fe Gazette* in 1880, with the arrival of the first Acheson, Topeka & Santa Fe train in Lamy. Even though Albuquerque and Las Vegas were on the main railroad line, and Santa Fe a mere spur, Santa Fe was nevertheless recognized as the capital of the territory. Then on January 6, 1912, New Mexico was admitted as the forty-seventh state of the Union.

The Manhattan Project: 1943

In 1943, Santa Fe became the address for a secret project in nearby Los Alamos called the Manhattan Project. The development and design of atomic and nuclear weapons was secretly achieved there under Manhattan Project director Robert Oppenheimer. These bombs brought the world into the nuclear age and abruptly ended WWII. Santa Fe figures directly in this story a bit later, when an English spy slipped nuclear secrets to the Russians under the Delgado Street bridge.

WWII. Santa Fe figures directly in this story a bit later, when an English spy slipped nuclear secrets to the Russians under the Delgado Street bridge.

Learning

Voltaire and Frederick at St. John's College

A Cerebral Salad

Studies the Civic and Ecological Environment
Executive Director, Cheryl Charles
Center for the Study of Community, Sol y Sombra, 4018 Old Santa Fe Trail

Founded in Santa Fe in 1993, the Center for the Study of Community focuses on the health of communities, from our personal relationships to those in civic settings to those including the ecological environment and all their interrelationships. The center convenes groups to address tough issues, conducts research, teaches skills of collaborative community problem-solving. Located at the personal home of Beth and Charles Miller, the center teaches about "natural guides to community building" by the examples in evidence of their extensive grounds, a private botanical garden and a permaculture center. The Windstar Foundation, established by John Denver in 1976, has recently co-located with the Center for the Study of Community.

One of the Largest Genetic Diagnostic Providers
Medical Director, Dr. Stirling Puck
Genzyme Genetics, 2000 Vivigen Way, (505) 438–1111, (800) 255–7357

Genzyme Genetics is one of the largest genetic diagnostic services providers in the world. They employ two hundred people, one hundred and fifty of whom are on the technical staff. The Santa Fe laboratory is an international prenatal diagnostics center with experts who identify chromosome patterns. Predictions can be made whether or not a pregnant mother's baby might be born with Down's Syndrome, a congenital disease that causes mental retardation. "This is no longer an esoteric test for women in the know," Dr. Puck said. "It is an amazingly accurate test which, if done sufficiently in advance, can help older pregnant women decide whether or not to have a baby." Tom Reed, the CEO of Vivigen, Genzyme Genetic's predecessor, told us that Dr. Puck is the daughter of the first U.S. human geneticist.

Studies Preservation of Native American Languages
Institute for the Preservation of the Original Languages of the Americas
713 1/2 A Canyon Road, (505) 820–0311

The Institute for the Preservation of the Original Languages of the Americas (IPOLA) helps perpetuate the languages of original inhabitants of the Western Hemisphere. Since "language is the primary vehicle of culture, it is a fundamental human right and the desire of Native American peoples to retain cultural identity with languages." Many such languages are in danger of extinction if they are not spoken by children. Because many languages have only a verbal form, countless sounds are being lost as are religious chants and songs.

IPOLA spearheaded a project at Santa Ana Pueblo to determine what would happen if their native language, Keres, was lost. This study has created an awareness that language and culture are inseparable. Joanna Hess, founder and president of IPOLA said, "Imagine going into a flower shop and seeing only one kind of flower to dress up your room."

One of the Largest Scientific Conferences
Keystone Symposia
P.O. Drawer 1630, Silverton, Colorado 80498, (907) 262–1230

These non-profit scientific conferences are held in Taos and Santa Fe throughout the winter; they bring 2,500 scientists from all over the world for conventions on molecular and cellular biology.

Home of the Most Famous Spy Story in History
Los Alamos National Laboratory
Los Alamos, New Mexico 87545, (505) 667–5061

In 1943 the U.S. government built a secret research lab, code-named the "Manhattan Project," at the former Ranch School for boys. Leading scientists met in Los Alamos in 1943. Two years later the test bomb nicknamed "fat man" was detonated at the Trinity Site in White Sands, New Mexico. What evolved from this secret research mission turned out to be the most famous spy story in the history of the world. Within twelve days, Soviet scientists already obtained a description of the U.S. test bomb which their spies stole right out from under the noses of American security officials. Four years later, in 1949, the Soviets set off an exact replica of our bomb. Within months, American code-breakers identified and sent to prison one of the Soviet sources at Los Alamos, the British physicist Klaus Fuchs.

In 1962, Los Alamos changed its status from a top-secret military base in order to sustain its work as one of the world's leading scientific research centers. With the Cold War over, Los Alamos National Lab's (LANL) is now dedicated to reducing nuclear danger and to enhancing scientific knowledge. Today Los Alamos is crucial to the development of nuclear energy for peaceful as well as for military purposes.

The Best Tri-National Public Policy Organization
President, John Wirth
North American Institute, 708 Paseo de Peralta Street, (505) 982–3657

"With globalization, North America is a leader in both economic integration and environmental protection. What is happening in our own continent is important in world terms as well as for the local community of New Mexico."—**John Wirth**, Gildred Professor of Latin American Studies, History Department, Stanford University

The tri-national public policy North American Institute presents papers about North American cooperation between Canada, Mexico, and the United States. They discuss environmental and economic impacts on the community as a whole and publish their findings. Institute president Professor John Wirth is married to Nancy,daughter of John Gaw Meem, the designer who popularized the Santa Fe style of architecture.

The Most "Responsible Tourism"
Ellen Bradbury, Recursos de Santa Fe
826 Camino del Monte Rey, (505) 982–9301

Recursos, resources or "responsible tourism," means learning. This non-profit local educational organization, founded in 1984 by former New Mexico Museum of Fine Arts director Ellen Bradbury, specializes in tours and seminars on various topics such as art, culture, history, and the environment of the Southwest and the Americas. Lectures and seminars on Santa Fe help develop an appreciation of the area's tricultural heritage and foods. Some popular programs include the Annual Writers' Conference (which attracts Pulitzer Prize winners), regional cooking courses, archeological tours and seminars on the Manhattan Project, a subject Ellen knows well: her father worked for the secret Manhattan Project, and her former father-in-law, Norris Bradbury, was LANL Director from 1945 to 1970. He is the only director who has served more than one quarter of a century.

The World Leader on "Complexity" Phenomena
President, Ellen Goldberg
The Santa Fe Institute, 1399 Hyde Park Road, (505) 984–8800

The Santa Fe Institute (SFI) is a private non-profit scientific research center founded in 1984 by a group of scientists associated with Los Alamos National Laboratory, some as employees (such as George Cowan and Nicolas Metropolis) and some as consultants (such as Murray Gell-Mann, its patron saint and 1969 Nobel Prize winner who named the subatomic "quark" after a line in Joyce's *Finnegan's Wake*.)

"At SFI (which has no secret projects) researchers from a great number of different fields—ranging from mathematics, computer science and physics through immunology, ecology, and evolutionary biology to economics, archaeology, and history—work together. They use a variety of theoretical approaches, including computer modeling and simulation, to study problems related to simplicity and complexity and to complex adaptive systems, ones that adapt, learn, and evolve the way living things do. Almost all the scientists are visitors, who spend periods of time ranging from a week to several years at SFI, which is now world-famous and attracts many of the finest minds on the planet. The seminars may be on fluctuations in financial markets, settlement patterns in the prehistoric Southwest, foraging strategies of ant colonies, or how the human immune system fights AIDS."—**Murray Gell-Mann, 1969 Nobel Prize winner**

To make Santafesinos (Santa Feans) more aware of SFI, the Institute offers public talks for the non-scientist by well-known scientists in residence. To get information about these lectures, call and ask to be put on their mailing list.

The **Prediction Company,** (505) 984–3123, founded by professors at the Santa Fe Institute, has developed computer software to predict what's happening in the futures and commodity markets.

One of the Best Resident Scholar Programs
Douglas Schwartz, President
School of American Research (SAR), 660 Garcia Street, (505) 982–3583

The School of American Research houses one the most important collections of Southwestern Indian art and artifacts in the world."— **Douglas Schwartz**, President

The School of American Research (SAR) was founded in 1907 by Edgar Lee Hewett as the School of American Archaeology. Leading Santa Feans were involved in amassing the "Indian Arts Fund" (IAF) collection of Southwest Indian art, the best of its kind in the world. One of these patrons was Amelia White, whose house on Garcia Street was given to the SAR in 1972. In 1972, IAF disbanded and deeded the collection to SAR. It is now housed in the School's Indian Arts Research Center. Many Indian artists use the collection for research and inspiration for their own work. The collection is constantly being expanded though gifts and bequests.

Doug Schwartz, who became president of SAR in 1967, started the resident-scholar program in 1973. It provides several nine-month all-expenses-paid residencies to carefully selected scholars. Also, three times a year SAR's advanced seminar program brings ten scholars together to discuss advanced anthropological research. The school conducts archaeological digs and sponsors seminars, lectures, and field trips. SAR Press publishes books for both specialists and the general public. The J.I. Staley Prize has been awarded since 1988 for the year's outstanding anthropological study. A $40 membership fee allows tour access to the collection at the Indian Arts Research Center, the school's annual report, the newsletter, and invitations to lectures and field trips.

Schools and Colleges

Perhaps the Most Intellectual College in the Country
President, John Agresto
St. John's College, 1160 Camino Cruz Blanca, (505) 984–6000

"St. John's College provides a great opportunity to enhance one's life, at any age. We learn to open our minds, to question and seek objective answers, providing a foundation for continuing expansion of our intellectual horizons."—**Mara Robinson,** Alumna, St. John's Graduate Institute, 1983

St. John's College is the third oldest higher educational institution in the country, founded by royal charter in 1696 as King William's School, and chartered under its present name, St. John's College, in 1784. (They celebrated their 300th birthday in 1996). It is the only school of its kind in the country with two campus—in Santa Fe and the original in Annapolis, MD, (410-263–2371). What makes the college unique is that the entire four-year curriculum is organized around about one hundred forum-style classes that emphasize reading the "Great Books" and then talking about them.

These books are the original teachings and thoughts upon which all Western education is based. Instead of learning Einstein's theories second hand, students actually read Einstein's 1905 paper on relativity and see for themselves why this was the foundation of modern physics.

St. John's Community Seminar Series is very popular and always sold out. If you sign up for *Virgil's Aeneid*, for example, you will get a list of recommended advance reading so that you, with your group leader, will be prepared to discuss the work. The Graduate Institute was started in 1967. A graduate program in Eastern Classics started in 1994. *"It is uniquely fullfilling to find an oasis of critical thinking in a place with so many compelling and distracting choices."*—**Juliana Seligsen**, 1996 Graduate Institute, St. John's College

The Best Hands-on Movie Making Center

College of Santa Fe, 1600 St. Michael's Drive, (505) 473–6011

The 1995 "America's Best Colleges" guide rated the College of Santa Fe among the top ten regional liberal arts colleges in the western United States.— **U.S. News and World Report**

The College of Santa Fe was rated as one of the 15 Bargain Colleges for 1995 in the Southwest and Mountain States.—**Money Magazine**

1991 Guide of America's Best Colleges said the College of Santa Fe was the eighth best liberal arts school in the West and an up and comer.— **U.S. News and World Report**

The Greer Garson Communications Center at the College of Santa Fe is one of the few colleges in the country that houses both professional and student movie production facilities. The new art center designed by internationally known architect Ricardo Legorreta of Mexico City includes the Anne and John Marion Center for Photographic Arts and the Visual Resources Center, and 100-seat lecture hall and 350-seat auditorium. The Marion Center for Photographic Arts at the College of Santa Fe will be one of the country's most state-of-the-art photographic schools.

The Only Congressionally Chartered College
Institute of American Indian Art (IAIA)
At the College of Santa Fe, 1600 St. Michael's Drive, (505) 988–6450

IAIA is the only federally chartered art college in the country for Indians and Alaskan natives. Some of the most successful Native American artists in the country have graduated from this college. The school's board of directors is appointed by the President of the United States and is confirmed by the Senate. The future if IAIA is in financial jeopardy because federal funding has been cut by fifty percent. Presently, if their money lasts, they are planning a new campus near Santa Fe Community College.

The Best Prep Schools for Gifted Native Americans
Native American Prep School
Pecos River Campus, Rowe, NM (505) 982–3365

"The youth who are educated at the Native American Preparatory School will not only be the leaders of their own tribes and states, but will also become effective architects of the future of our country."
—Richard Ettinger, founder of NAPS

NAPS is the best college-preparatory school for gifted and talented Native American students. The student body represents nine states

and twenty-three tribal entities. It is the only privately financed boarding school for Native Americans in the United States—one hundred percent of its student body receives financial aid. The board is committed to raising the money necessary to guarantee its mission of educating qualified students, regardless of their personal financial limitations.

The Only Accredited Hospice Program of its Kind
New Mexico Community College, Española, (505) 747–2100

Just outside Santa Fe you can earn a certificate in basic hospice care, death education, and grief counseling. The famous writer Elizabeth Kubler-Ross established this program in Española.

The Only Boarding School for the Deaf in New Mexico
New Mexico School For The Deaf
1060 Cerrillos Road, Santa Fe, NM 87503, (505) 827–6711

The School for the Deaf, grades one through twelve, has a statewide outreach program that enables preschool hearing-impaired children up to six-years-old to learn at home. The school also has various statewide outreach programs for kindergarten children in which deaf children are integrated with hearing children in a daycare center, and a joint program between the public school and deaf kindergarten children.

The Only Graduate School for Design Students
Santa Fe College of Design
Website: www.sfcd.org

This new college plans to open in 1998 at a still-undisclosed location. They will offer several master's degrees in design disciplines. Jan Morse-Schroeder is the new school's president. Check their web site for further information.

The Best Academic Bargain
Santa Fe Community College
6400 Richards Avenue, (505) 471–8200

SFCC offers the first two years of college free to Santa Fe's entire high school 1997 graduating class. But there is a catch: students must buy their textbooks, get to class, and complete a minimum classload of twelve hours a week for one semester with a minimum grade point average of 2.5—then the remaining semesters are free if they maintain their grades. The Santa Fe Community College is a great place to take computer and continuing education classes.

The Only Independent College Preparatory School
Santa Fe Preparatory School
1101 Camino Cruz Blanca, (505) 982–1829

The only sixth-through-twelfth grade prep school in Santa Fe; non-discriminatory, with substantial scholarships for those who fullfill its entrance requirements. Established in 1961, the thirteen-acre campus is located at the foothills of the Sangre de Cristo Mountains next to St. John's College.

A Two Year International Finishing School
United World College in Montezuma, NM, (505) 454–4200

Founded in 1982 by an American industrialist and philanthropist, the Armand Hammer United World College of the American West is one of nine such schools in a system called the International Council of United World Colleges. Their mission is to train its body of international students to be world leaders. It is a two-year "finishing school," or university prep, that emphasizes world relations.

Workshops

Academy Of Realist Art
5004 6th Avenue Northwest, Seattle, WA 98107, (206) 784–4268
For a brochure call (505) 793–1410

The drawing and painting workshops are in Santa Fe on a forty-acre Santa Fe estate. Gary Faigin teaches painting and his wife runs the workshop.

Anthropology Film Center
1626 Canyon Road, (505) 983–4127

Intensive summer and winter workshops on all aspects of the making of documentary films. Here you learn something about anthropology—the context rather than just the process of making documentaries. "Since visual anthropology is a required course for graduation in most European film schools, it should not be too much to ask for here," said Carroll Williams, director of this first film-making school in Santa Fe.

Elderhostel
75 Federal St., Boston, MA 02110–1941, (617) 426–8056

The program for elders fifty-five years or older has lectures and workshops on lots of subjects. The brochures tells you what kind of meals and accommodations are provided locally.

Santa Fe has three Elderhostel centers: the College of Santa Fe, Plaza Resolana at (505) 982–8539 or (800) 821–5145; Santa Fe Community College (505) 438-1254 sponsors the program at Glorieta Conference Center. You must sign up through the Boston office and ask for a catalogue.

Fechin Institute in Taos
Branham/Donner Ranch, P. O. Box 220, San Cristobal, NM, (505) 776–2622

The Fechin Institute features art workshops taught by professionals at a rustic mountain retreat eighteen miles north of Taos. Call for information about teachers, dates, and costs.

Ghost Ranch Conference Center
Abiquiu, N.M. (505) 685–4333
Plaza Resolana, Paseo de Peralta and the Old Taos Hwy., (505) 982–8539

Classes on many subjects can be taken at both centers sponsored by the Presbyterian Church. Call for brochures.

Mabel Dodge Lujan House Bed and Breakfast
P.O. Box 3400 Mirada Lane, (505) 758–9456 or (800) 846–2235

Art, literary, and spiritual workshops are held in this old Taos historic house, which has been converted into a bed and breakfast.

New Mexico Artists Association
R. 19 Box 90K Santa Fe, NM 87505 (505) 982–5639

These artists offer year-round workshops with more than forty artists who teach in their private studios one-on-one or in groups.

Santa Fe Art Institute
Kerry Benson
College of Santa Fe, 1600 St. Michael's Drive, (505) 473–6225

The Santa Fe Art Institute was founded in 1985 by the late Pony Ault and William Lumpkin, a noted architect and artist. It is the only art institute in Santa Fe where an advanced artist can study with a contemporary resident master. The school received a large grant from The Burnett Foundation. The resident "masters" include John Chamberlain, John Baldessari, Jennifer Bartlett, Lynda Benglis, Susan Rothenberg, Judy Pfaff, Donald Lipski, Elizabeth Murray, Janet Fish, Gregory Amenoff, Alexis Smith, Eric Fischl, Wayne Thiebaud, Larry Bell, Rudy Autio, Gregory Gillespie, Nathan Oliveira, Beverly Pepper, and Richard Tullis. Applicants submit a portfolio and are chosen by a committee. The "masters" make the final selection. John Marion, the institute's chairman, was chairman of Sotheby's Inc in 1975 and was one of the most successful auctioneers in Sotheby's history.

Santa Fe Glass Workshops
930 Baca Street,(505) 984–2236, or the Baca Street Studios,(505) 820–1854

All levels of glassblowing classes are available. Sculpture-casting and glassblowing by appointment year round.

Santa Fe International Academy Of Art
Hwy. 14, (505) 473–5350

SFIA is a visual arts school with on-going workshops in art for beginning and advanced students. Their impressive faculty offers graduate programs leading to a Master of Fine Arts.

Santa Fe Workshops
P.O. Box 9916, Santa Fe, NM 87504, (505) 983–1400 (for a catalogue)

There are over sixty one-week workshops from mid-June to mid-August held on the grounds of the Carmelite Monastery. Film-making and photographic workshops are taught by leading working professionals.

Valdez
1006 Marquez Place, (505) 982–0017

A monthly schedule of art workshops is offered throughout the year; they hold week-long seminars from June through October. Each October they begin eight-week art classes. All classes meet once a week.

Making Contact

There is no place in the country that has a greater diversity of people per capita than Santa Fe. The talented movie stars, media moguls, volunteers, educators, activists, scientists, business executives, politicians, singers, artists, and writers all get thrown in a pot and mixed with a constant supply of new people. The old saying, "Who would introduce the introducer if the introducer weren't introduced to you?" really applies here in Santa Fe.

Ambassadors

The New Mexico Amigos
320 Galisteo Street, Suite 302, (505) 982–3306

The Amigos are the official New Mexico good will ambassadors who travel annually throughout the country promoting Santa Fe. They started in 1962 to celebrate the 50th anniversary of statehood. They have 260 members statewide who are business or professional leaders. The first 120 people who sign up pay $3,000 to travel by chartered jet for seven days to various cities around the country. With the Governor, the Amigos make presentations, meet the governors of the states they visit, and "try and prove that New Mexico is one of our 50 states," says Gary Blakely, the Secretary-Treasurer.

Los Compadres
Santa Fe County Chamber of Commerce, (505) 988–3279

Los Compadres are volunteers that make up the public relations arm of the Santa Fe County Chamber of Commerce. They do ribbon cuttings, visit new businesses, and set up the monthly Chamber of Commerce meetings. Another branch of the Los Compadres, the Pancake Committee, puts on the Fourth of July pancake breakfast; one of the best local community family events on the Plaza.

French Consul of New Mexico

Gilles Milinaire, Rancho Viejo, Tesuque, NM 87574, (505) 989–8929

Gilles Milinaire, French Consul of New Mexico since 1991, took this position offered by the French Ambassador in Washington, D.C., to represent the French community in New Mexico and maintain cultural exchanges between France and New Mexico. He discovered that there was in the region a French presence in 1580 and a rich history of the passage of the French through this state. In March, 1996, Gilles Milinaire honored thirty-five New Mexican veterans on the 50th anniversary of D-Day. A senator came from Paris to decorate the veterans with medals and certificates in recognition for their role in liberating France. It was a very touching ceremony; many politicians and W.W.II veterans attended the event. A thirty-one piece band played anthems, military music, and music from the 40s.

Living Treasures

Santa Fe has 110 elder citizens who have made a significant contribution to Santa Fe. This program was started in 1984 by Mary Lou Cook who felt that the living treasures should be recognized for their deeds. In 1997 *"Living Treasures: Celebration of the Human Spirit"* was published to honor them.

Sister City Program

Staff Liaison, Mary Ellen Carroll
City Hall, 200 Lincoln Avenue, (505) 984–6592

The sister cities program promotes tourism and is valuable in a networking capacity. The executive committee for the sister cities program has meetings once a month.

Santa Fe has five sister cities: Hidalgo del Parral in Chihuahua, Mexico; Santa Fe de la Vega and Granada in Spain; Bukhara in Uzbekistan; Sorrento in Italy; and Tsuyama City in Japan.

Dubna, the previous sister city for Los Alamos, was built around an accelerator lab, like Los Alamos. On the occasion of the 50th anniversary of the Trinity Site, only scientists were allowed to go visit the Russian city. When the Cold War ended, Los Alamos selected another sister city—Aramas, near the Urals—because it is an academic research city much like Los Alamos. The City of Aramas sent a present to Los Alamos, part of an old Russian warhead, with a note that said, "Los Alamos, From Russia with Love."

Business

Nick Ault Private Investigations
200 West Marcy Street, Suite 146, (505) 986–5015

Nick, a former Santa Fe Police Officer and Special Agent for the Attorney General's Office, knows where to go and whom to contact discreetly for needed information. His associate, Jonathan Thornton, worked as a photojournalist for Reuters in Sarajevo, and he has all the technical and communication skills needed to get any sensitive job done. And he's good-looking, which helps! Chase Hamilton, is a former marine who was with FAST (Fleet Anti-Terrorism Security Team).

Santa Fe County Chamber of Commerce
510 N. Guadalupe Ste., (505) 988–3279

If you have a business here, it is important to join the the Santa Fe County Chamber of Commerce, which has 1,300 members and a directory of all members. Membership provides access to the mailing list. If you are self-employed with no employees, membership costs $230 a year. The chamber offers business seminars, a newsletter, many mailings, a radio show, and even access to medical benefits. They have different councils with separate meetings and specialists who speak on many subjects inlcluding education, the government, small business, tourism, infrastructure (which has to do with economic development, i.e. the railyard), and special projects. Members can go to any of these meetings, and they often feature important community leaders and state speakers and state representatives.

Santa Fe Community College Small Business Center
1600 Richards Avenue, (505) 471–8200

SFCC has a Small Business Development Center that provides seminars and workshops. Two full-time counselors are available to help free of charge. Many people write their business plans with the help of the center.

Santa Fe Convention and Visitors Center
Sweeny Center, Box 909,(505) 984–6760 or (800) 777–2489

The bureau is charged with the responsibility to attract tourists and convention groups to Santa Fe. They also will try to answer out-of-towners' questions.

Service Corps of Retired Executives (Score).
Montoya Federal Bldg. Room 307, 800–8–ASK

SCORE is a volunteer group of former business executives from all areas of business who give business advice without charge.

clubs

There are hundreds of clubs, special interest groups, and salons that meet regularly or when their members please! Check the *New Mexican* or *Albuquerque Journal* for weekly listings.

The Kiva Club

Computer Networking

New Mexico is one of the most advanced states in the development of computer technology. Did you know that Bill Gates started Microsoft in Albuquerque? Or that Intel's largest plant is in Rio Rancho. Los Alamos Labs has one of the highest concentrations of computer technology in the world, and Sandia Labs is just up the road.

New Mexico Internet Professional's Association
Hank LeMieux, President, www.nmipa.org

The NMIPA is a state-wide organization whose purpose is to provide a network of professionals to "expand the market for Internet-related services (connectivity, web design, web marketing, consulting, training, etc.) through a unified, orchestrated, industry-wide effort." They also sponsor educational projects for teachers, clients, businesses, and others. Among their other functions are political lobbying and out-reach to rural areas.

Santa Fe Macintosh Users Group
Meetings: Religious Science Building, 505 Camino de los Marquez
Hotline: (505) 474–SFMG (7364); www.nets.com/sfmug/

This is a wonderful, supportive group to belong to if you are a Macintosh user. They have 275 members, and 90 to 180 people attend each meeting. They produce an excellent printed newsletter for members. General meetings are on the first Wednesday of each month at 7 p.m. Meetings cost $3 for non-members; membership is $30 per year.

Royal City News
www.rcnews.com

Royal City News is an award-winning, monthly online community e-zine for and about Santa Fe. The beautifully designed web site contains local news and events, a calendar of Santa Fe happenings, historical notes, a comprehensive directory of local web sites, fiction, and much more. It is created by WebWorks and Cliff Simon.

Internet Service Providers

Santa Fe boasts one of the highest ratios of Internet Service Providers to residents. There are six providers with offices right here in town, several other businesses in Albuquerque and Los Alamos that provide local service, and several national providers with local numbers.

studio x
e-mail: connect@nets.com telephone: (505) 438–0505

Santa Fe Online
e-mail: human@sfol.com telephone: (505) 988–1720

Santa Fe Trail
e-mail: admin@trail.com telephone: (505) 983–4240

Roadrunner
e-mail: sysop@roadrunner.com telephone: (505) 988–9200

SISNA
e-mail: hbrand@sisna.com telephone: (505) 982–8309

Computer Network Service Professionals
e-mail: info@cnsp.com telephone (505) 986–1669

DirectNet Corporation
104 E. Marcy Street, www.directnet.com

DirectNet provides software, online tutoring, connectivity, and support to schools K-12, and it supports the One2One Learning Foundation. They have set up wireless ten-megabit networks all over the state to provide wireless Internet and Ethernet services to schools and business customers. Their technology is some of the most advanced in the country.

Web Site Development

Santa Fe boasts a number of professional web designers. John Tollett, a founding partner in West of the Pecos Web Design (www.westpecos.com), is co-author (with Robin Williams) of a best-selling book on web design, *The Non-Designer's Web Book*. He and his partner, Dave Rohr, are producing another book on web design, *The Web Designer's Design Book*, showcasing many of their professional web sites and design techniques. This company did the web site for the *Santa Fean* as well as my web site. Consult the yellow pages for other web design firms.

Robin Williams
www.ratz.com

Robin Williams is one of the most popular computer writers in the country. She has written more than a dozen computer-related books, most of them award-winning and best-selling, that have been translated into fourteen languages. Robin has a column in the Sunday business section of the *New Mexican* newspaper about what Santa Feans are doing on the Internet. She opened the first Internet cafe in New Mexico, was cofounder of the Santa Fe Mac User Group, cofounder of the New Mexico Internet Professionals Association, teaches seminars here and around the country, and is on several national advisory boards.

Tourist Information

New Mexican Infosource
(505) 820–6060 ext. 1400

A non-profit information and referral service funded through the city and the McCune Foundation, New Mexican Infosource continuously updates its database to provide information and a referral service to all the five-hundred human service agencies and programs in the Santa Fe area—including legal services or where to go if your husband is beating you up. A directory is available.

157

New Mexican Concierges Association
Nancy Eigenseld, Inn the Governors (505) 982–8333

Inger Boudouris, head concierge the St. Francis Hotel, is the only member in Santa Fe of the International Concierges Association, Les Clefs d'Or (The Golden Keys). Members of this organization wear the "keys" on the lapel of their uniform. In order to be a member you must pass a difficult test and work five years in a hotel; three of those years must be as full-time lobby concierge. Inger networks with colleagues in Les Clefs d'Or in thirty-three countries around the world. She is one of the founding members of the New Mexico Concierges Association. The group meets once a month at different restaurants and tell stories about the unusual requests they have received and fulfilled. They can find almost anything anyone asks for.

Plaza Information Booth
Bienvenidos, a division of the Santa Fe County Chamber of Commerce

Volunteers work at the tourist information booth located in front of the First National Bank on the Plaza. The booth is open during the summer months.

Public Lands Information Center
1474 Rodeo Road (505) 438–7542

A multi-agency information service about all public lands in New Mexico. Consult them if you and want to know anything about biking, hiking, boating, fishing, or anything about recreation areas in New Mexico. They will also tell you how to get there, where to stay, and what you need if you are camping out. They have books and maps you can take with you.

Santa Fe Welcome Center
New Mexico Department of Tourism
(505) 827–7400 or (800) 545–2040

Market Places

Jackalope

the 10 best

Artesanos Imports Company
222 Galisteo Street, (505) 983–5563.

A large variety of old Mexican pottery, glassware and tiles, furniture, lamps, and pots in the middle of downtown Santa Fe.

Farmers' Market
Director, Pam Roy
Sanbusco Center, (505) 983–4098

Open from June until the first Saturday in November on Tuesday and Saturday mornings from 7–11:30 and on Sundays from 9–1. It is not only the best place to buy fresh vegetables and fruits to the beat of the **Farmer's Market Band**, it is also the best place to be if you like to get an early start, get a cup of coffee, and catch up with friends you haven't seen in a while. The market enhances the regional agriculture of the area and brings fresh and locally grown produce to the consumer. Two distinctive vendors are the Martinez family, whose Zenitram firm (505) 581–4576 raises naturally-grown meat products that are outstanding, and Trujillo Family Farms, whose roasted green chiles give the market its enticing aroma. **The Farmer's Market Store**, on the north end of the Gross Kelly Building (43 W. Manhattan), is open all winter. It sells vinegar, dried floral arrangements, processed foods, and fresh soups. For information on the store call (505) 984–1010.

Jackalope Pottery
2820 Cerrillos Road, (505) 471–8539

This is the biggest marketplace, or "mercado," in Santa Fe. They have a gardening center, gardening seminars, a prairie dog home, and a furniture store, not to mention a huge selection of pottery. When owner Darby McQuade sold his small store in El Paso, Texas, in 1979, he agreed not to operate another similar store within 300 miles. Luckily, Santa Fe was 330 miles away.

Old Las Vegas Highway near Old Pecos Trail

This outdoor weekend market has different wonderful things every weekend: tamamori Indian pots, flagstone, rocks, and coyote fences. It is the second best place to get firewood (the first is Rios on Canyon Road).

Palace of the Governors under the Portal

Since the Museum of New Mexico was founded in 1909, it has worked to protect and advance traditional Southwestern Indian arts. The portal, or front porch, of the Palace of the Governors on the Plaza is reserved for the use of New Mexican Indian people to display and sell their handcrafted silver jewelry. Authenticity and quality is controlled by the tribes, the museum, and the city. Ask to see the maker's mark. Museum regulations require makers to put their mark on all pieces they sell. Since there is limited space the museum uses a lottery system to determine who is allowed to show on what day.

Sunset General Store
Old Las Vegas Hwy, (505) 982–6705

When Allen Jung bought this general store in 1993, it was a gas station, a liquor store, and a convenience store. Now, it is also a drug store, video rental center, and it has a sushi bar (often offering two for the price of one), hot Chinese food, a post office, Asian groceries, an automated teller machine installed by the Bank of Santa Fe, a wide selection of wine, and herbal medicine. It is probably as genuine as a general store gets.

The Trader Jack's Flea Market
Next door to the Santa Fe Opera

The flea market is open every weekend of the year except when it is snowing. People come from all over the world. *Art and Antiques Magazine* called it "one of the four best flea markets in the United States." It certainly is the best place to go if you are a die-hard, bargain-hunting shopper. In addition, you can get a massage, listen to music, people watch, have lunch, look at the beautiful view, grocery shop, and have your fortune told, all at the same time.

Tesuque Village Market
Tesuque, (505) 988–8848

Tesuque Market is a neighborhood restaurant, deli, grocery store, liquor store, gallery, and a local hangout, all in one.

"Tienditas" (little stores)

Johnny's Cash Store
John Armijo
420 Camino Don Miguel, (505) 982–9506

John and his father opened up the "tienda" together in 1946. Since then five generations of Armijos have helped at the store. His pork and chicken tamales are the most popular in town. They are delivered every morning fresh—$13 a dozen or $1.25 each. He has burritos and broasted chickens on Wednesdays.

Palace Grocery
Meliton and Yolanda Vigil
853 East Palace Avenue, (505) 983–9573

Yolanda has been running the little grocery store for thirty-five years, and her aunt and uncle ran it for thirty years before that. "We will stay here as long as we are able," Yolanda told me.

Museums

Support Groups

Friends of Contemporary Art (FOCA), Museum of Fine Arts, (505) 827–4452
Friends of Folk Art, Museum of International Folk Art, (505) 827–6350
Friends of Indian Art, Museum of Indian Arts and Culture, (505) 827–6344
The Palace Guard, The Palace of the Governors, (505) 827–4813

The Finest

Santa Fe's four state-run museums provide many outstanding exhibitions, lectures, educational programs and workshops, and year-round events. A one-day pass to all these museums costs $5, and a four-day pass costs $10. A ticket to one of them can be used at any of the other three. The four-day pass includes entry to the Georgia O'Keeffe Museum. New Mexico residents are admitted to any of these four museums for $1 on Sundays. For $50 a year a family can join the Museum of New Mexico Foundation (505) 982–6366, a non-profit private organization that raises money for the museums. Membership provides free admission to the museums plus a monthly newsletter listing all special events and seminars as well as a subscription to El Palacio (505) 827–4361, a quarterly that is the oldest museum magazine in the country (started in 1913).

"The Museum of New Mexico, perhaps more than any other single institution, has molded the character of Santa Fe. Without the foresight and hard work of the system's first director, Edgar L. Hewett, in the early 20th century, Santa Fe would not have become the art and cultural center it is today, nor would 'Santa Fe style' be a factor in preserving its history and architecture"—**Thomas A. Livesay**, Director, Museum of New Mexico

Museum of Fine Arts
Director, Stuart A. Ashman
107 W. Palace Avenue, (505) 827–4468

The oldest art museum in New Mexico was first established as a small art gallery in 1907 in the Palace of the Governors under the direction of Dr. Edgar Hewett. The present Museum of Fine Arts, built in 1917, is one of the best examples of Pueblo revival-style architecture. The architects, William and Isaac Rapp, studied the mission churches of Cochiti, Laguna, and Acoma pueblos. The synthesis of their research was the "New Mexico Building" built in San Diego for the Panama-California Exposition in 1915. This building was the prototype for the Museum of Fine Arts.

The permanent art collection contains approximately 8,000 works of art representing the Taos school of artists and other American artists such as Georgia O'Keeffe, William Penhallow Henderson, Gene Kloss, Jozef Bakos, and Gustave Baumann. It began as a regional museum which helped establish the Santa Fe artists in the 1920s. The museum grew with Santa Fe's sophisticated art community to become one of the leading museums of twentieth-century America in the West. There are ten to twelve shows a year that showcase regional artists. The **St. Francis Auditorium** is a performance center which can be rented for special events. The **Governor's Gallery,** located in the state capital, is an outreach facility of the Museum of Fine Arts, and it shows the work of local artists and exhibits the work by recipients of the annual **Governor's Award of Excellence.** Nominations are made through the State of New Mexico Arts Commission. The Governor and First Lady select the winners with the help of Terry Bumpass, the curator (505) 820–4198 and director Stuart Ashman.

Museum of International Folk Art
Director, Charlene Cerny
706 Camino Lejo, just off Old Santa Fe Trail, (505) 827–6350.

"Nobody is retired until they're dead."—**Alexander Girard**

The Museum of International Folk Art, founded by Florence Dibell Bartlett, opened to the public in 1953. With collections now numbering more than 125,000 objects from over one hundred countries, its holdings are larger than any other folk art museum in the world. In the **Bartlett Wing,** the museum presents important changing exhibitions on folk art interpreted in an historical and cultural context.

On permanent exhibit in the **Girard Wing** are approximately 10,000 pieces from the Girard Foundation Collection, the 1987 gift of Alexander and Susan Girard. An architect by profession, Mr. Girard himself designed the exhibition installation which opened in 1982.

The **Hispanic Heritage Wing,** which opened in 1989, has the finest collection of Hispanic religious art in the country. It represents

165

the museum's continuing commitment to the Hispanic community of New Mexico and the Southwest. It draws on the museum's extensive collection of Spanish Colonial and Hispanic folk art from the seventeenth century to the present. A changing gallery features the work of Hispanic artists who still use traditional artistic techniques.

The gift of the Neutrogena Collection by Lloyd E. Cotsen and the Neutrogena Corporation to the museum in 1995 brought to New Mexico a collection of 2,900 textiles and other objects. The new 8,000 square-foot Neutrogena Wing, opening in late August 1998, will allow visitors the opportunity to go behind the scenes to a collections area on the lower level.

MIAC/Laboratory of Anthropology
Museum Plaza, Camino Lejo & Old Santa Fe Trail, (505) 827–6344

The Museum of Indian Arts and Culture (MIAC) is pioneering a new approach to the display of Native American arts and culture by working in collaboration with native peoples to develop exhibitions and educational programming. "Here, Now, and Always," the Museum's new permanent exhibition now on view in the new **Amy Rose Bloch Wing**, represents this perspective. More than 70 Native Americans participated in the development and curation of the exhibit, which includes more than 1,300 objects from the museum's collections.

MIAC and the Laboratory of Anthropology, which together constitute a unit of the Museum of New Mexico, have a long and distinguished history. The Museum of New Mexico was founded in 1909. The Laboratory of Anthropology was founded in 1927 and funded by John D. Rockefeller as a research and collecting institution dedicated to anthropological study of the American Southwest. It merged with the Museum of New Mexico in 1947, and in 1987 the MIAC was opened to exhibit the Laboratory's collections and to further MIAC's mission of collaboration with Southwest Indian communities. The Laboratory of Anthropology and MIAC are located in adjacent buildings, and share their plaza site with the Museum of International Folk Art (also a unit of the

Museum of New Mexico). Close by is the Wheelwright Museum of the American Indian, a private museum.

Today the MIAC/Lab collection is recognized as one of the world's finest holdings of Southwestern United States Indian material culture, and it constitutes the most comprehensive collection in existence of ancestral and prehistoric material from New Mexico and bordering regions. There are over 65,000 individually catalogued archaelogical and ethnographic objects, 2,000 fine art objects, archival materials, and some 6 million artifacts and samples from archaeological excavations.

The Georgia O'Keeffe Museum
President, Jay Kantor
217 Johnson Street, (505) 995–0785
To arrange a tour of Georgia O'Keeffe's house in Abiquiu, (505) 685–4539

The newest museum in Santa Fe—the first museum in America devoted to a woman artist with an international reputation—opened in July of 1997. The museum houses the world's largest public collection of works by Georgia O'Keeffe, who is considered one of the most important twentieth-century artists. O'Keeffe lived part-time in New Mexico beginning in 1929 and took up permanent residency in 1949. New Mexican subjects dominated her work from her earliest visits until she stopped working in the 1970s. She had homes in Ghost Ranch and Abiquiu. She died in 1986 in Santa Fe. The 13,000 square-foot museum designed by New York architect Richard Gluckman features more than 80 O'Keeffe works, including paintings, sculptures, drawings, and watercolors. Barbara Buhler Lynes, author of the O'Keeffe *catalogue raisonne*, heads the Georgia O'Keeffe Museum Study Center.

The Georgia O'Keeffe Museum has a very unusual collaboration with the Museum of New Mexico, which enhances the entire museum system. Although the two museums share membership programs via the Museum of New Mexico Foundation, the Georgia O'Keeffe Musesum still remains a private museum. Hours of operation are Tuesday-Sunday from 10–5 and Friday from 5–8.

Anne and John Marion and the Burnett Foundation are the

museum's principal benefactors. In 1989 the Georgia O'Keeffe Foundation, directed by Elizabeth Glassman, acquired the majority of her assets including a large number of her paintings. In September of 1996, this foundation along with the Burnett Foundation contributed thirty-three paintings to the museum.

Her house in Abiquiu, a testament to her life and work, will be protected and become a part of the National Trust in a "co-stewardship" arrangement with the O'Keeffe Foundation serving as administrators. The Santa Fe Conservation Trust plans to protect the famous view from her house which was the inspiration for her work. If you are planning a tour of Georgia O'Keeffe's Abiquiu home, make your appointment as early as possible because the tours are booked months in advance.

The Palace of the Governors
Director, Thomas Chávez
On the Plaza, (505) 827–6483

Before New Mexico was even a state the Palace of the Governors was a museum. In the early days, in order to draw artists to Santa Fe, the musuem offered them studio space on the premise.

The museum collection includes more than 17,000 historical objects from the Spanish Colonial period, the Mexican American War, the American expansion along the Santa Fe Trail, and the transition from Mexican to American control and into the twentieth century. Be sure to see the the Segesser hide paintings, large buffalo-hide murals depicting Spanish colonial military operations. The museum is housed in the Palace of the Governors, which was built in 1610 (eleven years before the pilgrims landed at Plymouth) and is considered the oldest continuously occupied government building in the United States. Five governments have occupied this building: Spanish, American Indian, Mexican, Confederate, and the United States.

One of the best kept secrets of New Mexico is the unseen collection hidden in vaults and atmosphere controlled rooms. There is a costume room, furniture rooms, an arms vault containing ancient weaponry, a map room, a toy room, and a silver vault. You may have to pull some strings to see these collections.

Thomas Chávez offers a very popular lecture series beginning in January. The history lectures are at the Palace Meeting Room on Washington Street. The series of six lectures is a fund raiser for the Palace endowment. A series subscription is now $75; one lecture costs $15.

The Fray Angélico Chávez History Library and Photographic Archives
Director, Orlando Romero, (505) 827–6470

The new library in the Palace of the Governors, is a treasure trove of information and manuscripts of New Mexico history. It was dedicated to Fray Angélico Chávez, a New Mexican-born Franciscan who passed away in 1996. He wrote 23 books and was a poet, scholar, and painter. Thomas Chávez, historian and Director of the Palace of the Governors, is a nephew of Fray Angélico. The historical library has at least 15,000 rare books and thousands of letters, manuscripts, and edicts, some of which date back to the 1600s. The library has an impressive map and historical photograph collection. Their maps are used as visual aids for documentary film makers. One of the maps in the collection shows New Mexico as part of Texas. The library is an important international center of research. The library is run by Orlando Romero, who has written several books and is a valuable resource—he can get any seemingly unobtainable question answered!

Institute of American Indian Arts Museum
108 Cathedral Place, (505) 988–6211

IAIA houses works of Indian artists who have taught or studied at the Institute of American Indian Arts located at the College of Santa Fe. IAIA is the only federally chartered art college in the country for Indians and Alaskan natives. The school's board of directors is appointed by the president of the United States and is confirmed by the Senate. The museum's mission is to present "Indian Art through Indian eyes." It is the largest and most comprehensive contemporary Indian art museum run by American pueblo peoples and Alaskan Natives in the country. There is also a gallery displaying works by current students.

Federal funding for IAIA has been cut by fifty percent, which puts its future in financial jeopardy.

El Rancho de las Golondrinas
Director, George Paloheimo
La Cienega, 20 miles south of Santa Fe, (505) 471–2261
Tour office (505) 471–4169

Now a living history museum, this historic rancho was founded in the early 1700s when it was acquired as a royal purchase by Miguel Vega y Coca. Las Golondrinas was an historic "paraje," or stopping place, on El Camino Real, the Royal Road to Mexico City. The last encampment before reaching Santa Fe, it was an oasis where travelers could rest themselves and their animals after their six-month journey north.

The 200-acre museum opened on the site in 1972 after existing buildings were restored and authentic structures erected on old foundations and related buildings, were brought in from other sites. Thirty-three buildings including an eighteenth-century placita house with a defensive tower, nineteenth century dwellings, blacksmith shop, school house and Penitente Morada, and are all authentically furnished. They come alive during festival weekends when historically clothed interpreters bake bread in outdoor ovens (*hornos*), weave, spin wool and demonstrate the many other activities of daily life in Spanish Colonial New Mexico.

The museum season runs from April 1 to October 30th. Call the museum for hours, admission fees, and special events.

Santa Fe Children's Museum
1050 Old Pecos Trail, (505) 989–8359

The children's museum was opened in 1988. They have exhibits which teach children about science with hands-on demonstrations. Recently, they built with a $250,000. grant from the Howard

Hughes Foundation "Earthworks," the museum's outdoor environmental classroom.

The Wheelwright Museum
Jonathan Batkin
704 Camino Lejo, (505) 982–4636

Mary Cabot Wheelwright's interest in religion brought her to the Southwest around 1918 when she was about forty years old. She collaborated with a friend, Haa'steen Klah, a famous Navajo medicine man (and great-grandson of a famous Navajo war chief) who had mastered the complex system of the rituals, ceremonies, and sacred sandpaintings of the Navajo culture. Wheelwright and Klah had been introduced by Arthur and "Franc" Newcomb who owned the Newcomb Trading Post. For fifteen years they gathered information about these ceremonies, neither one speaking the language of the other. Since the original sandpaintings were always destroyed after the healing ceremonies of a patient, Franc memorized them and later, with permission, reproduced them so this knowledge would not be lost. The original museum was designed by William Penhallow Henderson in 1937 (the year Klah died) and built by Mary Cabot Wheelwright to house this collection and to help preserve and foster Navajo spiritualism. The museum is a ceremonial "hogan"—an eight-sided home with its entrance facing the rising sun. Unfortunately the sandpaintings are not on display. Today the museum features changing exhibitions of traditional and contemporary Native American art. The Case Trading Post is a replica of a Navajo trading post, and it offers antique and current works of art, rugs, and pottery and many books on related subjects.

Outdoor Sports & Adventures

Bare Hunting in the Pecos Wilderness

An Outdoor Mecca

Active outdoor people love Santa Fe because there is so much to do in the area year-round. New Mexico has the most diverse scenery, and the widest array of cultural and natural wonders of most places in the world. Six of the world's seven life zones, or varieties of terrain, are found in this state.

Adventure Centers

Blue Hole Dive Shop
141 South 5th Street, Santa Rosa, NM 88435, (505) 472–3370

There are around three thousand certified scuba divers in Santa Fe. The Blue Hole is the best place in the state to dive. People from all over the Southwest come here to dive.

The National Rifle Assocation's Whittington Center
Raton, New Mexico, (505) 445–3615

The NRA's Whittington Center is one of the premier hunting and shooting facilities in the United States. Located on thirty-three thousand acres, Whitington caters to virtually all the shooting sports. For those interested in hunting, the Whittington Center holds seasonal hunts for elk, bear, deer, and turkey and other wild animals. Competitor housing, cabins, RV facilities, and primitive camping are available at very reasonable rates for those interested in spending the night.

Philmont Scout Ranch
The National High Adventure Base of the Boy Scouts of America
(505) 376–2281

The Philmont Ranch was given to the Boy Scouts in 1938 by Oklahoma oilman Waite Phillips, who died in 1964. The one hundred and thirty thousand acre spread is next door to Ted Turner's Vermejo Ranch. Philmont offers year-round activities for Boy Scouts;

There are fifty primitive camp sites where trekkers can camp out for the night. Scouts are taught the basic skills professional rescuers use including orienteering. The ranch is considered one of the best places to hunt wild turkey, elk, bear, and other feathered and four-legged critters. Outsiders are welcome to hunt there for a hefty price. For $325 scouts can chose from 27 different training itineraries. Philmont is one of three adventure camps in the country run by the Boy Scouts.

St. John's Search And Rescue
Director, Herb Kincey, (505) 984–6000 or (505) 984–6135

There are about 100 members of this volunteer organization— fifty are students at St. John's College and the other fifty are Santa Fe residents. Founded in 1971 by Herb Kincey, Jim Carr, and Istvan Fehervary, the team began as a school-sponsored activity and an extension of an emergency first-aid course that Kinsey taught. It quickly became an indispensible service for the community. The volunteer ground rescue team assists in searching for downed aircraft and lost hikers. They work with other emergency units if needed. Members of this team have to be competent outdoorsmen and have all the technical and leadership skills to survive in the wilderness and save lives.

The Santa Fe Climbing Gym
835 Early Street, Suite A, (505) 986–8944

Some people feel more comfortable learning how to climb indoors. The Climbing Gym offers a number of programs specifically designed for climbing outdoors. They go to White Rock or Las Conchas, and such trips cost $175 for a full day and $100 for a half-day. You can take climbing lessons for $10 a class.

The Santa Fe Mountain Center
Route 4, Box 34C (505) 983–6158

The center offers seventeen day wilderness expeditions, rope courses, backpacking, rock climbing, rappelling, and white water rafting. Hands-on training and experience teach young people their strengths and weaknesses.

Biking, Hiking and Camping

Mountain biking is one of the countries most popular outdoor sports. In Santa Fe, **New Mexico Mountain Bike Adventures** will take you anywhere in the state, and they can accommodate groups on six-day camping trips. The company also runs mountain biking tours out of Silver City. Call (505) 474–0074 or (505) 264–5888 for information. Park your car at Ft. Marcy Recreation Complex and ride fifteen miles up the Ski Basin Road. You begin at 7,040 feet and end at 10,300. **Santa Fe Century** winds through historic communities of Madrid and Galisteo. Call Willard Chilcott (505) 982–1282 for information. Another biking resource in Santa Fe is to join the **Sangre de Cristo Cycling Club** (505) 466–7434.

Santa Fe and New Mexico probably has the best hiking and camping of any state. There are more than 78 million acres of public land. Fabulous for hiking, camping out! Most of the state and national parks operate on a first come first serve basis. But you might be able to get reservations on Forest Service campgrounds if you call (800) 280–CAMP.

Santa Fe is a very healthy state. If you don't make use of the outdoor, you might be frowned upon! One of the best hiking trails is up the Winsor Trail, starting in Tesuque. It is scenic, not hard, and if you want to walk your dog or go with friends, then take a picnic and have lunch next to the stream.

Otherwise, make an investment in the book *Hikes in New Mexico* by Harry Evan by calling (800) 898–6639.

Fishing —— by El Pescador

High Desert Angler

435 S. Guadalupe Street, (505) 98-TROUT

The first thing you should do if you're thinking about doing some fly-fishing while in Santa Fe is to visit the High Desert Angler.

It has all the merchandise you could want, including accessories in all price ranges, and it can outfit you fully on a rental basis. Most importantly, it's just fun to be there and talk fly-fishing with the knowledgeable staff, that enjoys working with you. They have up-to-date information on all the rivers and lakes because so many of the locals call in their reports after a fishing trip. Owner Jan Crawford is widely acknowledged as one of the best anglers, and certainly the premier woman angler in the area, and she's twice as nice. In fact, you should consider the High Desert Angler your Santa Fe fishing headquarters. Since I go there more often than I fish any given river or lake, I count it as my favorite "fishing" spot.

Just as important is the book *Fly-Fishing in Northern New Mexico*. It's the atlas and bible of the local fishing fraternity. Each section is written by an expert on that particular area and includes everything you want to know about the places it covers. And of course, the High Desert Angler carries it.

Pecos

The closest river to Santa Fe is the Pecos. You can catch trout inside the town, less than thirty minutes from Santa Fe, or you can drive up the Pecos Canyon road and fish any number of spots for the next twenty miles. Much of the water is on private property, and the public stretches are sometimes crowded, but there are always some quiet areas, particularly if you are wading. The river is heavily stocked with rainbows and is primarily a put-and-take fishery for the bait fishers, but there is a stable spawning population of wild browns for the fly-fishing enthusiast.

San Juan

In northern New Mexico (near the Four Corners area, you'll find that the first four miles of the San Juan River below Navajo Dam, is one of the great trout streams in the U.S. It's three and a half hours from Santa Fe, but you won't be disappointed. You can float the river with a guide or wade it on your own after you get to know where the monsters are. Twenty-inch rainbows on a size 20 or 22 fly are not uncommon. Parts of the river get crowded, but there is plenty of fish for everyone—about six thousand trout per mile. It's essentially all catch-and-release (with barbless hooks) in the special regulations section, which is about 3 miles long.

Chama

The little town of Chama, one hundred miles north of Santa Fe, has an incredibly beautiful and luxurious hideaway resort called the Lodge at Chama (it used to be called Chama Land and Cattle Company). There are 14 lakes, from 8,000 to 11,000 feet, on 32,000 acres, and a superb lodge with 11 rooms. Only one group fishes a lake, along with a guide who gets you over the rough mountain roads in a big four-wheel drive vehicle. Once there, you'll catch rainbows, browns, cutthroats, and sometimes brookies, depending on the lake you choose. These are big, healthy, and heavy fish in the 16 to 24 inch range. You can fish from the banks or have the guide take you out in a rowboat with an electric motor. Naturally, it ain't cheap.

The Rio Grande

The Great River, which has its headwaters in Colorado not far from Creede, is exciting but can be a challenge. It is fishable all year except when it's too muddy or during peak run-off, when it is more suitable for river rafting. Some of the best fishing starts near Pilar, about 50 minutes north of Santa Fe, (and the drive there is beautiful). There is good fishing from Pilar up to the river's confluence with the Little Rio Grande. Farther north, near Taos, the river has cut a deep gorge in the rock, and fishing the Box of the Rio Grande Gorge is an experience in climbing and fishing that every fit person should try. The fishing can be very rewarding, but the climbing is demanding. Another ten miles north the Hondo runs into the big river, and that's a place for fun fishing without the strenuous climb.

Indian Ponds

At least five of the Indian pueblos, all within an hour from Santa Fe, have one-to-five acre ponds that are stocked mainly with rainbows but also with catfish and crappie. Santa Clara has four ponds along the scenic twelve-mile Santa Clara Canyon drive. San Ildefonso has the closest pond, and there are usually some residents for company and conversation. Nambe has the biggest lake, San Juan has two ponds, and Picuris is a bit out-of-the-way. Day and season rates are reasonable at all of these ponds, but it's worthwhile to check the status of the lakes before you go.

Jemez River

The Jemez Mountains are located north of Albuquerque and west of Los Alamos, where there are streams for all types of fly-fishing; meadows, canyons, pocket water, and all kinds of water on the Jemez river. What's the most fun is fishing for small (by Western standards), wild, wary mountain brown trout all along the East Fork. Easy access makes the more popular sections crowded at times, but evenings and weekdays are perfect times to fish in the Jemez. There are good campgrounds, and Bandelier is only a short drive. In addition to the Jemez itself, there are many streams worth exploring, many of them never crowded—the San Antonio, Rio de las Vacas, Peralta Creek, Rio Frijoles, the Cebolla, and the Guadalupe. Of these, my favorite is the San Antonio above Fenton Lake, which provides fine stillwater fishing, particularly if you are addicted to the float tube.

Jicarilla Apache Indian Reservation Waters

On the way to the San Juan River at Navajo Dam, you go to Chama and turn left. The town of Dulce is twenty-five miles down the road. It is the headquarters of the Jicarilla Apache reservation, which, among other things, has five trout-fishing lakes in the fifty to ninety-acre range. You don't need a New Mexico fishing license,

but you have to have a tribal fishing permit. You can get one
(they're not expensive) at the Tribal Game and Fish Office in
Dulce, at the Best Western Inn in Dulce, at the High Desert Angler
in Santa Fe, and at some other fishing shops in Northern New
Mexico. The best of the lakes for big, powerful rainbows is Stone
Lake, and the anglers who like to go out with a belly boat—sorry,
float tube—consider Stone Lake to be among the best. Bank fishing
is also productive here. There are other lakes, such as La Jara,
Mundo, Hayden and Burford (Stinking), but you should get up-
to-date information on how each is doing at any given time.

179

Rio do los Pinos and the Conejos River

The Colorado border is a little more than two hours north of Santa Fe, and there are two fine trout streams that run near it. Los Pinos is fished mostly from the New Mexico side. It offers fine dry fly fishing and is loaded with all kinds of trout. The Conejos is on the Colorado side, and you need a Colorado license to fish there. It's a gem. Get your license in Antonito, which, by the way, is the northern terminus of the Cumbres and Toltec narrow-gauge railway. The Chama River also has excellent fishing if your taste doesn't drive you to the luxury of the Lodge at Chama.

McAllister Lake

If you happen to be in Santa Fe when the season opens at McAllister Lake (it's one of the few lakes with a definite seasonal opening), it's worth your while to drive to Las Vegas, New Mexico with your float tube, to fish deep for the monsters who have been feeding all winter. The lake gets a lot of use later on, but the early season can be a joy. Watch out for the wind, though; Las Vegas, like all of Northern New Mexico, can be windy in the spring.

For current fishing reports call 800-ASK FISH
Also check the Department of Fish and Game
(505) 827-7885 or visit their web site at www.gmfsh.state.nm.us

Golf

"Golf used to be an elite country club sport—not really available in Santa Fe. New Mexico is desert country, and water remains precious. Accordingly, golf—benefiting from the use of "gray water" for irrigation—has just come to the area and just at the time that golf is becoming a sport for everyone. The only requirement is traveling to the course, arranging a starting time, and paying the price.

Two public courses are now available in Santa Fe; two private clubs exist; and public golf is readily available in nearby Los Alamos, Taos, and Albuquerque. But be careful if you are new to the area and are not used to the altitude. At 7,000 feet the views are fabulous, but don't attempt to walk the course if you are not fit." —**Luther Hodges**

Pueblo de Cochiti Golf Course

5200 Cochiti Hwy., Cochiti Lake, Cochiti Lake, NM 87083
(20 minutes south of Santa Fe)
(505) 465–2239 or (505) 465–2230

"One of America's Top 75 Affordable Courses"—**Golf Digest**

This public, very beautiful Robert Trent Jones, Jr. designed course is difficult but fun and fair. Bring plenty of golf balls. The Duke of Bedford lost a ball in the top branches of a pine tree here.

Las Campanas Santa Fe

Club House Drive, (505) 989–8877

Two Jack Nicklaus-designed 18-hole courses make the club the most expensive and exclusive in New Mexico. Membership is available only to those who purchase lots in the huge development. In addition to the two golf courses, facilities include riding stables, a John Gardiner staffed tennis club, an elaborate fitness center, and a 30,000 square foot, hacienda style clubhouse that has a bar

GOLF

Golf New Mexico Reservations
800-776-7669 ext. 540

and banquet facilities.

Even though the second golf course will be completed by the year 2000, beware of the slow, crowded play of golf at this club. Be prepared for rounds consuming in excess of five hours.

Quail Run
3101 Old Pecos Trail, (505) 986–2222

This private club has a true country club atmosphere, and it can be joined for the price of a golf membership. The club has a 9-hole, as well as two tennis courts, a fitness center, a full restaurant, banquet facilities, and a festive bar.

Regarding their golf—"*If you don't hit it straight it's a ball eater*"— **Jill Potter**

Santa Fe Country Club
Airport Road, 87502-2865, (505) 471–0601

This 18-hole semi-private course just west of Santa Fe and near the Villa Linda Mall offers beautiful views of the Ortiz, Sandia, Sangre de Cristo and Jemez Mountains. It is a "very forgiving" course and the club has always allowed the public to play. Another public course, operated by the City of Santa Fe, is opening in 1998.

University of New Mexico Championship Course
3601 University Blvd. S. E., Albuquerque, NM 87131–3046, (505) 277–4546

This very impressive long course, considered the best in Albuquerque and the most challanging in the Southwest, is ranked in the top twenty-five public golf courses in the nation according to *Golf Digest Magazine.*

Horses—

BLURB!

The Juan Tomas Hounds Hunt
("The Royal Order of the Fallen")

...and an Ass

"Tubak"

My great aunt Gladys Butler lived at 1120 Canyon Road until her death on January 15, 1949. There she had a stable attached to her bedroom in which lived a goat and a burro named Tubak who was a house-trained alcoholic. "Tubak would come in the house for Aunt Gladys's cocktail parties and guests would feed him drinks. Afterwards Tubak and the goat would chase each other through the house. Soon he became a mean drunk, and everytime he got mad he would take a chunk out of Aunt Gladys's favorite French chair. After guests stopped giving him drinks he developed a new habit. He followed them to their cars to get a buzz from the exhaust."—**Francesca Bliss**

"I used to ride by Gladys's house on my donkey—in the old days when Canyon Road was not paved. Tubak would be romping in the courtyard with the Scottish deer hounds."—**Donald Murphy**

THE STRAIGHT POOP

New Mexico has been one of the most multifaceted equestrian communities in the U.S. since the sixteenth century when the Conquistadores introduced horses to the American Southwest. New Mexico has all sorts of riding stables and breeders scattered around the state. If you want to see the wilderness areas, there is no better mode of transportation than horses. For a list of outfitters that offer pack trips call the **New Mexico Department of Game and Fish** at (505) 827-7911.

Breeders—

Annon's Equestrian Center
James Mits Annon & Robyn Cloughley Annon
2442 Cerrillos Road #134, (505) 984-9767

For the past fifteen years, members of the Annon family have been working with registered Spanish Barbs and Mustangs—examples of the historic horses of the conquest and colonization of Hispanic America. Currently Mits and Robyn are boarding, riding, training, competing, and giving lessons at the facilities in the village of Agua Fria. The Spanish Barb stallion, Lukachukai, and four of his offspring are there, along with a variety of other sport horses. The results of the breeding program conducted by the Annon's over the years are spread throughout northern New Mexico and on the West Coast. The Spanish barb is the ideal young person's horse: small, quick, smart, and tough.

Olivia Annon Tsosie is currently researching the characteristics and influence of equestrian practices in the Hispanic colonies of North America, and she is an active supporter of the binational Camino Real project.

La Estancia Alegre
Barbara Windom (505) 852–2883

Barbara's stables are on the Rio Grande River half way between Taos and Santa Fe. Here she breeds Peruvian pasos, the only naturally gaited breed in the world which can guarantee its gait to 100% of its offspring. Their unique four-beat lateral gait makes the Peruvian horse one of the smoothest riding horses in the world. One of her horses was in the 100-mile Tevis race, one of the best endurance races in the country. These horses are also known for their gentleness.

Los Trigos Ranch
Ginny Cowles, Rowe, NM 87562, (505) 757–2334

Los Trigos Ranch in Pecos is one of the most beautiful places on the Pecos River—like the movie *A River Runs through It*. Norwegian Fiords are friendly and gentle three-gaited horses ideal for young or inexperienced riders. They are happiest when they are working, and they can be taught to drive carts. They have the same characteristics of the primitive wild Przewalski horse from which they are believed to be descended—they are khaki colored and look like zebras without their stripes.

Twin Willow Ranch
Manager, Steve Tremper
Ocate, NM, (505) 666–2028

Twin Willow Ranch breeds performance quarter horses to be ridden in competition "cutting and reining" events. Cutting horses are used by cowboys to ride the cattle. In this competition the horse has to go through certain exercises that have to do with moving cattle. Reining refers to completing a series of specific patterns and movements in an arena's course. Twin Willow Ranch sells their yearlings and two-year-olds at cutting and reining sales in Oklahoma and Fort Worth. Owner Nancy Dickenson's dream since she was seven years old was to have a working horse ranch. Her ranch is located in a beautiful valley in Northern New Mexico.

Competitions

The Downs at Santa Fe

27475 W. Frontage Road, on I-25, (505) 471–3311

The most picturesque of the states three race tracks is owned by the Pojaoque Indians (the others are in Ruidoso and Albuquerque). It is located ten miles south of downtown Santa Fe on I-25. There is simulcast racing every day except Tuesday. A schedule can be obtained at the racetrack.

Event at the Downs

For more information call Abel Davis (505) 982–1040

Dressage is an Olympic sport that is one of the most important horse events in the West. At this two-day event with three competitions, there are 112 competitors from 12 states. Jane Silverman says, "It is the ultimate test of athleticism, trainability, and bonding between a rider and his horse. The first event is dressage, which is a training method to devise and promote suppleness, and it warms the horse up. In dressage, the horse and rider perform a pattern of movements that are judged. It focuses and attunes the horse for the second event where the horse and rider are judged on the execution of jumps on a two-to three mile course. This is a dangerous event where strength, bravery, and boldness are needed. In the third event the horse again changes its focus, and he must be collected again for the stadium jumping performed in a jumping arena. The events go from collection to explosion back to collection."

Polo
Eric Oppenheimer, (505) 820–7859 or (505) 583–2389

The Santa Fe Polo Club plays at the polo fields that used to be owned by Jim Alley—now called Rancho Oso Rio. They play every weekend during summer season. Polo players who have recently moved to Santa Fe are Charles Kokesh and Michael Butler.

Polocross
Sam Silverman, (505) 984–3002

In 1989, a small group met at Tomasita's and formed the first Polocross (a cross between polo and lacrosse, or "cowboy polo") team in Santa Fe. Eventually this team evolved into one of the top teams in the country. It plays in Anton Chico at a cowboy ranch owned by Danny Byrd near Las Vegas, NM. This group was successful because they incorporated trained breeding horses with polocross. The season in Las Vegas opens in June and ends on Labor Day; games are held every Sunday at 1:30 p.m.

Rodeo de Santa Fe
(See Annual Events)

Hunts & Rides

Chimayo Chile Ride
Talissa Ralph and Durt Sickafus, Rt. 1 Box 28
Santa Cruz, NM 87567

This is a fifty-mile or twenty-five-mile endurance ride where elevations range from 5,500 to 8,700 feet. The ride is regulated by a national endurance riding group which requires pre-ride veterinary inspections. The rules require horses to be at least five years old for the fifty-mile ride and four years old for the twenty-five mile event. Riders come from all over the state.

Chuck Wagon Riders
Paul Follmer, (505) 852–4447 or (505) 753–2383
Jim Mazza (505) 753–3698

This men-only ride, held annually the end of June, is one of the most popular rides in New Mexico. About 100 men from all over the country attend this three to five day event. The cost for membership and administrative fees is $50. The basic cost for the catered meals and lodging is $450 if you have your own horse. Although many members bring their own horses, they can be rented for an extra $350. Transportation to the start-off point is not included in the cost.

Challenge New Mexico Ride
Recreation Director, Chris Wuerhane
1570 Pacheco Street, Suite E6, (505) 988–7621

In October, Challenge New Mexico (CNM) sponsors a ride for the benefit of their organization whose membership is made up of individuals and families with disabilities. The half or full-day ride at Forked Lightning Ranch (which used to be Greer Garson's) is a popular and easy ride. The fifty dollar donation includes a BBQ and prizes.

Juan Tomas Hounds Hunt
Co-masters: Helen Krueger (505) 898–4607 and James Nance (505) 854–2805

This is the oldest "fox hunting for coyote" group in the state. They wear the traditional red coats worn only in the fanciest of hunting clubs, and follow the hounds in the traditional manner of the Masters of Fox Hounds of the Association of America. The Royal Order of the Fallen is an exclusive group who fall from their horse. They are known as the "fallees." The Secretary keeps track of who has fallen and the "fallees" bring a bottle per fall to the two biggest social events of the year. The formal Hunt Ball is held each year in Santa Fe or Albuquerque. The club, which started more than twenty-six years ago, is two-thirds Albuquerque riders and about one third Santa Fe riders. Their hunt breakfasts and approximately thirty rides take place from October to March each year. They host the Pony Club, a national organization founded in England that teaches children the management of horses and horsemanship.

Rent-a-Ride

There are very few places to rent a horse for pleasure riding. Most people own their own horses.

Bishop's Lodge Stable
Bishop's Lodge Road Tesuque, (505) 983–6377

Guided trail rides are offered mornings and afternoons daily. The cost for a ninty-minute escorted ride is $25.

Rancho Encantado
State Road 22, (505) 982-3537

One of the advantages of staying at Rancho Encantado if you like to ride is that you have full use of the riding facilities for only a nominal extra charge. There are regular rides scheduled at 9:30, 12:30, and 5:30 everyday. Trail rides cost $45 for non hotel guests. A private ride costs $55. Residents can board their horse here for only $700 a year if the horses are made available for the daily rides. Robert Redford boarded his horse here until last year.

Trainers

Goose Down Farms
HC 75, Box 55
Gallisteo, 87540, (505) 466-8771

Goose Down Farms is one of the best training centers dedicated to the development of horses and riders for the sport of Combined Training or Eventing. On 350 acres, Goose Down Farms boards and trains horses for these competitions.

TTEAM
Linda Tellington-Jones,
TTEAM Headquarters, P.O. Box 3793, Santa Fe 87501

Jones is a world-class horse trainer and founder of the Tellington Touch Equine Awareness Method (TTEAM), a holistic training methodology for horses. Since most training problems stem from the animal's physical tension or pain, Linda alleviates this tension with special therapeutic techniques.

Santa Fe Colores
Terry Berg
200 Camino Colores, R.R. 14, 87505, (505) 473–0905

Terry Berg and Kenny Laymen do Western reining and English equitation. Reining is a Western form of dressage where riders are scored by points on precision, speed, and beauty of pattern.

Hunting

The goal of hunting season is to provide recreation and also to control the wildlife population.

The Department of Game and Fish
408 Galisteo Street, (505) 827–7911

Divison of Wildlife
(505) 827–7885

The following outdoor stores specialize in equipment which you will need for hunting trips.

Active Endeavors, 301 N. Guadalupe Street, (505) 984–8221

Base Camp, 121 W. San Francisco St., (505) 982–9707

Outdoorsman of Santa Fe, 506 Cordova Road, (505) 983–3432

Ron Peterson's Guns, 509 Airport Road, (505)471–4411

Wild Mountain Outfitters, 541 W. Cordova Rd., (505) 986–1152

The Official State Mammal
The state legislature selected the black bear as the state's official mammal on February 8, 1963. **Smokey the Bear**, *the most famous bear in the history of the United States, a cub from New Mexico was found in a tree after a forest fire.*

Most of the major New Mexico mountains have black bears, the smallest species of bears in North America. If you plan to go bear hunting, get forest maps from the individual forests. **The Forest Service Regional Office** (505) 842–3292 in Albuquerque will provide you with the necessary maps and phone numbers. The most successful place to hunt for bear is in the Jemez Mountains. The Department of Wildlife monitors how many bears have been killed in different areas. A bear license costs $30 for residents and $140 for non-residents and can be purchased at any sporting goods store.

The most sought-after game is the deer and elk, the largest of New Mexico's big game species. Licensing can be complicated. There are over 300 vendors from private and public state properties. Because there are limits on the number game licenses issued, there are drawings—and the winners get to hunt on public lands. (The application deadline for bighorn sheep is April 15, for elk the deadline is May 13th, and for antelope, June 13th). If you miss the draw the best hunting is to get a land owner permit. The Department of Game and Fish have a list of these ranchers, two of whom are listed below.

Lodges and guiding services

The Valle Grande
(800) 456-6620

The Valle Grande, also known as Baca Location No. 1 and Valle Caldera, is unique because it is one of the largest dormant volcanos, or *calderas,* in the world. A *caldera* is formed by the collapse of a volcanic cone. The success of the elk herd is attributed to the abundant grasses and lush hills. Valle Grande receives about 120 permits each year for hunting.

Vermejo Park (Raton)
Vermejo Park Ranch
Drawer E, Raton, New Mexico 87740 (505) 445-3097

Ted Turner bought the 578,000-acre Vermejo ranch from Penzoil. It has an international reputation for elk hunting. The ranch's main lodge, which can accommodate seventy-five people, looks like Yellowstone with no people. Prices range from $290 a person per day to $3,600 a person per day for exclusive use of the lodge. Fall hunting expeditions cost from $1,850 for a turkey hunt to $12,000 for an archery hunt for elk. The success rate on elk hunts is about 95%. There is an abundance of other wildlife and 183 species of birds—including the only ptarmigan population in New Mexico.

Rafting and Kayaking

For a listing of rafting companies call the Bureau of Land Management (BLM) 224 Cruz Alta Street, Taos, NM 87571 (505) 758-8851
Reservations in Santa Fe, (505) 983-6565 or (800) 338-6877.

The state's most popular whitewater rivers are the Rio Grande and the Chama. There are many commercial rafting companies which offer half-day, full-day or overnight trips. When spring weather melts the mountain snow packs, the *Box* is the most exciting place to go when the water level peaks. The Box is 17 miles of the river ending in Pilar. Class 6 rapids are unnavigable— the Box is class 4 in the system of measuring rapids. The cost for a one day Box run ranges from $60 to $75. A half day on the Racecourse below Pilar is between $25-$50. Remember, you can't get out of Box Canyon even if you have a broken leg so it is best to use all safety precautions—wear your helmet! The only time I have ever been on the Box, was a terrifying experience. The boat, with eight people in it, flipped on a rock just above a rapid called *car wreck*.

For a recording on river information, call the Bureau of Land Management in Taos at (505) 758–8148. If you are planning your own trip, get the essential *New Mexico Whitewater: A Guide to River Trips.* It is available for $3 from the the New Mexico State Park and Recreation Division, Box 1147, Santa Fe 87503

Downhill Skiing

Ski New Mexico (505) 982-5300
www.skinewmexico.com

There are many ski resorts in New Mexico. The ones within two and one half hours from Santa Fe are as follows:

Angel Fire
(800) 633–7463 for reservation

This 2,200-foot vertical 26 miles east of Taos has 50 runs for novice to advanced skiers. The Legends Hotel is located at the base of the lifts.

Pajarito
(505) 662–5725

They are open about three days a week. It is best to call ahead to make sure they are open. It is popular because there are no lift lines. The peak is 10,441 feet, the base elevation is 9,031 feet. The ski lifts—one quad, three doubles, one triple, and one single—are never crowded. They have thirty-seven runs—30% expert, 50% intermediate, and 20% beginners. The ski resort was started as an activity for the scientific community of Los Alamos during the 1940s.

Red River
(800) 348-6444

This was once a gold-mining town founded in 1869, thirty-six miles northwest of Angel Fire was founded in 1869. The 1,500-foot vertical has forty runs and lodging for 4,000 people. It has 40 runs and lodging for 4,000 people. Children under 12 ski free when accompanied by an adult skier.

Sandia Peak
(800) 473–1000 for reservations
(505) 242–9133

Sandia Peak in Albuquerque is one hourdrive north from Santa Fe. You can access it from the east side of the mountain or from the west side where you can take the tram—the longest one in the world—at an extra cost. There are twenty-five runs. The peak is 10,378 feet and the base is 8,678 feet.

Santa Fe Ski Basin
(800) 776–7669 for accommodations
(505) 982–4429

The last day of the ski season, "Surfin Santa Fe," ends with a splash with live music and Hawaiian dress. Skiers competing in the Slush Cup Challenge try to get across Lake Totemoff without getting wet and without a boat!! Its a wild and funny event.

Santa Fe Ski Basin, conveniently located only 16 miles from town, is ranked among the top 10 highest elevation ski areas in the country—12,000 at the peak and 10,350 at the base. There are 38 runs—40% expert, 40% intermediate, and 20% beginners. Fortunately for residents, Santa Fe has the short lift lines on weekdays which is why it is still one of the best kept secrets. The

Totemoff on the deck of the mid-mountain lodge is one of the most fun places to people watch and have lunch. If you have small children, put them in charge of Lucy Huckabee, director of the **Chipmunk Corner.** The cafeteria at the bottom of the hill is popular. The toughest run at Santa Fe is Big Rocks. Benny Abruzo, the areas general manager picks First Tracks.

One of the largest ski fund-raisers in the country is the Jimmy Heuga Ski Express, which raises money for multiple sclerosis. For information call (505) 983–5615.

Sipapu
(800) 587-2241 for reservations
(505) 776-2291

Sipapu is one hour and 30 minutes from Santa Fe, just before Taos. They have 20 runs—30% expert, 50% intermediate, and 20% beginner. The peak is 9,065 feet and the base is 8,200 feet.

Taos Ski Valley
(800) 776–1111 for reservations
(505) 776–2291

Taos Ski Valley is not only the biggest and best known ski area in New Mexico but also known internationally. The peak is 11,819 feet and the base is 9,207 feet with 72 runs—51% expert, 25% intermediate, and 24% for beginners. It is one and a half hours from Santa Fe. Their ski package includes three gourmet meals a day. Highlands University in Las Vegas, NM, offers an excellent ski program in Taos.

Cross-Country & Telemarking

Telemarking is a combination between downhill and crosscountry skiing. Some good cross-country skiing is on the Windsor Trail near the Santa Fe Ski area, the William's Lake Trail near the Taos ski area and the Chama Community track area north of Chama. For information on areas to cross country ski in the Santa Fe and

"The first ski lift in town opened in 1936 at the location of the Evergreen Restaurant. People used to get there on horseback. The original group, the 'Sierra de Santa Fe,' were Howell Ernest, Ned Wood, Ferd Cook, DD Lord, Jack Watson, and myself. We got the money together, and for $60,000 we built the lodge and the chairlift. The chairs were army surplus chairs which came out of airplanes. I changed the name from Aspen Basin to Santa Fe Basin because people might be disappointed to be here instead of Aspen."—**Buss Bainbridge**

Carson National Forests call the U.S. Forest Service, headquarters in Santa Fe (505) 984–6940 Taos (505) 758–6200. For information about the Jemez Mountains call the Los Alamos Chamber of Commerce (505) 662–8105 or (800) 444–0707.

The Southwest Nordic Center
Doug MacLennon
P.O. Box 3212 Taos, N.M. (505) 758-476.

Rent a "Yurt"—a circular shelter with a covering stretched over a framework. The advantage of staying in a yurt is that you can get rid of your gear and ski unencumbered. The yurts are located at the southeastern end of the San Juan Mountains. The area was chosen because of the reliably excellent snow conditions, spectacular scenery and the varied terrain. Yurts have skylights and two windows. One is equipped with wood-burning and cooking stoves, lanterns, two bunkbeds, and cooking utensils. Doug owns and operates the yurts by permit from the Rio Grande National Forest and removes them at the end of each season. A group can rent any of the four yurts, which sleep six people on foam mattresses. You may choose a guided tour to the yurt, or if you are experienced at routefinding then you may choose an unguided tour.

Tennis— is my Racket

by Gladys Heldman

By Gladys Heldman

Ian Bedford, The Duke of Bedford

After giving up tennis for 50 years, he picked up a racket 7 years ago and has been going at it every summer in Santa Fe ever since. He took up tennis when he was 73—and he is now 64. He plays doubles every Sunday, rain or shine (because he plays indoors). He is a wonderful competitor, quite strong on serve and volley, and if he continues to improve at the same rate, he will win Wimbledon at the age of 90.

Tom Udall, New Mexico Attorney General

Tom is young, handsome, hard hitting, and on the way up, both politically and on the tennis court. He's good enough to take a club title in singles or doubles and/or to win a congressional election. He is extremely fair on the court ("Good shot!" "Take two!" "Ace!") and is in great demand as a doubles partner by all good Democrats.

Frank Ortiz, Former Ambassador

Frank will play at the drop of a hat. He adores the game and has improved considerably in the last couple of years. His favorite partner was former United States National Champion Frankie Parker, who was his houseguest five years ago. The two Franks made a fearsome combination even though their combined age was over 140 (Frankie Parker died in 1997 at age 82).

Serge Gagarin, Russian Prince

Serge is another promising "comer." He is 75-plus, although he leaps and runs like a kid of 60. Although he is small of stature, he always follows his serve to the net, perhaps because he enjoys the challenge of tearing back to the baseline to retrieve the lob over his head. He is full of good spirits, win or lose.

—**Gladys Heldman** has been publisher and owner of *World Tennis Magazine* for 22 years. This Santa Fean is the founder of the Virginia Slims circuit and started Women's Professional Tennis in 1970. Gladys has two cats "Virginia" and "Slim."

The Best Places

For a small town like Santa Fe, the tennis facilities are incredible and the number of good players is astonishing. Among those who have competed at Wimbledon are Claudia Monteiro (the head pro at Las Campanas), Rocky Royer (the head pro at Sangre de Cristo), Tim Garcia (a lawyer), Julius Heldman (a fly fisherman) and Gladys Heldman.

The Bishop's Lodge
Bishop's Lodge Road, (505) 983–6377

There are four Omni tennis courts at Bishop's Lodge, which is a well-known resort open all year round. The tennis courts, however, are open only from mid-April to mid-October. The pro is Jeanette Hadi, who has been teaching here for seven years. Anyone can sign up for the ninty-minute tennis clinics ($18 an hour per person) or to play in League matches of Men's, Women's and Mixed Doubles ($65 for 8 weeks). There is a small club for outside memberships, but because the facilities are limited, the rates are not publicized.

Club at El Gancho
Old Las Vegas Highway, (505) 988–5000

El Gancho has a tennis stadium (clay) plus one other clay court, five hard courts, and two indoor courts. There are two pools (one indoor, one outdoor), a full-service restaurant, and a complete gymnasium. Initiation fees in 1996 for a family were $600 and monthly dues were $128.

The Club at Las Campanas
132 Clubhouse Drive, (505) 995–3500

The two hard and two clay courts are for members only. The initiation fee is a minimum $200,000 (the cost of a lot), for which one gets the use of the courts, the pool, the golf course, the clubhouse, and other facilities in the works, including a second golf course and, perhaps, more courts. The tennis courts and shop are under the management of John Gardiner, and the head pro, Claudia Monteiro, was a finalist in the French Mixed Doubles Championships and was ranked in the World's Top 100 in singles. She is currently the Southwestern Women's Doubles and Mixed Doubles Champion. Her pupils, of whom I am one, adore her.

Quail Run
3101 Old Pecos Trail, (505) 986–2222

If you buy one of the beautiful condos at Quail Run, you are entitled to use all the facilities (tennis, golf, gym, pool, restaurant) at no extra cost. There are also 500 outside memberships for those who want to play golf, tennis, swim, etc. A 1996 Family Membership, which provides the use of all the facilities except for golf, costs $2,500 (initiation), $130 (deposit), $130 (monthly dues), and $35 (minimum food and beverage charge). With golf included the cost was $3500 (initiation) and $178 (dues). Quail Run has two hard courts. The pro is the athletic, talented Pat Narvaiz.

Rancho Encantado
State Road 592, (505) 982–3537

This hotel-resort has two courts and they are available to outsiders at the rate of $35 an hour (private lessons) and $15 an hour for either singles or doubles. The pro is the popular Sonny Martinez, who has been teaching at the hotel for 19 years. He was twice City Clay Court Doubles Champion in the Men's 35 division. Although there are no tournaments at the hotel, Sonny plans clinics and League play for future years.

St. John's College
1160 Camino de la Cruz Blanca, (505) 984–6000

The three hard courts at St. John's College are always open to the public, winter or summer, without charge. A small donation to the college, earmarked for the courts, is not necessary but is appreciated. No reservations are needed. The hours tennists may use the courts are posted. For example, the nearby Prep School has the use of the courts on Tuesdays afternoons from 1:15 to 1:45 and on Thursday from 2:30 to 3:30. St. John's students and faculty do have primary rights to the courts, and the public is expected to respect these priorities.

Sangre de Cristo Racquet Club

1755 Camino Corrales Road, (505) 983–7978.

Sangre de Cristo is a beautiful facility with six hard courts, one indoor court, and a swimming pool. The fees for a family membership were $800 in 1996 and monthly dues were $102. One can have lunch in the shade while watching sweating contestants battle it out in the blazing sun. The head pro, Rocky Royer, is a stand-out. He was ranked in the Top 100 of the World and was ranked no. 5 in the United States in Men's 35's division in 1995. Rocky also won the Southwestern Clay Courts several times. He and Claudia Monteiro are a fearsome twosome in mixed doubles.

Santa Fe Community College

6401 Richards Avenue, (505) 471–8200

The William C. Witter Fitness and Education Center has six asphalt tennis courts that are available to anyone enrolled in a fitness course at the center. The center has a swimming pool, indoor and outdoor tracks, a resistance training center with weights, and three outdoor gyms.

Santa Fe Country Club

P.O. Box 22865, Airport Road, (505) 471–3378

Santa Fe Country Club has three hard courts plus a full-service restaurant, a swimming pool, and an 18-hole golf course. A family can either join for $1,000 and pay monthly dues of $85, which entitles them to all the privileges of tennis, golf, swimming, and the restaurant, or one can use just the tennis facilities at $10 per court per hour for singles or $15 per court per hour for doubles. The head pro, a lovely gal named Debbie Romero, has won 10 City Singles and Doubles and six Mixed Doubles titles over the years.

Shellaberger Tennis Center

College of Santa Fe, 1700 St. Michaels Drive, (505) 473–6144.

Shellaberger has seven courts and an active tennis program of League matches, clinics, and tournaments. The head pro is Mike Bachicha, a very good player who was captain of the Oregon State team. Family memberships are $450 with monthly dues of $45. If one doesn't join, one can play all day for $5, although such guest privileges are limited to five visits a year per player.

Private Courts

Clark Hulings (hard court), Gerald Peters (clay court), Chuck Diker (hard court), the Heldmans (indoor), Eddie Gilbert (hard court), the Don Merediths (hard court), and Laura Rossi (hard court).

Public Courts

There are 27 public courts in Santa Fe. For more information, call (505) 984–6864.

People Watching

Celebrations Restaurant

The Most Diverse Places

Santa Fe and its people have a "look," which makes the city the ultimate laboratory for people watching. Locals struggle to be themselves, and tourists want to look like natives. All of Santa Fe's eccentricities are at play here.

The Most Popular Neighborhood Hang Out
Celebrations Restaurant and Caterers, 613 Canyon Road, (505) 984–8904

Lunch inside is a social affair with all the Canyon Road-Eastside regulars. The outside patio is the best place to watch people walking up and down Canyon Road, one of the oldest streets in the country. Owner Sylvia Johnson and Manager "Veikko" make neighbors feel especially at home.

The Best Place to People Watch if you are Homesick
Eldorado Court Lobby, 309 W. San Francisco Street, (505) 988–4455

The Eldorado, the largest convention hotel in town, is bound to have a concentration of eastern, midwestern, western, and southern professional people who have never been affected by Santa Fe. This can be comforting if you are homesick.

The Best Place to Hang Out Saturday Mornings
Farmers' Market. Sanbusco Center

Here you can see everyone in town and shop for all of your healthy, environmentally correct home-grown vegetables and fruits every Tuesday and Saturday (more customers)starting at 7 A.M. Have coffee and pastries and listen to musical groups play.

The Best Place to Go if You Are Gay
The Drama Club, 125 N. Guadalupe Street, (505) 988–4374

The bar is gay every night but Wednesday, which is "trash disco night." There is a small cover charge when they have live entertainment.

The Best Meeting Place at The Flea Market
On Taos Highway next to the Santa Fe Opera

The outdoor food stand at the flea market, north on the Taos Highway next to the Opera, is the best meeting place and rest-stop for exhausted bargain hunters. Locals see almost everyone they know here because it is one of the most fun things to do on Fridays, Saturdays, and Sundays whether you shop or not.

The Most Discriminating Shopping Place
Kaunes (pronounced Connies), 511 Old Santa Fe Trail, (505) 982–2629

This is where discriminating people who are in a rush shop for their groceries—no matter what the cost! It is one of the smallest, most expensive, but friendly gourmet grocery stores in the country. It's conveniently tucked between two of the best neighborhoods, and on the corner of two major streets, on which everyone must pass at least once a day.

The Best Place to People Watch Without Being Seen!
The Ore House balcony, 50 Lincoln Avenue, (505) 983–8687

Weather permitting, the balcony overlooking the Plaza is the perfect perch from which to watch all the activity on the Plaza without being seen; happy-hour is from 4:30 to 6:00 p.m. A favorite drink is the margarita, and the chips and salsa are free.

The Best Multi-Cultural People Watching
The Plaza

You have all the multi-cultural things at play here: Indians under the portal, tourists gawking, shoppers shopping, and hippies congregating. There are many things to do, benches to sit on, and museums to visit. Get one of "Roques *carnitas*" from the cart on the corner of Washington and Palace. A *carnita* is made of marinated thinly sliced top round steak. It is grilled on an open fire with sliced green chile and onions, topped with home-made salsa and served in a flour tortilla. It is very messy; get plenty of napkins. Or get a frito pie from The Five and Dime General Store. Go to Fajita's Alley on Palace Avenue (opposite Cathedral Park) and get a fajita. Or go to Haagen Daz for dessert, it has to be one of the most popular in the country and theyhave one of the best bakeries in Santa Fe right there. Sit next to the window where there are two seats facing the Plaza. Or go sit in the park. Ride your bike and bring a picnic lunch if you can't afford any of these places.

Seeing the Most Environmentally Correct People

Wild Oats, 1090 S. St. Francis Drive, (505) 983–5333 and
Wild Oats, St. Michael's Village West, (505) 473–4943
Alfalfas, 333 W. Cordova Road, (505) 986–8667

These health food grocery stores are very popular because everyone in Santa Fe is so health conscious. During the summer you can sit outside. They have the best bulletin boards in town. Both stores offer cooking courses, take-out food, salad bars, regular groceries, and Alfalfa's has an excellent cafeteria. People who shop at these kind of places buy exactly what they want no matter what it costs. You can eat and shop at the same place. Their large assortment of tester bottles are fun to try.

Performing Arts

The Santa Fe Symphony and Chorus

The Santa Fe Opera

General Director, John Crosby
Associate General Director, Richard Gaddes
Post Office Box 2408, 87504–2408, (505) 986–5900 or (800) 280–4654
http://www.santafe opera.org

A Proven History

The Santa Fe Opera was founded in 1956 by John Crosby who had become familiar with the area because his family had vacationed here from New York and he had gone to the exclusive Los Alamos Ranch School which became the secret "Manhattan Project" headquarters the year before he graduated in 1943. Santa Fe was already an artistic and literary community but the musical element was missing. Crosby's dream—he was thirty at the time—was to build an opera in the northern hills of Santa Fe. When Crosby told Miranda Levy, one of Santa Fe's artistic elite, about his new opera venture, she contacted her good friend composer Igor Stravinsky at his home in Los Angeles. Stravinsky is often called the greatest composer of the twentieth century. Crosby's plan for the first opera season was to produce Stravinsky's *The Rake's Progress*. Miranda, who said "Crosby is a genius," had no difficulty getting Stravinsky to come to Santa Fe and meet him. Stravinsky supervised the production of *The Rake's Progress*, and the first season of the Santa Fe Opera opened in the summer of 1957. The tickets were $5. It was a great beginning for the opera and for Santa Fe because the first season was well received and well reported in the international press. There was a sudden demand for tickets and for more information about Santa Fe. Stravinsky returned for five more seasons between 1959 and 1963.

A former artist here, a world famous dancer, film star, narrator and stage director Briggitta Lieberson Wolfe, formerly known as Vera Zorina, now resides permanently in Santa Fe.

The Opera Facilities

The first opera house built in 1956 cost $112,000; it burned to the ground in July of 1967, ten years after it opened. By the opera's twelfth season, the second opera house was built at a cost of $2,200,000, providing three times the seating of the first, a total of 1,889 seats. It was the only opera house in the country that had an open roof. You could see all the way to Los Alamos behind the stage. The third opera house, started at the end of the 1997 season and finished before the 1998 season, cost $19 million. In an amazing act of civic pride and international fame, the money was raised to erect the new opera house before the old building was razed! The new theater increases seating capacity by 269 seats.

The Management: A Year Round Operation

Running the opera is a full time, year-round job despite the short performance season. It is run like a large corporation with a board of directors and a foundation board. The annual budget is $8 million. Two-thirds of the audience (and the money) comes from outside of Santa Fe and one-third from Santa Fe.

Nancy Zeckendorf, a former ballerina and president of the opera until 1996, "has the energy of a mountain goat," Miranda Levy said. "She knows how to collect money and be charming at the same time. I don't know what we would have done without her. She was the one who got the corporations interested. She started the gala and has always been its chairman."

Miranda Levy says about John Crosby: "He had a clear vision, he knew exactly what he wanted. He is talented about money and music. He is a remarkable business man and extraordinary with numbers. To date he is America's longest reigning opera manager.

Richard Gaddes, associate general director and considered heir apparent, worked with Crosby for many years then left briefly to start the Opera Theatre of St. Louis. "Everyone missed him so much he had to come back," Miranda Levy told me.

"Richard brings many talents to the opera—artistic, audition, administrative, and artistic background as well as a solid relationship with John Crosby. He brought the community to the opera." Nancy Zeckendorf said. Gaddes produced Benjamin Brittens' *Noah's Flood* in the church of Santa Maria de La Paz. The production involved over 300 children and was widely acclaimed as an extraordinary community project of the opera.

The Costume Shop

Costumes for most productions are made in the Santa Fe Opera costume shop. It is supervised by professionals and costumes are created by young apprentices who are learning the trade. They have a complete wig department with hundreds of all periods, and a complete shoe department. One former costume designer, Patton Campbell, teaches costume design in New York. Their costumes are often rented to other opera companies.

The Most Elegant Social Event Of the Summer

The four-day Gala Opening Celebration in late June which kicks off the opera season is one of the most important social events of the summer. This gala raises operating money for the opera and helps to finance the Apprentice Program, one of the oldest and best training opportunities for young professionals in the world, The Opera Ball kicks off the event. It is the most elegant and formal party of the year with Mike Carney's New York band playing.

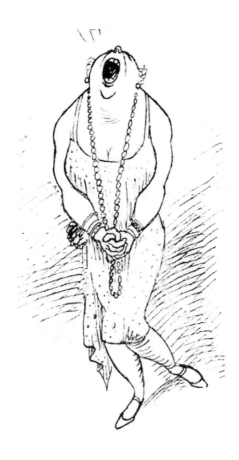

Dance

The Largest Spanish Dance Company in the Country
Maria Benitez's Estampa Flamenca, (505) 982–1237
Benita's Caberet: Hotline and Reservations, (505) 992–5814

The largest and best Spanish dance company in the country is choreographed and directed by Maria Benitez. Teatro Flamenco included Jose Greco, who danced with her company in 1986. She also directs Segunda Compania, another dance troupe, and has a summer International Spanish Dance Workshop here in Santa Fe. Santa Fe has been Maria's summer home for at least twenty-two years. She has been nominated for the National Medal of Arts, the country's highest arts honor conferred on twelve Americans each year by the President of the United States.

A Famous Dance Program for Children
Artistic Director, Catherine Oppenheimer
National Dance Institute of New Mexico
Box 831, Tesuque, NM 87574, (505) 983–7646

Jacques d'Amboise, who had an extraordinary career with the New York City Ballet from 1949 to 1984, founded the National Dance Institute (NDI) in 1976 to help children in the inner-city schools develop confidence and a sense of achievement. Today NDI-NY serves over 1,000 children a year in twenty-five schools in the New York area. D'Amboise has won numerous awards for his work in arts education, including the Kennedy Center Award for Lifetime Achievement in the Arts in 1995. In 1995, Catherine Oppenheimer, an accomplished dancer with the New York City Ballet and the Twyla Tharp Dance Company, founded the National Dance Institute of New Mexico along with her mentor, Jacques d'Amboise. Their program, which is in seven schools and in the School for the Deaf, keeps more than 400 children dancing each year.

Newest Group: The Santa Fe Ballet
General Director, Henry Holth
Santa Fe Festival Ballet, P. O. Box 1695, S.F., (505) 232–2710
Tickets (800) 905–3315

The Santa Fe Ballet presented its premiere season August of 1997 at the James A. Little Theater on the campus of the New Mexico School for the Deaf. The ballet features live music by the Santa Fe Pro Musica chamber orchestra and imports well-known performers. Choreographers whose works are produced have thus far included Alex Ossadnik, George Balanchine, John Clifford and Catherine Oppenheimer, director of the National Dance Institute. The ballet company provides workshops for advanced ballet students and ballet teachers at the College of Santa Fe and the University of New Mexico.

Musical Groups

The Best Place to Spot Celebrities

To Benefit Santa Fe Cares, P. O. Box 1255, (505) 986–3820
Lensic Theater, 211 W. San Francisco Street

An annual fun and unique concert in July featuring the best of
Santa Fe's performing arts at the Lensic Theater. Tickets sell out
fast so get your tickets early. In 1997, Lauren Bacall took the role
of emcee and the Lensic Theater was filled with movie stars,
illustrious locals, and out-of-towners. Santa Fe Cares provides direct
services for counceling and education for the prevention of AIDS.
Santa Fe Cares also sponsors (and you must get someone to sponsor
you) the AIDS Walk in October, and the Ski for Life in February.

One of the 10 Best Chamber Music Festivals in the U.S.

Executive Director, Eric Volmeer
Santa Fe Chamber Musical Festival, Ticket Reservations (505) 982–1890
640 Paseo de Peralta, Box 853, (505) 983–2075

The music festival is one of the most popular annual musical
events of the summer in Santa Fe and considered one of the best
Chamber Music festivals in the country. They have terrific, world-
famous musicians who play both traditional chamber pieces as
well as modern pieces, swing, and jazz. Performances run from
July through August.

Produced Sounds of Santa Fe

Executive Director, Jerome Nelson
The Santa Fe Desert Chorale
P.O. Box 2813, (505) 988–2282, summer (800) 244–4011

The Santa Fe Desert Chorale is one of the top forty fully professional
chamber choruses in the United States. They recruit nationally for
twenty to twenty-four singers. The season runs six weeks in the
summer and two weeks in December. They perform at the
Sanctuario de Guadalupe, the Loretto Chapel, and St. Francis

217

Auditorium. In addition to their many recordings, they have produced and participated in many American and world premiers. Their first commercial compact disc, *Sounds from Santa Fe,* is available on the Musical Heritage Society label.

One of the top 10 bluegrass festivals
George Butterfield, (505) 298–3080
Santa Fe Bluegrass & Old Time Music Festival
Rodeo Grounds, Rodeo Road, (505) 438–6230

One of the top ten bluegrass festivals in the country held in late August. The two-day, three night mini-festival with banjo, fiddle, guitar, mandolin, old-time bands, and bluegrass competitions has been in Santa Fe for at least twenty-two years. Performers come from all over. Saturday night a nationally known bluegrass band performs. Some twenty-three to thirty bands performing non-stop from noon until 7 P.M. and about 120 to 125 performers participate. Each has a chance to play three songs, each is judged and ranked, and the winners delight in the praise (as well as the prize).

The Orchestra without a Conductor
Concertmaster, Ralph Morrison
Santa Fe Pro Musica, 320 Galisteo Street, Suite 502, (505) 988–4640

In a season that runs from October to May, the concertmaster leads from his violin. Performing without a traditional conductor, this virtuoso chamber orchestra has established a reputation for musicality and precision. The Pro Musica Chamber Ensemble performances in historic Loretto Chapel at Christmas and during Holy Week are tradition beloved both by visitors and residents.

The Largest Santa Fe Musical Group
The Santa Fe Symphony and Chorus
P.O. Box 9692, NM 87504–9692, (505) 983–3530

The Santa Fe Symphony, the largest of the Santa Fe musical groups, was founded thirteen years ago by Greg Heltman, who is its current president. The symphony plays at Santa Fe's largest auditorium, Sweeney Center (capacity: 900). Outstanding artists who have been presented by the symphony include pianist Andre Watts, soprano Marilyn Horne, conductors Elmer Bernstein and Stuart Robertson, the late Dinah Shore, and jazz musicians Eddie Daniels and Dave Grusin.

The Symphony has one unusual way of raising money at the same time that it provides a delightful "insider's" tradition. An individual can join the Symphony Club for $500 for twelve months. This entitles the member to attend ten buffet-musicales at ten different Santa Fe homes. The musicales vary; a string quartet, a piano recital, a small chamber group or perhaps a harp. The symphony starts its season in September and finishes in April.

Theater

The Largest Circus in the World
Carson and Barnes Big Top Circus

The largest circus in the world comes to Santa Fe every spring for three days. When it is laid out flat, the tent covers a space as big as three football fields Four elephants pull up the huge tent in only forty minutes.

The Only Dinner Theater in Santa Fe
La Casa Sena Cantina, 125 East Palace, (505) 988–9232

La Casa Sena has live Broadway show tunes sung by the waitpersons as you eat. Shows nightly are at 6 and 8 p.m.

Hissing and Booing are Required
The Fiesta Melodrama, Santa Fe Playhouse, 142 E. DeVargas, (505) 988–4262

During the annual fiesta weekend in September, the Fiesta Melodrama is an excuse to let loose at local characters and everything in Santa Fe. Nothing (and nobody) is sacred.

The Best Place to See Touring Comedians
Santa Fe Comedy Club, Ramada Inn, 2907 Cerrillos Road, (505) 471–3000

The Route 66 Comedy Allstars, a touring group of five New Mexican comedians, performs year-round every Thursday, Friday, and Saturday.

One of the 10 Best Plays of 1996—The New Mexican
Artistic Director, Judith Joseph
Santa Fe Theatre Company, P. O. Box 2504, (505) 982–1441

The Santa Fe Theater Company is more than five years old. They mount original productions like *Wit,* the only play chosen by both the *New Mexican* and the *Reporter* as one of the ten best plays of 1996. Performances are held at the Armory for the Arts.

One of the Best International Theaters in the U.S.
Santa Fe Stages, Greer Garson Theatre at the College of Santa Fe
1600 St. Michael's Drive, (505) 982–6683

One of the best international theater companies in the United States, Santa Fe Stages hosts an international theater festival with productions at the College of Santa Fe and at adjacent Weckesser Studio Theater. The theater group, financed by Sallie Bingham— poet, playwright, and offspring of the Louisville *Courier Journal* family—has already given $750,000 and pledged $2 million annually until the year 2000. One of the conditions of the pledge is that Martin Platt, a renowned director, run the theater group and that he be allowed the artistic license to present whatever plays he selects.

The Best Outdoor Festival for the Whole Family
Managing Director, Mary Bush
Shakespeare in Santa Fe, 355 E. Palace Avenue, (505) 982–2919

Shakespeare in Santa Fe was established in 1987 by the Board of Directors of the Witter Bynner Foundation for Poetry, Inc. at the recommendation of Steven Schwartz, the founder. A collaborative effort with St. Johns College, the professional summer outdoor Shakespeare festival takes place in July and August on Friday, Saturday, and Sunday evenings. Pre-show activities begin at 6 P.M. with picnicking, wandering minstrels, jugglers, and other entertainment. There is a fabulous buffet catered by Wild Oats, of salmon and vegetarian dishes, and it even has hotdogs for children. The show starts at 7:30 P.M. Performances are held at St. Johns College.

The Best Performing Arts Teaching Center for Children
Director, Wayne Sabato
Santa Fe Performing Arts School and Company
1050 Old Pecos Trail, (505) 982–7992

The Santa Fe Performing Arts School manages the armory as a performing arts center for non-profit organizations. The school has intensive courses for children and teenagers. The building was constructed in 1940 and was the home of the National Guard's

221

200th Coast Artillery Regiment. During World War II, the 200th was the primary military unit on the Bataan Death March. The armory has a military museum.

The Oldest Continuously Active Theater in the West
Executive Director, Catherine Owen
The Santa Fe Playhouse, 142 E. DeVargas Street, (505) 988–4262

The former Santa Fe Community Theater, this oldest continuously active theater west of the Mississippi changed its name in 1997. The 100-seat theater hosts its own productions.Other theater groups rent their facilities, so productions are constantly on stage throughout the year. The theater was founded in 1922 by writer Mary Austin and friends.

A Year Round Theater
Director, David Olson
Theaterwork, 1336 Rufina Circle, just off Cerrillos, (505) 471–1799

This theater was founded in 1979 outside of Minneapolis by David Olson who has had twenty years experience as artistic director of theater. They have a full season of productions year-round. This dynamic national organization sets up theater producing not only their own works but also plays by local artists. They have community outreach programs and apprenticeships for young people. They are known for drawing stories out of the community. During the month of May they have a series called Women of the Arts. In February of 1998, for example, they honor the memory of local veterans with a performance on the Bataan Death March. There are over one hundred veterans in New Mexico who are survivors of Bataan.

Restaurants

There are approximately 230 restaurants in Santa Fe. There are about 10,000 people who work in local Santa Fe Restaurants. There are more fine restaurants per capita than any other city in the world. One of the phenomenons of Santa Fe is that people say they come here for cultural reasons and to sightsee but when asked what they enjoyed most about Santa Fe, they mention the restaurants. Santa Fe is one of the top 25 American Restaurant Cities according to, among others, *Money Magazine* and *Playboy Magazine*—**Al Lucero,** President, The Santa Fe Restaurant Association (505) 983–7929.

The Most Time-Tested

The Most Formal
The Compound, 653 Canyon Road, (505) 982–43▓3

The Compound is located in an old adobe landmark house that was completely overhauled by Alexander Girard, designer of the world-famous Museum of International Folk Art Museum here in Santa Fe. The secret of Girard's genius is achieving beauty out of simplicity. The impeccably served continental cuisine caters to sophisticates who like formal dining.

Most Secrets Were Shared on Their Dance Floor
El Nido Restaurant in Tesuque, (505) 988–4340

The wonderful ambiance and the consistently good food make El Nido popular with the locals. Great steaks and fish. In 1942, scientists assigned to the "Manhattan Project" in Los Alamos went there to drink and dance. (Do you think they knew it was a brothel then?) Sit in the front room where you can see everyone!

Unfortunately Billy the Kid Worked in the Kitchen
La Plazuela in the La Fonda Hotel, 100 East San Francisco Street, (505) 982–5511

La Fonda, at the end of the Old Santa Fe Trail on the Plaza, has the only restaurant in Santa Fe that regularly serves ostrich meat. The historic courtyard dining room is full of old Santa Fe charm. It is always crowded with politicians and locals. Billy the Kid worked in the kitchen on the site of the former La Fonda—the old Exchange Hotel. He was gunned down by Sheriff Pat Garrett on July 14, 1881.

Santa Fe's Most Famous Gambling Saloon
The Palace Restaurant, 142 W. Palace Avenue, (505) 982–9891

This was the site of Dona Tules' famous gambling saloon and house of ill repute! Owner Lino Pertusini has decorated one of the oldest restaurants in town in plush turn-of-the-century decor. The Palace specializes in Northern Italian cooking. It is a hangout for politicians and locals who have been "regulars" for years. A favorite is the Caesar salad, which is made at your table. The outside patio is a local's favorite during warm months. Alfonso, the most popular bartender in town, knows all the ghosts in (and out!) of all the closets. The Palace is one of the best places to spend New Year's Eve.

The Most Time–Honored Restaurant
The Pink Adobe, 406 Old Santa Fe Trail, (505) 983–7712

The Pink Adobe, one of the oldest restaurants in town, opened in 1944. The decor, the cozy rooms, and owner Rosalia Murphy's cheerful style of putting on a local art show are all features that attract people to the "Pink." It's an institution and a part of old-time Santa Fe. Rosalia's trademark is her hot French apple pie with hard sauce and hot brandy (sold at Kaune's Grocery Store), and also her Steak Dunnigan, topped with a green chile sauce and mushrooms.

On The Plaza Since 1918
The Plaza Cafe, 54 Lincoln Avenue, (505) 982–1664

The Plaza Cafe is Santa Fe's oldest restaurant. The current owner, the Beneranda Razato, bought the down-home restaurant in 1947. They'll be happy to show you a page from a 1918 *New Mexican* featuring an advertisement for the Plaza Cafe. The Plaza Cafe serves a mix of Mexican and American food. On Friday night they have Greek specialties. A popular, less expensive on-the-Plaza restaurant.

Haute Southwestern

Haute Southwestern: Indigenous, regional ingredients crossed with Southwestern chili and corn and incorporating the sweet, tart, and hot flavors of Asia.

The Only 4–Diamond and 4–Star Restaurant
Anasazi Restaurant, Inn of the Anasazi, 113 Washington Avenue
(505) 988–3236

Santa Fe High Style: The Anasazi Restaurant, located in the Inn of the Anasazi, has been awarded the American Automobile Association's Four Diamond Award for four years in a row. Everything on your plate is visually stunning. The library is a small, intimate, and cozy place to eat. The wine cellar is popular for private parties. *Bon Appetite* awarded the Anasazi their "Restaurant of the Month Award."

The Finest Paintings
La Casa Sena, 125 E. Palace Avenue, (505) 988–9232

The restaurant is located in an historic house built by Major Jose Sena in 1860. The outdoor patio, surrounded by shops, is the largest patio and one of the nicest for summer dining by day or night. Inside, the paintings loaned from the Gerald Peters Gallery add to the elegant ambience of the restaurant.

The Only Native American Restaurant
The Corn Dance Cafe, Hotel Santa Fe, 1501 Paseo de Peralta Street
(505) 982–1200

The only Native American restaurant in Santa Fe—indigenous foods of the North Americas. They should win an award for the most riveting entrees—kick-ass buffalo chile and little big pies. Their game meats, such as buffalo and venison, are a specialty.

The Most Media Attention
Coyote Cafe, W. Water Street, (505) 983–1615

Innovative Southwestern cooking in a contemporary casual room. Mark Miller is one of the best celebrity chefs in the country, and he has done more than anyone else to put Santa Fe on the culinary map. Coyote Cafe has the best counter to sit at and chat as you watch meals being prepared. **The Coyote Cantina,** upstairs, is a good place to go if your mind is set on Coyote food, but you don't want to spend as much as the Cafe charges.

The Most Historic Building
Geronimo, 724 Canyon Road Road, (505) 982–1500

In one of the oldest buildings on Canyon Road, this restaurant has a wonderful ambiance and is very popular with the locals. The outdoor patio on the Canyon Road side is a great place to people watch. Geronimo has won the "best entree" award three years in a row and the "grand prize" award for two years at the annual Taste of Santa Fe charity event.

The Most Elegant
The Old House Restaurant, 309 W. San Francisco Street, (505) 988–4455

Candlelight, a fireplace, and beautiful furniture make this restaurant quaint, quiet, and appealing. The Old House serves the best lamb chops in the world. They have the convenience and good fortune of being located in the grandest hotel in the city.

Combines French and Southwestern Flavors
Ristra, 548 Agua Fria Street, (505) 982–8608

Ristra is unique in the restaurant scene by the way it combines the French and Southwestern spirits in its approach, ambiance, and cuisine. Housed in an historic home, the intimate surroundings are warm and casual, yet elegant.

The Only Place There's an Antique Water Well
Santacafé, 231 Washington Avenue, (505) 984–1768

You have to circumvent the antique water well in the bar in order to get to the bathroom. "Contemporary American" with spring rolls as their trademark. The top restaurant in the city according to Zagat's 1995 rating. Santacafe has been awarded the Distinguished Restaurant Award from *Condé Naste* magazine. The historic setting of the Padre Gallegos house contains one of the city's most visually relaxing outdoor patios.

Native New Mexican

The Best Cabaret
Cantina Casa Sena, 125 Palace Avenue, (505) 988–9232

The Cantina serves traditional New Mexico food and sandwiches at dinner while the waiters and bartenders sing songs from Broadway and light opera. They don't take reservations unless there are six or more people in your party.

The Best Sopaipillas
Guadalupe Cafe, 422 Old Santa Fe Trail, (505) 982–9762

A sopaipilla, which looks like a blown-up piece of bread, is wonderful served with honey as an accompaniment to the meal or served as a meal in itself when stuffed with meat or chicken. Breakfast here is very popular with the locals. If you don't go early on weekends you will have to wait in line. Recommended by the *New York Times*.

The Best Margaritas in the World!
Maria's New Mexican Kitchen, 555 W. Cordova Road, (505) 983–7929

Marias is the only place a strolling mariachi plays every night. Declared the "best in the West" in 1953 by the Nashville *Tennessean*, it's a great place to go with a group because it has a cantina ambiance, it's cheap, and lots of fun. The fajitas and burritos grande are grand and so are the seventy varieties of margaritas. Al Lucero, its owner and manager, won the 1997 Restauranteur of the Year Award, the 1997 Best Margarita in Santa Fe from the *Santa Fe Reporter,* and the 1997 Best Margarita in New Mexico from *Crosswinds Magazine.*

The Only Mexican Restaurant
Old Mexico Grill, 2434 Cerrillos Road, (505) 473–0338

This wonderful and genuine Mexican (not New Mexican or Tex/Mex) ambiance, with tiles behind the grill and a painting by Elias

229

Rivera, was rated number one as "the best Mexican Restaurant in the state" by Zagat's Survey. Mexican specialties are the pipian, the mole poblano, and the fajitas.

The Most Eclectic Breakfast
Pasquales, 121 Don Gaspar Street, (505) 983–9340

The community table here is a great place to meet new people if you don't know too many people already. One of the favorites is Huevos Motulenos—blue or yellow corn tortillas with eggs, black beans, goat cheese, friend bananas, and home made red chile. The sourdough pancakes and waffles are also delicious. Get there early or wait in line.

The Best Inmates "Food Night" Program
The San Marcos Cafe, Hwy 14, (505) 471–9298

The penitentiary is only four miles away from this cafe. Inmates on good behavior are allowed to pool their money and order from their choice of Santa Fe restaurants. A favorite is the San Marcos burrito.

The Best Red Chile
The Shed, 113 1/2 E Palace Avenue, (505) 982–9030

The restaurant is housed in a seventeenth-century hacienda. The colorful murals on the walls, painted by Shelby Matis, make this restaurant one of the most attractive in town. Specialties are the red chile enchiladas with blue corn tortillas. Their sister restaurant, **La Choza** which serves exactly the same food, is on Cerrillos Road.

The Best Quesadilla Breakfast
Tecolote Cafe, 1203 Cerrillos Road, (505) 471–0611

Try Tecolote's New Mexican breakfast with scrumptious double bacon-and-egg burrito and fabulous hash browns.

The Best Chalupas
Tia Sophia's, 210 W. San Francisco Street, (505) 983–9880

Relatives of the Tia Sophia's crowd also own **Tomisitas** and **Diegos** respectively so the family really knows New Mexican cuisine. A very popular place for breakfast—try the breakfast burrito.

The Only Restaurant In An Old Convent
La Tertulia Restaurant, 416 Agua Fria, (505) 988–2769

The convent on the "Camino Real"—the road which connected Mexico City to Santa Fe—was constructed in 1926 for Dominican nuns who taught at the Guadalupe Parish school next door. The Ortizes opened the restaurant in 1972 and it has been a family-run restaurant ever since. A noteworthy mural has been preserved. The Old Santa Fe Association gave La Tertulia an award for their careful restoration. Their signature dish is paella, and their special drink is Sangria.

The Best Fajitas
Tiny's Restaurant and Lounge, 1015 Pen Road, (505) 983–1100

Tiny's has dancing on Friday and Saturday nights. Tiny plays the accordian on request, and Betty never forgets a name. Tiny's is particularly popular with politicians and locals.

The Longest Lines
Tomasita's Cafe, 500 S. Guadalupe Street, (505) 983–5721

The wait for a table can seem interminable, but patience has its rewards. Have a margarita or two while you're waiting. *The Santa Fean* "Best" poll voted Tomasita's the best place for margaritas and chile. Specialties are enchiladas, chile rellenos, and burritos.

Continental (No Chiles)

The Best Pasta
Andiamo! 322 Garfield Street, (505) 995–9595

Although they specialize in pasta dishes, they serve chicken, steak, and fish specials daily. It is one of the few restaurants where both of the owners are working in the kitchen and on the floor. Dinner only from Wednesday through Monday, not open for lunch.

Their Wood Burning Brick Oven Makes Great Pizzas
Babbo Ganzo, 130 Lincoln Avenue, (505) 986–3835

Southwest Airline's *Spirit Magazine* in 1994 named Babba Ganzo one of the top five Italian restaurants in the country. A romantic, aesthetically attractive, quiet, very popular, Tuscan–style Italian trattoria with dancing every Wednesday night.

The Best Bistro Food In Town
Bistro 315, 315 Old Santa Fe Trail, (505) 986–9190

The menu is displayed on a blackboard that is brought to the table. Bistro 315 is most "cozy by necessity" because of its size. Serving the best classic provincial French food in town, they are famous for their squash blossom beignets. This is a restaurant in which it is difficult to make a dining decision because everything is so good.

The Biggest And Best Display Of The Best French Pastry
Le Cafe, in the Desert Inn, 311 Old Santa Fe Trail, (505) 982–7302

This is one of the best French bakeries and restaurants in Santa Fe. Because you eat facing two long cases of French pastries, it is hard to resist their fabulous desserts. No shortage of free parking: a rarity in Santa Fe.

The Best Lobster Specials
Fabios, 329 W. San Francisco Street, (505) 984–3080

Fabios is a romantic, popular Italian restaurant with white table-cloths and Florentine specialties. The menu specifies quantity, which allows you to downsize your portions if you are dieting. For example you may order one, two, or three lamb chops.

The Most Romantic
Julians Italian Bistro, 221 Shelby Street, (505) 988–2355

The tables are far enough apart to have a private conversation here. Candlelight and several fireplaces make this an attractive place to go for a romantic interlude. Owner Lou McLeod won the Restauranteur of the Year Award for 1996 given by the New Mexico Restaurant Association.

The Best Lamb Osso–Buco
Osteria D'Assisi, 58 Federal Street, (505) 986–5858

Come enjoy Northern Italian cuisine by chef Bruno Pertusini. One favorite dish is the lasagne bolognese. My favorite is their tuna fish salad. Bruno is the brother of Leno, owner of the Palace Restaurant.

The Best Homemade Ravioli
Il Piatto, 95 West Marcy Street, (505) 984–1091

Il Piatto has a variety of seafood and meats on their menu, and it's served in a cozy, sunlit room. It is very popular with the downtown locals.

Italian Language Cassettes in the Bathroom
Pranzo Italian Grill, 540 Montezuma Street, (505) 984–2645

One of the most popular and reasonably priced restaurants in town. A great place to go after the movies. Be sure to have a reservation. But while you are waiting, visit the loo—this is a great time to learn Italian!

HOME STYLE

The Most Popular Place for Politicians
Bull Ring, the Interstate Plaza Bldg., (505) 983–3328

The most popular place with politicians and the downtown business crowd. A great place to go if you are a hungry meat-eater. Their chicken salad with caesar dressing is spectacular. You must ask for it because it's not on the menu.

The Most Eccentric
Cafe Oasis, 526 Galisteo Street, (505) 983–9599

Everything in this funky restaurant (except the food) was made from "found" things. The beautiful mosaic courtyard was done by Adam Steinberg with shard remains of pots, bottles and pieces of glass; the tables were made from wooden cable spools. A health food restaurant and a popular place for breakfast.

The Most Religious Music With "Hangover Stew"
Carlos' Gospel Cafe, 125 Lincoln Avenue, (505) 983–1841

This is where the religious greet, eat, and meet because Carlos likes gospel music. The food is cheap and most popular with hippies and the local downtown business group. The atmosphere is relaxed and the menu is fun. Specialties include "Hangover Stew." You can split a peanut butter sandwich and an Alice B. Toklas, a Gable and Lombard, or just have a half of a sandwich.

The Most Startling Bathroom
Celebrations Restaurant, 613 Canyon Road, (505) 989–8904

Breakfast and lunch are served all day, every day. Dinner is served Wednesday–Saturday. Sylvia and "Veiccho," the owner and manager, mingle with local guests and make people feel as though they are in their own homes. The patio is a great place to watch the Canyon Road traffic go by.

Eastsiders stop here during a morning run, or dog walk. It is the only place on Canyon Road where you can get a full breakfast at 7 A.M., read the paper, take a dog (hide it under the table), and see your neighbors. No matter how many times you have been in the bathroom it is always electrifying because "the man in the bathroom" (not a real man, alas) has been rearranged in a different position.

The Best "New Age" & Bakery Combo
The Cloud Cliff Bakery, 1805 2nd Street, (505) 983–6763

A hippyish restaurant with good, healthy cuisine and contemporary art on the walls. It has one of the best bakeries in town with speciality breads.

The Best BBQ
The Cowgirl Hall of Fame, 319 S. Guadalupe Street, (505) 982–2565

This is a very popular restaurant and saloon all in one. They have entertainment nightly. Their BBQ is cooked on an open fire pit. Their $1 beer night on Tuesdays is popular with the young crowd.

The Most "Countrified"
Harry's Road House, Old Las Vegas Hwy., (505) 989–4629

A river runs through the rustic multi-layered outside patio and chickens and geese are quack in the barnyard adjacent to this rustic restaurant. Particularly popular for breakfast on weekends, so try to get there early to avoid a wait.

Downtown Balcony Dining
Jack's, 135 West Palace Avenue, on the Top Floor, (505) 983–7220

"Modern American Cuisine with influences from French, Italian and Asian styles" is how Jack describes the food at one of the city's hottest new spots. Jack's is the only downtown restaurant where you can dine balcony-top with spectacular views of city landmarks, mountain ranges, and sunsets. Write while you eat, since crayons and paper adorn your table. Best freebie: a memento game of 'jacks' to play on the sidewalk on the way home.

The Best Place to Eat if You Can't Afford the Opera
The Opera cafeteria for lunch during Opera season

Go to the cafeteria and hang out there while the divas are practicing. This way you can hear them sing without leaving the cafeteria. It is best to go with someone who is connected to the Opera.

The Only Real Diner in Town
Pantry Restaurant, 1820 Cerrillos Road, (505) 982–0179

One of the most popular, reasonably priced breakfast spots and hangouts for blue-collar locals.

The Best Game
Pinon Grill, 100 Sandoval Street, (505) 988–2811

"New Western" cuisine with smoked quail and mixed wild game grill.

The Best Place To Go After A Workout At El Gancho
The Steaksmith at El Gancho, Old Las Vegas Highway, (505) 988–3333

The steaksmith serves simple food and good steaks.

The Best Onion Roll in Town
Vanessie's of Santa Fe, 434 W. San Francisco, (505) 982–9966

Simple, classic good food with large portions; entreés include a rack of lamb, and a whole chicken. Everything is à la carte. The onion roll is the best in town. Piano players entertain after 8 P.M.

Funky American
Willie's on Water Street, 409 West Water Street, (505) 982–0008

Willie's is a comfortable restaurant that is low on pretense and expense and high on value and quality. They serve regional American dishes for fair prices. The Caesar salad is excellent!

The Highest Pies
The Zia Diner, 326 Guadalupe Street, (505) 988–7008

A very popular for lunch spot is this popular home–style restaurant. The best green–chile meatloaf in town and fabulous home–made desserts. Very popular with the movie crowd, the Zia is consistent, serves large portions, has great hamburgers and serves bread from its fabulous bakery. A specialty is the homemade fruit pies. It is great place to go before or after a movie at the Jean Cocteau Theatre.

ORIENTAL

The Most Contemporary Inventive Chinese Cooking
Chow's, 720 St. Michaels Drive, (505) 471–7120

Creative dishes such as Santa Fe mushu and spinach pesto dumplings make this Chinese restaurant stand out from its competitors. The winner of the *Santa Fean's* poll for the best Asian food.

The Best Sushi
Masa Sushi, 927 W. Alameda Street, (505) 982–3334

"Masa" is friendly and will make anything—even if it is not on the menu.

The Longest Sushi Bar
Shohko Cafe, 321 Johnson Street (505) 983–7288

Excellent sushi bar and tempura.

The Best Teriyaki
Sukura, 321 W. San Francisco Street, (505) 983–5353

You can take off your shoes and eat in a private room sitting on the floor or sit at the sushi bar or at a regular table. The yellow tail and salmon teriyaki is excellent.

A Spiritual &
New Age Mosaic

HEADACHE

Santa Fe is a haven not only for seekers, new agers, hippies, and free-thinkers but it's also a melting pot for many religious and spiritual groups. 1998 marks the 400th anniversary of the founding of the Catholic church in New Mexico and New Mexico's 400th birthday, New Mexico's first opportunity for a big centennial observance (1898 passed unnoticed). Don Juan de Oñate, who founded New Mexico in 1598, might be considered the George Washington of New Mexico. For information on *Cuarto Centennial* activities call (505) 983–3811 in Santa Fe.

The Land of Enchantment is rich with a variety of spiritual values and cultures, from the Native Americans who honor their Great Spirit, to the Franciscans who built their first Christian church in 1598, to the other religious faiths that gravitated to New Mexico because of its stunning and transcendental natural beauty. — **Michael J. Sheehan,** Archbishop of Santa Fe

FROM A — Z

Santa Fe is the international center of New Age healing because of preexisting spiritual powers here and the availability of schools, practitioners, and a variety of native herbs and natural medicines.

The National Institute of Health's Office of Alternative Medicine believe that conventional medicine is important for emergencies and acute illnesses but less successful in treating chronic health problems. Now more than thirty percent of all Americans seek alternative medicine.

A as in **Acupuncture.** Santa Fe is known as the country's "acupuncture capital." Robyn Benson (505) 986–1089 and Fiquet Duckworth (505) 982–9626 are two of the most reputable acupuncturists/herbalists in town. In addition there is the **Southwest Acupuncture College Clinic** (505) 988–3538 and the **International Institute of Chinese Medicine** (505) 473–5233. **Archaeoastronomy** or sun watching at Chaco Canyon. The Anasazi must have had some knowledge of astronomy. Certain structures or sites, such as the "sun dagger," were built by the Anasazi for the sole purpose of predicting astronomical events such as the summer solstice. The **Ark Books,** 133 Romero Street, (505) 988–3709, is the best resource bookstore in Santa Fe for anything holistic, New Age, natural, and spiritual. **Astrocartography.** Fifty years ago people only traveled widely if they were explorers or were rich. Today everyone travels, but because of the high divorce rate and job changes people are often suddenly thrown into different lifestyles than previously achieved. Your focus and your location often change at the same time. Astrocartography (or relocation astrology) gives you a blue print, or verification, based on your individual natal chart about where you will be happiest in the future. It also gives a map of your past locations. Ariel Guttman (505) 984–8330 wrote a fascinating book called "The Astro-Carto-Graphy Book of Maps" with Jim Lewis. **The Astrological Forum,** 320 Agua Fria Street, (505) 988–3254 brings professional astrologers, teachers, and students to Santa Fe to create a better understanding of the art and science of astrology. Go to their fun annual December meeting and get an astrological preview of the new year by the most recognized people in the field.

B as in **Janine Burke** (505) 983–8001, a transformational psychotherapist specializing in the rapid clearing of anxieties, various phobias, traumatic memories, and addictive urges. **Fred Brown** wrote the book, *Money and Spirituality.*

C as in **Carmelite Monastery,** 49 Mt. Carmel Road. Church services every day at 7 A.M. (in the winter at 7:15 A.M.) at their small chapel next to St. John's College. **Chaneling** as in Patti Levey (505) 474–8378. **Chimayo Pilgrimage** is the annual Good Friday trek to the Sanctuario de Chimayo. The holy dirt is said to have healing powers. Maybe you need a **colonic** hydrotherapy. Call Martha Flannery, (505) 983–8722 or Sorrell Page, (505) 988–3076. **Crystal Healing** with Carla Lamesch (Fax: 505-982-1023) a trained psychotherapist from Europe who moved here ten years ago and studied with Jane Ann Dow, a well-known crystal healer. Carla mastered the technique of healing with crystal energy.

D as in **Dar al Islam,** (505) 685–4515. The Islamic community in the hills of Abiquiu was started in 1979 by a handful of Muslim converts who got a grant from a Saudi businessman to start a model religious community. The 30,000 square foot stucco mosque sits on top of a hill where it can be seen from miles away. The **Day of the Dead** is a Latin American tradition observed in Santa Fe on October 31st. It is a believed that if you place a picture of someone who has passed away on a shrine, the spirit of the dead will come to visit for two days. The **Deva Foundation** (505–757–6752) does energetic healing work.

E as in **E.T. Encounters in Roswell.** The universe holds such infinite possibilities—it is hard to imagine that we are the only living beings it holds. According to a Newsweek poll, forty-eight per cent of Americans think UFOs are real and another forty-eight think there is a government plot to cover up their existence. In New Mexico, this percentage is probably higher because of an incident in 1947 which received world wide attention. The fiftieth anniversary of this event coincided with the first successful landing on Mars on July 4, 1997. **Very Large Array** (VLA) is fifty miles west of Socorro, N.M. The Y-shaped array of twenty-seven antennas

The Roswell Incident—1947

is well known to astronomers because they form one of the world's best radio telescopes. The array can extend as far as thirteen miles in three directions to capture interstellar radio waves which can take faint sounds from millions of light years away and produce images of them. The array has been featured in many movies about communicating with outer space including *Contact* starring Jodie Foster.

F as in **Friendship Club,** 1915 Rosina (505) 982–9040 or (505) 982–8932. There are seventy-five twelve step meetings a week in Santa Fe.

G as in **Chris Grissom,** who founded the Light Institute in Galisteo, specializes in past life regression therapy (505) 446–1975.

H as in **Joan Halifax,** a Buddhist visionary who founded the Ojai Foundation in California and the Upaya House, a Buddhist study center on Cerro Gordo Street in Santa Fe. The **Harmonic Convergence** was held at Chaco Canyon on August 16 and 17, 1987 (August 16th is the birthday of my second set of twins, an astrological event in itself!). The Harmonic Convergence happens when the planets fall into a particular alignment at a time set by the Mayan calender, sending a message to get your ducks in a row.

I as in **Indians.** Many Native Americans live in pueblos where they make sand paintings, go to sweat lodges, chant, eat special herbs, fast, beat their drums, and dance—all for religious and mental and physical health reasons. Amazingly enough, it is the Native American people from New Mexico who have continuously inhabited the same sites as their ancestors did before the arrival of the Europeans in the sixteenth century. **International Institute of Chinese Medicine** (505) 473–5233, is a nationally accredited acupuncture school that offers a master's degree in Oriental medicine.

J as in the **C. C. Jung Institute of Santa Fe** (505) 455–7156, a certified analysis training institute.

K as in **Kiva**, a sacred shelter used by Pueblos for ceremonial rites and gatherings. Four points of a kiva represent the four seasons, the four directions, the four ages in a persons's life, and the four obligations to a tribe. The circle in the center represents unity of all things. **Kinesiology** is the study pursued by Chaz Schatzle, (505) 982–1554.

L as in the **Lama Foundation** a non profit spiritual retreat on 110 acres in Lama, NM. The Hondo fire destroyed it in 1996 but it is slowly rebuilding itself. The **Light Sanctuary** was built at the Armand Hammer United World College because of its dedication to bringing together international students to share ideas and beliefs.

M as in **Massage.** The New Mexico Academy of Massage and Advanced Healing Arts (505) 982–6271 qualifies students for a massage therapy license. **The Monastery of Christ of the Desert.** The monastery is located on 375 acres right on the banks of the Chama River in a peaceful setting 14 miles off the main road from Ghost Ranch. Monks live a monastic and contemplative existence of work, meditation, prayer, study, and silence. They operate a gift shop, a community store, and a thrift shop at 1609 St. Michael's Drive. Uncharacteristicaly, the monks advertise their wares on the World Wide Web (e-mail: scriptorium@christdesert.org and internet: http://wwwchristdesert.org/pax.html). Amen.

N as in **The Nizhoni: The School for Global Consciousness** (505) 466–4336 is a school that utilizes the Light Institute's work.

O as in **Ortho-Bionomy,** a gentle method of releasing acute and chronic pains. Call Vhristina Montes de Oca (505) 986–9939. **Ocamora Foundation** in Ocate (505) 666–2389 is a popular Buddhist retreat near Mora.

P as in *Penitentes* are part of the Order of St. Francis brought into New Mexico by the early Franciscan Fathers. They express their empathy with Christ's suffering on the cross by doing penance. The *morada* is the church of the *Penitentes*. During Easter week they have special exercises in the *morada* that might be scary to anyone not directly involved. The *Penitentes* keep their rituals and beliefs private. They tried to emulate the suffering of Christ on the Cross to remind everyone how Christ suffered to atone for our sins. The Penitentes went into hiding until 1947 when the Brotherhood was officially accepted as a cultural offshoot of the Catholic Church.

Q as in **Quarks**—discovered by Nobel Prize winner Murray Gell-Mann who lives here, and **Quartz**—no two are alike. Watch out for **Quacks!**

R as in **Reiki** healer, a natural method of healing based on chakras, which allow us powerful access to our own inner healing ability. Judy Beatty (505) 988–3465 is one of the best. *The Reporter* has one of Santa Fe's most popular astrologers. "Everyone in Texas reads it."

S as in **Santa Fe Chamber of Consciousness** (505) 466–4552, a networking venture in Santa Fe's alternative community. It offers free discussion and internet demonstrations. *The Santa Fe Sun* is the most important paper to read about the new age activities. The **Sikh** community (505) 753–5881, north of Espanola, is the religious authority for the Sikh religion in the Western hemisphere. The Seiks don't drink or smoke. **The Southwestern College of Life Sciences** (505) 471–5756 specializes in transformational studies and aura balancing. **St. Michael** is the healing saint who is usually pictured with a blue flaming sword that chases away the evil spirits. Santa Feans can chase the evil spirits out of their houses by trimming their windows in blue or turquoise. **Eetla Soracco** is some sort of visionary. **Jay Scherer Academy of Natural Healing** (505) 982–8398 qualifies students for a massage therapy liscense.

The Spirituality Institute, (505) 473–6390. Brother Brian Dybowski at the College of Santa Fe puts on a five-week program of spiritual study. He believes that psychology, philosophy, medicine, and spirituality are all interrelated. "In the 70s, some people tried to separate psychology from spiritualtiy, but people don't respect that artificial bountry." **The Institute for Engaged Spirituality**, run by Wayne Muller and Bread for the Journey is an annual summer conference held at St. John's College and it is dedicated to examining our spiritual practices to see what affects our spiritual growth and capacity to be loving, generous, and kind (505) 438-

4696. In addition consider the **Santa Fe Business & Spirituality Conference** (505) 989-4094 and **Claude Saks** (505) 988–3510, a certified meditation teacher, the author of two books, and, and a student of a master Taoist for twelve years. **Santa Fe Institute for Medicine and Prayer** (505) 820–5479 is a nonprofit corporation founded in 1995 by physicians Larry Dossey and Anthony Rippo. Its mission is to bring back the sacred into the practice of medicine. The institute operates a program at the Cancer Treatment Center at St. Vincent Hospital in Santa Fe. Their effort is based on the scientific evidence of more than two hundred studies demonstrating the effectiveness of contemplative and meditative prayer.

T as in **Tibet.** Santa Fe is one of twenty three cities in the country who offered resettlement communities for Tibetans in 1992. The Dalai Lama is the spiritual head of Tibetan Buddhism worldwide and the political leader of Tibet. Despite the overwhelming odds against the reestablishment of Tibet as a country, he teaches the importance of spirituality and nonviolence for which he was awarded the Nobel Peace Prize in 1989. Project Tibet director, Paljor Thondup, 403 Canyon Road, (505) 982–3002.

U as in **Upayah Center,** 935 Alto Street (505) 982–5049 houses three schools: the World Learning Academy, the Aqua Therapy Institute, and the Jay Scherer Institute.

V as in **Vitamins, Virgins, Vampires, and Vision Quest.** Santa Fe has all but one of these!

W as in the book ***Who's Who in the Healing Arts*** is a directory (505) 984–0878 of healing practitioners. **White Crane Studios** (505) 820–0583 is a healing arts center that offers affordable classes in Tai Chi.

X as in **X-Factor**—vital life force so evident in Santa Fe!

Y as in **Santa Fe Community Yoga Center** (505) 820–9363.

Z as in **Mountain Cloud Zen Center,** on Old Santa Fe Trail just 1 mile south of the Zia Road, (505) 988–4396, and the **Zodiac,** which can be read at the Zia Diner in the evening.

Tours

Organized Tours

Santa Fe has organized daily tours, ghost tours, historic walking tours, art walks, open-bus tours—or you can design your own tour.

A Boot About Santa Fe
Carla and Allan Jordan, (505) 988–2774

An hour and a half history tour of Santa Fe's old churches. Leaves from the Hotel St. Francis at 9:45 A.M. and 1:45 P.M. daily.

Afoot in Santa Fe
Inn at Loretto Hotel, 211 Old Santa Fe Trail, (505) 983–3701

Daily historic tours with Charles Porter depart from the Inn at Loretto Hotel. The two and a half hour tours leave at 9:30 a.m. and 1:30 P.M. daily, with a 9:30 A. M. tour on Sunday. The cost is $12 per person. No reservations required. Children under 12 no charge.

Anthony Atwell
Route 7 Box 127C Santa Fe 87501, (505) 982–6373, (800) 235–8412

Tony takes people to galleries and acts as an art consultant and broker. You pay a fee ahead of time to go on art tours with him. One-day tour fee is $150 for a group of five.

Behind Adobe Walls Tour
(505) 983–6565

The Santa Fe Garden Club was founded in 1939 to raise money for education, conservation, and beautification projects in Santa Fe through its annual fundraiser, "Behind Adobe Walls"—a tour through some of Santa Fe's most beautiful gardens and houses. Tours begin in July.

Fiesta Tours on the Plaza
Leaves from Palace at Lincoln, (505) 983–1570

A fifteen-passenger van owned by city counselor Frank Montano run at 10 A.M. and 12, 2, 4, and 6 P.M. daily for hour and a quarter sightseeing trips of historic Santa Fe. The cost if $7 for adults, $4 for children.

Ghost Tours of Santa Fe
Allan Jordon, 2009 Pacheco Street, (505) 988–2774

A walking tour of less than one mile in radius from the Plaza takes you to twelve documented haunted locations in downtown Santa Fe. The tour guide offers you ninety minutes of entertaining tales that mix local legend, folklore, and history. A theatrical guide in costume tells about the ghost of La Posada, Julia Staab, whose portrait hangs above the fireplace in a first-floor sitting room. Guests who rented Julia's former bedroom were driven out of the room by unexpected and incessant flushing of the toilet.

Loretto Line
Charles Porter, Inn of Loretto, 211 Old Santa Fe Trail, (505) 983–3701

Loretto Line has a one hour and fifteen minute ride around historic Santa Fe for $9. There are daily trips to Taos from April through October which leave at 9 A.M. and cost $60 per person.

Recursos de Santa Fe
826 Camino de Monte Rey, (505) 982–9301

Recursos de Santa Fe specializes in tours and seminars on art, culture, history, and environment of the Southwest and the Americas. Ellen's unique background allows her to tailor the tour to the special needs and interests of each group. Your leader has lived in Santa Fe for many years and worked as a former director of the New Mexico Museum of Fine Arts. Whether you want to go on a cooking tour of Santa Fe, study the world of Georgia O'Keeffe, attend a writing conference, or study birding in the Bosque, her trained guides, leaders in their field, can take you there with enthusiasm. She has worked with such organizations as the Whitney

Museum of Modern Art, the Smithsonian Institution, the Chicago Institute of Art, and many college and university groups.

Santa Fe Detours
107 Washington above Hagen Das, (505) 983–6565

This is one of the oldest tour companies in Santa Fe. They arrange tours to almost anywhere and have daily trips to Taos and they pick up at the hotels. For **Roadrunner** motorized tours, (505) 983–6565, For $8 an adult you can ride around on the Roadrunner, an open-air bus, and see Historic Santa Fe in just one hour and fifteen minutes. The Roadrunner departs from the Plaza at the corner of Lincoln and Palace avenues several times daily (9, 11,3, and 5). No reservations are required.

Walking tours are offerd by the same company at 9:30 and 1:30 daily for $10. You cover two miles in two hours. Call the number above for meeting details.

Southwest Seminars
Allan Osborne, 219 De La Vaca, (505) 466–2775 or (505) 988–5089

Allan, a cultural historian, lectures on Southwest history and gives walking tours of Santa Fe and custom tours for groups all over Northern New Mexico. "Americans call it the Southwest, Spain called it El Norte, Native Americans call it the center."

Pedicabs
Tamara Singer (505) 984–1187

Pedal-Cabs, Santa Fe rickshaws with cheerful, well-informed pedalling drivers, are like over-sized (but licensed) tricycles that ferry people to restaurants, shopping, and on sight-seeing trips around town.

Archeological Tours

Santa Fe, located in the center of the American Southwest, and north of Mexico, could be considered the archaeological capital of the United States where the most important ancient and modern native cultures were focused.

Arroyo Hondo

Arroyo Hondo Pueblo, perched on the edge of the 125-foot deep Arroyo Hondo, is one of the "best reported sites in the Southwest," according to Douglas Schwartz, head of the "dig" and Director of the School of American Research.

The twenty-five year research on this thousand room, fourteenth century Pueblo, described in Doug Schwartz's book, is on-line for scholars to use worldwide. The property where the site is located is owned by the School of American Research and maintained as an archaeological resource forever.

Bandelier National Monument

"Slept until 9 A.M. with bedbugs"—**Adolph Bandelier's** first journal entry from Santa Fe

Adolph Bandelier was one of the most significant figures in the early history of anthropology and archaeology not only in the Southwest, but also in Mexico and South America. Bandelier—pioneer, archaeologist, and ethnologist—discovered Frijoles Canyon on October 23, 1880 on his quest to learn the history and culture of the Southwestern Indians. The ruins of Tyuonyi and others are in the Frijoles Canyon where nomadic hunters, ancestors of today's Pueblo Indians, lived from about 1200 to 1500 A.D. Some pueblos had as many as 500 to 1000 rooms. Their descendants live in the Pueblos of San Ildefonso, Santa Clara and Cochiti. There are sixty-five miles of ancient trails, abandoned villages and wilderness. Bandelier's ashes were the first to be allowed scattered at the ruins near Los Alamos bearing his name.

250

Chaco Canyon

Chaco Canyon, considered "America's Stonehenge" and the "state's most recognizable Indian ruin," is a remote and spectacular prehistoric ruin. The Anasazi deserted Chaco Canyon 800 years ago, but the prehistoric ruins still standing are one of the most extraordinary stone villages in the United States. One of the larger buildings at Chaco Canyon, Pueblo Bonito, was probably the largest apartment-house in the world. It covered three acres, stood four stories high, and had 800 rooms—how amazing these people were! The ancient Anasazi could predict the seasons simply by watching the way the sun or moon would shine through a tiny crack in a door or window. Chaco Canyon is ranked with the Pyramids of Egypt and Peru's Machu Picchu as a World Heritage Site.

Coronado State Monument

These ruins of the Kuaua Pueblo are a great example of the Rio Grande pueblos. It was built around 1300 A.D. using coursed adobe bricks with large multi-storied room blocks around three large plazas with underground kivas. It was peopled by Tiwa-speaking Indians, descended from the Anasazi, ancestors of today's Indians at Sandia and Isleta Pueblos. They were farmers and hunted for small game. Some of their glazeware pottery has been found around the entrance of the Sandia Cave. There is a reconstruction of its famous square kiva with seventeen layers of frescoes, the first extensive prehistoric mural art found in New Mexico (one can enter through the smoke-hole ladder). There is a small museum with a cultural exhibit and a self-guided interpretive trail.

Indian Petroglyphs State Park

The petroglyphs were drawn on volcanic boulders at the edge of an old lava flow that is one half to a million years old. They were made by descendants of the Anasazi from 1100 A.D. to the early 1600s. There is a driving loop with places to get out and walk, a picnic area and toilets. Dinosaur bones dating back 225 million years compose the most complete and some of the earliest found. The fossils belong to a three foot-long theropod, a meat-eater that ran on its two hind legs.

Jemez State Monument

Excavations at Giusewa reveal a pueblo at least 300 years older than its church, San Jose de los Jemez, built in 1627. The church was about 111 feet long and 34 feet wide, the windows made of selenite (translucent form of gypsum) and had an octagonal defense tower 42 feet above the altar. A monastery with a small private chapel and part of a stairway have been found. The museum has reproductions of the cave frescos, a rarity in New Mexican religious art.

Pecos National Monument

Farming groups consolidated at the Pecos River between 800 to 1100 A.D. some pueblos grew to nearly 700 rooms. These multi-storied room houses were built around a large central plaza with kivas (one can go into several). It was built to be a fortress with no outside windows or doors and a perimeter fence. It became an important trade center due to its location between the pueblos of the Rio Grande valley and the Great Plains nomadic Indian tribes. There are interpretive trails amongst the ruins of the pueblo, mission church and its convent, plus a National Parks visitor's center with a museum and short movie of its history.

*Seismosaurus, one of the world's largest dinosaurs, was excavated from federal land near San Ysidro in New Mexico beginning in 1995. The dinosaur was brought to the **Museum of Natural History** with its fossilized bones still encased in rock; this animal roamed New Mexico during the Jurassic era about 150 million years ago.*

Puye Cliff Dwellings
Santa Clara Pueblo, (505) 753–7330
Closed in winter.

Puye Mesa has a large pueblo on top of the mesa and two levels of cliff dwellings below. The pueblo was built of blocks of tuff (lightweight, porous, volcanic rock easily shaped by the stone tools) in the thirteenth through fifteenth centuries. It contained up to 1000 rooms in multistoried roomblocks terraced back in a quadrangle around a large courtyard. A road leads up the mesa where you can park, walk through the ruins, and explore the caves carefully (or one can go up to the caves from the center below). There are toilets, fresh water, and a picnic area.

Salinas National Monument
Go south beyond Albuquerque on I–25, right on route 60 to Abo about 9 miles west of Montainair, then 8 miles north of Mountainair to Quarai and then 26 miles south of Mountainair on NM 14 to Gran Qivira.

Salinas Monument comprises three major archaeological sites. Abo has yet unexcavated mounds of the Tompiro Pueblo and the ruins of the Franciscan Mission, San Gregorio de Abo. This church had high vaults, sandstone walls, and huge hand-carved timbers that were dragged from the Manzano Mountains. Pinon nuts were an important cash crop, and watermelon and grape seeds (from the Old World) have been found. One can only view the ruins from the fence, as they are unstable. At Quarai, the Spanish consolidated the Saline missions to facilitate their administration. The Church of the Immaculate Conception and its convent were built about 1628. There is a visitor's center with historic and prehistoric artifacts, a reconstructed model of the site, an interpretive trail, and picnic area. Gran Quivira was the largest of three pueblos built by the Tiwa-speaking Jumanos. These people gradually disappeared due to starvation, health and sanitary conditions, or perhaps they were killed or enslaved by the Apaches. The remaining population joined other pueblos or migrated to El Paso. One can see masonry ruins of the pueblo and its roomblocks, kivas, and plazas, and the San Buenaventura Mission. There is a self-guided walking tour and rangers at the visitor center which features archaeological and historic exhibits.

The Cerrito Site
Go north on US 84–285 for 30 miles north of Española, left on NM 96, between Abiquiu Dam and Rte. 84.

The earliest known site of Navajo Indians in New Mexico is along the shores of the maximum pool created by Abiquiu Dam, with remains of seventeenth-century hogans and sheep pens. This area attests to the use of the valley by nomadic hunters-and-gathers as early as 3000 B.C.Native Americans called Apaches de Navaju by the Spanishwere nomads who probably migrated from the Great Plains and stayed about one hundred years before moving westward. This is the only Navajo archaeological site in the southwest that has been set aside as a public monument.

Design Your Own Tour

There are many places to explore which are within an hour in any direction from Santa Fe. Have fun locating pueblos and archeological sites of interest on the map on the next page. For starters, go to Abiquiu, Taos, Madrid (along with Cerrillos). Don't miss the places in between!

One of many places to which you might meander is **Abiquiu**, not even mentioned on many maps (including my own!) which is about 45 minutes from Santa Fe.

Abiquiu: Go north on U.S. 84-287 to Espanola and turn west on NM 84 towards Chama for about 23 miles. Just past Espanola is the San Juan Pueblo and across the Rio Grande are the foundations of **San Gabriel**, the first Spanish capital of New Mexico.

Then you'll pass Hernandez, an almost extinct town, made famous by Ansel Adams in his photograph, "Moonrise." The country that Georgia O'Keeffe painted and loved is all around Abiquiu. The sandstone cliffs have amazing colors. If you want to see Georgia O'Keeffe's house you will have had to make those arrangements way in advance at the Georgia O'Keeffe Foundation office, (505) 685–4539. The **Abiquiu Inn** (505) 685–4378 is on Route 84. Just beyond the inn is a real country store which sells everything from saddles to wash tubs. Pass through typical Western towns until you arrive at the Presbyterian Church's **Ghost Ranch Study Center**. Further down the road is the **Ghost Ranch Museum** with displays of the area's geology, natural history, even a small zoo with local animals. The approach—a bumpy 14-mile road in a beautiful setting on the Chama River—to **Christ of the Desert Monastery** is nearby. Just beyond the museum on the main road is **Echo Amphitheater**: where you can (surprise!) hear yourself talk. If you have time, travel another 30 minutes through the Chama River Valley to Los Ojos to the **Ganados del Valle,** a non-profit community organization that assists businesses which use the region's agricultural resources.

Perhaps you're drawn to the spirituality of Chimayo? Go north on 84-285 for about 14 miles then turn right on Rte 503 in Nambe for about 8 miles then take a sharp left on Rte. 520 to Chimayo for about 2 or 3 miles. The **Rancho Chimayo** is the perfect place to stop for lunch either coming or going.

Search for your own routes and pleasures. Let me know what you find.

Day Trips

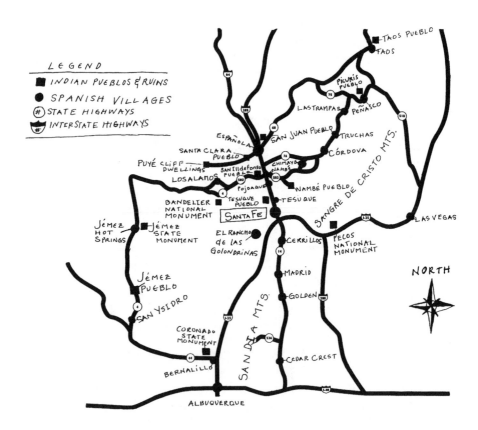

LEGEND
- ■ INDIAN PUEBLOS & RUINS
- ● SPANISH VILLAGES
- (#) STATE HIGHWAYS
- (#) INTERSTATE HIGHWAYS

TAOS PUEBLO
TAOS
PICURIS PUEBLO
76
LAS TRAMPAS
PEÑASCO
518
84
285
66
SAN JUAN PUEBLO
TRUCHAS
ESPAÑOLA
SANTA CLARA PUEBLO
CÓRDOVA
PUYÉ CLIFF DWELLINGS
76
CHIMAYÓ
NAMBÉ
SANGRE DE CRISTO MTS.
SAN ILDEFONSO PUEBLO
LOS ALAMOS
502
501
NAMBÉ PUEBLO
POJOAQUE
4
TESUQUE PUEBLO
TESUQUE
BANDELIER NATIONAL MONUMENT
I-25
LAS VEGAS
JÉMEZ HOT SPRINGS
JÉMEZ STATE MONUMENT
SANTA FE
EL RANCHO de LAS GOLONDRINAS
CERRILLOS
PECOS NATIONAL MONUMENT
NORTH
14
JÉMEZ PUEBLO
MADRID
4
SAN YSIDRO
GOLDEN
285
CORONADO STATE MONUMENT
I-25
SANDIA MTS.
536
44
BERNALILLO
CEDAR CREST
I-40
ALBUQUERQUE

Watering Holes

"To see and be seen,
To do and be undone."
—Alexander Pope

A Sampler

Although most of the hotels have some sort of entertainment, Santa Fe, with its high-desert location, is always short of liquid refreshment. Santa Fe has many unique and lively watering holes, which are popular for age, gender or cultural reasons.

The wateriest "hull" belongs to Santa Fe resident Gregg Bemis. The Lusitania, a bit inaccessible, rests in 300 feet of water off the coast of Ireland. Bemis hopes to solve the mystery of why the Louistania sank in 18 minutes May 7, 1915.

Most of Santa Fe's restaurants and hotels have bars, some with entertainment. But the following places allow you to get out of your hotel and test Santa Fe night life!

Four Santa Fe Brew Pubs

Currently there are four Santa Fe breweries. **Wolf Canyon Brewing Company** (505) 438–7000, **Santa Fe Brewing Company** (505) 424–3333, **Blue Corn Cafe and Brewery** (505) 984–1800 and (505) 428–1800 for Villa Linda Mall and the **Second Street Brewery** (505) 982–3030

The Only Strip Joint in Santa Fe
Cheeks, 2841 Cerrillos Road, (505) 473–5259

Live entertainment with lots of dancing girls happens seven nights a week. This is more popular with tourists staying in hotels on Cerrillos Road than for locals who probably don't want to be seen there.

The Best Salsa Dancing
Club Alegra, on lower Agua Fria near Siler Road, (505) 471–2324

One of the most popular things to do on Friday night—if you can get in—is to go salsa dancing at Club Alegra. Father Frank Preto, known as the salsa Priest from Agua Fria Church, has a popular salsa band that plays at Cafe Alegra to a very local crowd. If you don't know how to dance to salsa, take the free lessons offered before the band begins. On Saturday and Sunday nights they have live Mexican music, which is very popular with locals.

The Best Bar Menu
Tom and Anthony Odai
Catamount Bar, 125 E. Water Street, (505) 988–7299

One of the most fun bars for young people because they have live bands, pool tables and a good bar menu. Bands play on Tuesday, Friday and Saturday nights. The upstairs bar is classier with better brands of liquor, cigars, an outside balcony, and six pool tables, which can be rented for $10 an hour. The food is simple, good, and cheap.

The Best Sports Bar with Casino Gaming
Cities of Gold, 14 miles north of Santa Fe on Hwy.84/285, (505) 455–3984.

They have a happy hour, $1 draft beer, ladies' night, pool tournaments, and shuttle service to Cities of Gold Casino. Call for more details.

The Best Cantina with a CD Mix of Music
Coyote Cantina, 136 Water Street, (505) 983–1615

People go there to drink or to eat on the rooftop of the Coyote Cafe. A great perch from which to people watch. The food is primarily Mexican.

$1 beer night on Tuesday
Cowgirl Hall of Fame, 319 S. Guadalupe Street, (505) 982–2565

Live music every night, great BBQ, and a great hangout if you are looking for an authentic man! A busy patio and popular bar make this a popular place to go year round.

The Only Gay Bar in Town
The Drama Club, 125 N. Guadalupe Street, (505) 988-4374

This is one of the best places to dance in town. Trash disco night on Wednesday is a very mixed crowded night. The rest of the week it is mostly a gay bar. On Tuesdays and Thursdays there is live music. A rock theater band plays selections from Broadway musicals on Thursday nights at 9 P.M. Once a month on Friday night there is a stand-up comedy show with a gay or lesbian comic. There is a small cover charge when there is entertainment.

The Most Authentic 'Santa Fe Style'
The Dragon Room Bar at the Pink Adobe
406 Old Santa Fe Trail, (505) 983–7712

This is one of Santa Fe's most popular bars, and they serve free fresh-popped popcorn. Rosalia, its owner, and a painter, monitors the restaurant from her round corner table in the Dragon Room and gives the "Pink" its personality. On Friday nights there is standing room only; on weekends there is wonderful guitar music.

The Best Tapas In The Oldest Bar
El Farol, 808 Canyon Road, (505) 983–9912

This was once an artist's headquarters, where Alfred Morang painted murals on the wall in the 1820s in exchange for drinks. It was, and still is, one of the most fun, rowdy, and popular bars for everyone whether you are a cowboy, a movie star, or a local, or even a tourist! Every night there is music and dancing on a tiny dance floor. The restaurant is known for its "tapas" (Spanish "delectables").

The Best Dive
Evangelos Cocktail Lounge, 200 W. San Francisco Street, (505) 982–9014

With a bar upstairs and a smoky pool room downstairs, this lounge is very popular with young adults.

The Biggest and Most Centrally Located Bar
La Fonda Bar, on the Plaza, 100 E. San Francisco Street, (505) 982–5511

The La Fonda became involved with the Manhattan Project during WWII when Col. Boris Pash posted an intelligence man at the front desk and two of his intelligence men in the bar—**Sam Ballen**

The La Fonda is and always was a great place to meet because it it the closest hotel to the Plaza where so many events take place. The Fonda Bar is open seven nights a week and it features different bands every night. On weekdays they serve hors d'oeuvres at the bar at 5 P.M.

The Best Sports Bar In Town
The Green Onion, 1851 St. Michael's Drive, (505) 983–5198

This is the best place to go on St. Patrick's Day and hear Irish music and the best place to be on Super-Bowl Sunday.

The First Gambling Table And The Best Bartender
The Palace Restaurant Bar, 142 W. Palace Avenue, (505) 982–9891.

The late J. I. Stahly was known for his impromtu limericks.

> At the Palace in Old Santa Fe,
> They drank to the toast of "Ole!"
> They guzzled good gin
> Right up to their chin,
> Then decided to call it a day.—**J. I. Stahly**

The Victorian bar with "bordello" wallpaper original in the 1960s was the site of Donna Tulles' gambling table—the first in Santa Fe. Alfonso Alderette, who has been at the Palace since 1983, is the most popular bartender in town. He always gives you more than you bargained for! A painting of a young girl with an Indian war bonnet is in the bar. Ramon Rice, the artist, actually painted a boy, then he added breasts to make the boy look like a girl.

Good Live Music
El Paseo, 208 Galisteo Street, (505) 992–2848

Good live music with a young crowd in a confined area makes this place, with friendly bartenders, a cozy and popular place.

The Best Country Western Music
Rodeo Nights, 2911 Cerrillos Road, (505) 473–4138

Rodeo Nights is a good place to go with a group. It is an authentic country western dancing place. They have free dance lessons on Monday nights from 7 to 9 P.M. Wednesday night is ladies night.

The "Closest Thing to a London Gentleman's Club"
The Staab House Bar at La Posada De Santa Fe, 330 E. Palace Avenue
(505) 986–0000

Its historic setting has a Victorian ambience with leather chairs, a painting with a sporting scene by Randall Davey, a fireplace, and reading lamps. One of the most popular bars in town for locals. La Posada is the former home of Julia Staab whose ghost roams around the grounds.

The Best Piano Bar
Vanessie's of Santa Fe, 434 W.San Francisco, (505) 982–9966.

Doug Montgomery and Charles Tichner play the piano for a lively crowd of locals and tourists. If you like sing-alongs or impromptu singing from the audience, this is the place for you.

Western Wear

The clothing scene in Santa Fe is volatile because of the competition from chain stores such as Eddie Bauer, Banana Republic, the Gap, Ann Taylor and J.Crew. There are two factory malls south of town. In addition the Santa Fe area is filled with stores, galleries, markets and pueblos where you can purchase Indian fashions, accessories, jewelry, and Southwestern clothing.

Southwestern Chic

"Santa Fe style means wearable art, western and fiesta fashions fringes and beads, bandanas and baugles, ethnic and handwoven, suede and leather, panchos, broom skirts and ribbon shirts, and cowboy and Indian clothing. All of these styles can be worn with a wide variety of Western accessories; concho belts, Indian jewelry, chaps and boots, shawls, bolos and squash blossoms. Santa Fe chic can also be jeans worn with your finest jewelry or your finest clothes."—**Cheray Hodges**

Santa Fe clothing stores are just as diverse as its population and the range of social events during the year.

Autobody Express, 519 Cerrillos Road, (505) 438–4877. Fred Imus, the brother of the *Imus in the Morning* Imus, has affordable men's shirts and clothing. They have women's hats and mens casual wear and western wear. **La Bodega**, 667 Canyon Road, (505) 982–8043, has fabulous clothing designs by North American artists and clothing from Guatemala as well as wonderful old authentic Navajo jewelry. **Bodhi Bazaar**, 500 Montezuma Street, (505) 982–3880 sells the most contemporary high fashion of any other clothing store in Santa Fe; its affordable designer clothing is casual and dressy. **Nancy Boucher**, 418 Montezuma Street, (505) 989–1131 makes custom clothing with vests and jackets and pants made out of old rugs, leather, and suede. **Char**, at 104 Old Santa Fe Trail, (505) 988–5969 sells fine suede clothing, exotic leather handbags and boots and jackets for men and women. **The Costume Salon**, is at 631 Old Santa Fe Trail #3, (505) 988–9501—if you are tired of all the costumes in your closet, then rent something different for every occasion, whether it be halloween or the opera. **Dewey Trading Company**, On the Plaza, 53 Old Santa Fe Trail, (505) 983–5855 is the source for blankets and the famous Pendleton virgin wool men's shirt which evolved in 1924. **Faircloth Ltd.**, 228 Old Santa Fe Trail, (505) 982–8700 carries contemporary custom clothing. **Fourth World Cottage Industries**, 2nd floor, 102 W. San Francisco Street, (505) 982-4388 makes clothing from fabulous vintage or antique fabrics and carries antique furniture and beautiful hats. **French Rags**, Eldorado Hotel, (505) 988–1810 sells fabulous clothes made in California with richly patterned jacket and coats that are sophisticated and wonderful for traveling. **Hop-A-Long Boot Company**, West of Richards Road on Rodeo, (505) 471–5570 carries second-hand cowboy boots, hats, shirts and collectibles. The best non-Western men's clothing stores are Robert Bailey, Harry, and Lancaster York. **Robert Bailey**, 150 Washington Avenue, (505) 983–8803 has a men's clothing store "as nice as anything on Rodeo Drive." Their mock turtlenecks and custom-made blouses are popular with both men and women. **Harrys,** on Galisteo and Water, (505) 988–1959 has Italian men's clothing, and some women's too. **Lancaster York**, 121 A E. Palace Avenue, (505) 984–1577 carries men's clothing from casual to dressy (no suits), with a dash of Southwestern thrown in. Nicole Miller socks make wonderful gifts because they are theme-oriented—doctors socks for doctors, etc. **Judy's Unique Apparel**, 714 Canyon Road, (505) 988–5746 has been a local favorite for 20 years. Judy's is a truly unique boutique with a handcrafted flair, featuring original local designers and clothing from around the world. Everything including her collection of jewelry is reasonably priced. **Natalies**, 503 Canyon Road, (505) 982–1021, has been called the "Hermes of the western." Her designer Western jackets and boots are for the well-heeled. Her embroidered, rhinestone jackets have a Hollywood cowboy look. She is also strong in belts, buckles and designer cowboy boots. **Mimosa-Ortega**, 52 Lincoln Avenue, (505) 982–5492 stocks Southwestern clothing—velvets and leather and beaded jackets and vests, and shirts with silver buttons. **Origins**, 135 W. San Francisco Street, (505) 988–4626 is the most fabulous store to see, whether you can afford it or not! It features imported and locally made one-of-a-kind clothing and jewelry. **Pinkoyote**, 315 Old Santa Fe Trail, (505) 984–9971 is the perfect place to buy simple loose fitting clothes, then create what look you want with accessories. **Michael Robinson Inc.**,1003 Canyon Road, (505) 988–3127 shows the most unique wholesale showcase in Aspen and Santa Fe. He sells hand embroidered and tooled sheerlings and cashmeres here and to Bergdorfs, Neimans, and Saks. He features one-of-a-kind artists like Ford Ruthling and Deborah Clare. **Santa Fe Dry Goods**, 55 Old Santa Fe Trail, (505) 983–8142 carries men's and women's classic and casual sports clothing with a Santa Fe twist, featuring some of Barbara Hester's old Navajo antique textile clothing. **Santa Fe Weaving Gallery**, 124 1/2 Galisteo, (505) 982–1737, displays the work of twenty different fiber artists, knitters, and silk artists from New Mexico and around the country. About one-half of these are local New Mexicans, including Susan Summa who knits limited editions and one-of-a- kind sweaters. In **Simply Santa Fe**, On the Plaza, (505) 988–3100, the majority of clothes typify Santa Fe style: chenille sweaters, velvet, boots, wonderful jewelry, and vests and blouses constructed from table linens. **Jane Smith Ltd.**, 550 Canyon Road, (505) 988–4775 has chic and expensive Western designs and fashions for clothing, boots, and furnishings. Her fabulous sweaters with Western designs are her trademark—no one else has them! **Spirit of the Earth**, 108 Don Gaspar Street, (505) 988–9558 shows lots of regular everyday clothes, and features lamb suede clothing for women. **Susan K's**, 229 Johnson Street, (505) 989–8226 is the perfect place to buy an outfit at the last minute for that opening of the Opera or to find fancy jackets that will dress up any outfit. **Timbavati**, 125 Lincoln Street (505) 988–4200 shows simple, sophisticated clothes that go anywhere! Ewa Kielczewska's simple patterns for dresses and tunics are chic. **Vivi of Santa Fe**,117 Galisteo Street, (505) 984–3114 features long sleeveless chenille vests and sweaters as well as kilim rug vests with deerskin backs. **Wild Things**, 216 Garfield, (505) 983–4908 has ethnic, vintage, wild, and "trippy" clothes are as much fun as her restaurant, the Cafe Oasis! **Yarrow Collection**, 223 W. San Francisco Street carries its own line of shearling coats bought from designers around the country.

Accessories

The Bolo Tie, the official state tie is a braided coil or string with matching tips held together by a piece of jewelry. In 1987, the New Mexico State House of Representatives voted to honor the bolo tie by declaring it the official state tie. The resolution states *"....in New Mexico there is a tradition of an excellent decorative tie, allowing individual eccentricity and individual flair while providing a dash of elegance. All rules of any body politic of the state is hereby directed to recognize that he who wears a "bolo tie," wears the official state tie or neckware of New Mexico and that he shall be welcomed at all events or occasions when the wearing of a tie is considered if not mandatory, then at least appropriate."*

Desert Son, 725 Canyon Road, (505) 982–9499 carries silver buckles ranger sets, tip sets and leather belts made to order. **Caballo** and **East West Trading Company** share the same space at 727 Canyon Road, (505) 986–3489. Together they have hand-tooled leather belts or gold belt buckle studded with rubies, concha belts, Rockmount cowboy shirts with pearl snaps, vests made of old Navajo rugs, Chimayo wool coats, and miscellaneous boots and hats. **Lucchese Boots**, 203 Water Street, (505) 989–7959, are well known throughout the Western world. **The Monte Cristi**, 118 Galisteo Street, (505) 983–9598 or the custom shop: 322 McKenzie Street. Their specialty is Panama hats and unique hat bands. **Packards Indian Trading Store**, 61 Old Santa Fe Trail, (505) 983–9241. One of the best places to buy Western accessories and jewelry. **James Reid, Ltd.**, 114 E. Palace Avenue, (505) 988–1147 for popular contemporary silver jewelry and belts. **Santa Fe Boot Company**, (505) 983–8415. You can get top of the line lizard flame-stitched boot made by Tony Lamas. **The Square Deal Boot Shop**, 304 Johnson Street, (505)982–6469. David Gallegos makes his own boots which start at $550. **Tom Taylor Co.**, La Fonda Hotel, (505) 984–2232. Unique buckles and leather belts and custom made boots. **Wind River Trading Company**, 113 E. San Francisco, (505) 982–1592/989–7062. They give discounts at this largest store for jewelry and silver and turquoise accessories.

The Sparkle of Gold & Silver

*Designs and manufactures their own jewelry

Stores that design gold and silver contemporary jewery are as follows: **Antony/Williams***, (505) 982–3443. **Nancy Brown Custom Jewelers***, 111 Old Santa Fe Trail (505) 982–2992. A gallery of contemporary jewelry featuring designs by Nancy Brown. **deBella Jewelers***, 100 E. Palace Avenue, (505) 984–0692. Award winning designs in platinum and gold. **Canyon Collections***, (505) 982–7808. Works in gold and unusual stones by Michael Kneebone. **Fairchild & Company***, 110 W. San Francisco Street, (505) 984–1419. Fine gemstone jewelry—on the cutting edge of design. Nedra Matteucci's Fenn Gallery shows **Richard Tang***, 31 San Juan Ranch Road, (505) 986–1000. A master designer who incorporates fine gems and artifacts from his own collection into a contemporary 22k gold setting. **Dell Fox Jewelry***, 435 S. Guadalupe Street, (505) 986–0685. Ancient and classical Greco-Roman designs—"jewelry with passion." **The Golden Eye***, 115 Don Gaspar, (505) 984–0040 carries international award winning imaginative work in gold and unusual gemstones by Nora Pierson. **Gusterman Silversmiths***, 126 E. Palace, (505) 982–8972. Three generations of silversmiths! **Jett**, 110 W. San Francisco Street, (505) 988–1414. He shows Robert Morris who is Donna Karan's designer. **Jewel Mark,** 228 Old Santa Fe Trail, (505) 820–6304. They represent contemporary designers Doris Panos, Damiani, Seidengang, and Frederica. **James Kallas Jewelers**, 503 Old Santa Fe Trail, (505) 986–1955. **Lewallen & Lewallen***, 105 Palace Avenue, (505) 983–2657. Handcrafted whimsical jewelry in gold and silver. **Luna Felix Goldsmith***, 116 W. San Francisco,(505) 986–1296. Award winning 22k granulation. **Miraposa Gallery**, 225 Canyon Road, (505) 982–3032. They respresent mostly New Mexico and regional jewelers. **Ornaments**, 209 W. San Francisco Street, (505) 983–9399. One hundred and fifty contemporary and traditional artists from all over the country. **Romancing the Stone***, 133 W. San Francisco Street, (505) 988–4477. Owner Donuta represents a broad span of elite designers. Go see the original designs at **Running**

Ridge Gallery, 640 Canyon Rd. (505) 988-2515. Fun, fine, whimsical, and very wearable gold and silver jewelry. **Santa Fe Goldworks***, 66 E. San Francisco Street, (505) 983–4562. They feature designs by David Griego. **Spirit of the Earth**, 108 Don Gaspar Street, (505) 988–9558. Contemporary jewelry designed by Tony Malmed. **Teresa Vorenberg***, 656 Canyon Road, (505) 988–7215. She designs her own contemporary jewelry in gold and silver and shows jewelry of world-wide designers.**Things Finer,** La Fonda Hotel, (505) 983–5552. Estate and contemporary jewelry. They show **Dian Malouf**, who searches the planet for the most unusual pieces and incorporates them into her one-of-a-kind jewelry, especially her legendary large rings—highly collectible for those "in the know."

INDEX

TO ORDER

$19.95 plus tax
If you don't have any stamps
call toll free
(888) 269-2504
fax: (505) 988-5035
e-mail:adobe@thorntonsbest.com
web address: www.thorntonsbest.com

If you have a stamp
304 Delgado Street, Santa Fe 87501